Pricing for Profit

Pricing for Profit

LEN ROGERS

Basil Blackwell

Copyright © Len Rogers 1990

First published 1990

Basil Blackwell Ltd
108 Cowley Road, Oxford, OX4 1JF, UK

Basil Blackwell, Inc.
3 Cambridge Center
Cambridge, Massachusetts 02142, USA

British Library Cataloguing in Publication Data

A CIP catalogue record for this book is available from
the British Library.

Library of Congress Cataloging in Publication Data
Rogers, Len
Pricing for profit / Len Rogers.
p. cm.
ISBN 0-631-16994-6
1. Pricing I. Title.
HF5416.5.R64 1990
658.8'16--dc20
90-33757 CIP

Typeset in 11 on 13 pt Palatino by
Archetype, Stow-on-the-Wold, Gloucestershire
Printed in Great Britain by
T. J. Press Ltd, Padstow, Cornwall

Contents

Contents

Contents

Contents

Contents

Contents

List of exhibits

List of exhibits

Preface

One business activity that causes more discussion and dissention then any other is the process of arriving at a price for a product or service.

In a shrinking world of expanding markets and faster communications, price is rapidly becoming the most important component in the marketing mix. Often it is the leading question in business negotiations because, if suppliers are competent, price signposts the quality, delivery and service the customer can expect, thus perpetuating the adage: 'You get what you pay for.'

Pricing procedures range from the utterly basic 'cost plus x per cent' to the theoretical, often hypothetical regions of academic discourse. No matter how tortuous and protracted the deliberations, eventually a price has to be decided.

For many years a useful framework for setting a price has been a consideration of the range between floor-price and ceiling-price, that is, determining the level between what it cost and what we can get for it. Hence we have become accustomed to 'high-price' and 'low-price' strategies depending whether we have priced towards what the market will bear, or what it cost to produce and deliver.

Another widely held concept has been that price determines the level of profit. It doesn't. It is an essential factor in the profit equation but has to be linked with the equally vital component of sales in the determination of an acceptable profit.

A sale is also a purchase: they are two aspects of the same transaction. To put it simply, if we want to increase sales, we should aim to increase purchases. To consider pricing from the purchasing point of view is in line with modern business thinking called marketing.

In this book I have introduced a different approach to pricing for profit by considering the three main components of price: basic cost, oncosts, profit.

Each of the three is subject to varying pressures from internal and external factors, including production methods, employees, trade unions, suppliers, direct and indirect competitors, customers, shareholders, taxation, officialdom, and one's colleagues with whom one is working to establish a price. By exploiting the possibilities of each of the three components, a different pricing structure can be constructed.

Although all the methods and computations in this book can be transferred to the reader's own work situation using an ordinary calculator, if these pricing procedures are adopted in earnest, the use of a personal computer will be invaluable. Simple tables are given which remove much of the tedium of number-crunching and, to save the reader spending endless hours devising the formulae, these are included in a form ready to insert into the PC software.

The software I have used is Symphony from Lotus. However, it is *not* necessary to have this particular spreadsheet because the formulae work equally well in the original Lotus 1-2-3 which was introduced in 1983. Users of other spreadsheets will find little difficulty in modifying the formulae to suit their particular software.

I have avoided using formulae that are too complicated. My editor, Richard Burton, pointed out the occasional error in unit figures of some of the totals. This is due to the rounding of the several places of decimals which are automatically held in the program during the calculation of a formula such as: @SUM(A12..A18) If these minor discrepancies are not acceptable, and you are using Symphony release 2.0, then instead of formatting cells to a number of decimal places insert @ROUND(before the formula, and after it add a comma, the number of decimal places required, and a closing bracket. This will avoid errors in the final figure of summations. Thus, the previous formula rounded to the unit figure with no decimal places becomes: @ROUND(@SUM(A12..A18),0) Obviously, if two decimal places are needed, it becomes @ROUND(@SUM(A12..A18),2)

ACKNOWLEDGEMENTS

I wish to thank the editors of *The Economist*, *Business Week*, *Financial Times* and *Sunday Times* for some of the news items and references made in the book.

Len Rogers
Luxembourg, 1990

1

Pricing and marketing

THE IMPORTANCE OF PRICING

There are two reasons why we put a price on something: we want to sell it; we want to make a profit. If we want to make a large profit, we set a high price, but we may find that we cannot sell it at a high price. To be reasonably sure that we will sell it, we set a low price. When sold, the profit we get makes us wonder why we bothered, and if we set the price so low to be absolutely sure of making a sale, we stand a good chance of losing money.

Whether we are talking of a tiny one-man or one-woman business, or a large complex organization, no matter how simple or elaborate the procedures, these two main aims, sales and profit, are fundamental to every pricing policy, strategy, tactic and decision. Selling and profit aims are often in conflict, and the overall pricing problem that confronts anyone wishing to sell something is the explicit or implicit resolution of this conflict.

Set the price too high and insufficient sales result; set it too low and inadequate profits are made or opportunities of making greater profits are lost. This is why few people relish the thought of having to set a price for a product or service, and those responsible for constructing overall company pricing policies often approach the task with reluctance.

Pricing holds a central position in the corporate affairs of a company because pricing decisions are a major factor in determining the volume of business the company will achieve, its position in the market compared with competitors, and its total sales, revenue and profit.

MARKETING AND PRICING

Before the 1960s companies were mainly concerned with the production of goods and services – the development of manufacturing skills in mass-production techniques and then mass-production of components and multi-assembly of finished goods.

Since the 1960s a wide variety of product ranges has become available: if a particular product does not satisfy the customer there is ample choice from which other purchases can be made. Gradually the customer has become a dominant force in the market, exercising critical influence on sales and thus on the production of goods and supply of services.

Pressures on selling the output at ever keener prices, and in the face of increasing competition, have created the need for dynamic sales and marketing managers. Today, and certainly in the expanding future markets of tomorrow, the pressure is on pricing – pricing to sell and pricing to make profits.

To focus a company's activities on customers, their needs, wants and desires, is fundamental to marketing thinking. The real purpose of a company's endeavours is not to produce goods but to sell them. And to sell them at prices in such quantities that the resulting profits will keep them in business and enable them to expand. Pricing is the profit-generating activity in business and is a major tool in marketing.

COMPETITION AND PRICE

This continuing battle in the market-place in the pursuit of sales and profits is evident everywhere – in the smallest item we buy, the weekly shopping basket of goods, the occasional major household or office purchase, in the large capital investments.

Even our daily intake of food is subject to competitive pricing. All the supermarkets, delicatessens, convenience stores, chain stores, garages, delivery services, manufacturers of microwave meals etc. are competing to fill the customer's stomach. Faced with this competition, fast-food suppliers in the late 1980s slashed prices as though burgers were going out of fashion. In October 1989 Wendy's cut prices by 6 per cent, Hardee's by 17 per cent, Kentucky Fried Chicken by 18 per cent, Taco Bell by 25 per cent, and McDonald's by a whopping 47 per cent.

In many cities, such as Trier (Germany), Toulouse (France), London (UK) and Luxembourg, McDonalds held their prices, but with the occasional localized promotion. In other locations they experimented. In Chicago you could have a quarter-pounder for 99 cents when the local Chicago Bears football team won, but a deal on French fries when they didn't. In New York it was a meal with a movie – videos selling for $5.99 when you bought your burger.

The personal computer boom of the 1980s peaked in 1987 and slowed at the start of the 1990s. Despite the significant steps in networking, the dramatic improvements in computing speeds and miniaturization that gave light-weight lap-tops greater power than desk models of only a year earlier, sales sagged. Month after month, advertisements for the latest computers using the most advanced chips announced lower and lower prices; some even adding, 'price on application, because prices are too low to print'! This cut-throat pricing to stimulate sales succeeded only in depressing profits to near zero growth.

In the heavy capital investment area, Japanese pricing tactics became even more spectacular. Fujitsu Ltd landed a contract in late 1989 to design a computer system in Hiroshima by bidding 1 yen.

Earlier the same company and NEC Corp both bid 1 yen to design a library computer system in Nagano Prefecture; they had to draw lots for the contract. Fujitsu won, as they had with the toss of a coin two years previously, when they and another company both bid 1 yen to design a telecommunications system in Wakayama Prefecture. In the intervening period, apparently with no other bidder in the race, Fujitsu won a similar contract with a bid of 10,000 yen.

Students of marketing will recognize the early 'Polaroid' problem here: you can sell the camera at a high price and the special film at a low price, or give the camera away for peanuts and make money on the film.

PRICING POLICY

A company should have a pricing policy to guide executives responsible for setting prices, irrespective of whether it is explicitly recorded or implicitly understood. Pricing policy may be developed generally, for product groups, or for specific products.

All pricing activities – setting a price for a new product, revising the price of an existing product, raising it to cover increased costs, lowering it to combat competition, dropping it to penetrate a particular market, coping with the vicissitudes of business such as in the early 1990s – should be carried out within the general guide-lines of company pricing policy.

Pricing policy and pricing strategy are confused in some companies but, to distinguish them as they are discussed in this book, pricing policy includes the general principles a company proposes to follow in its pricing activities, and pricing strategy is how it is intended that the policy will be implemented.

A company's policy could be to price its products in line with their high standard of manufacture, and not to offer heavy discounts. Pricing strategy would be the plans, campaigns and methods used to implement the policy with specific types of products to particular groups of customers.

A general pricing policy may be observed in the marketing operations of many companies – clothes with a well-known label, personal computers, branded footwear, jewellery, pens, perfume etc. Because the products are made to a high specification, the company wishes to create and maintain a high-quality image. This is achieved by a high-pricing policy, an avoidance of discounting and price cutting, and often a sustained publicity programme with messages or slogans such as: 'When it has to be the best', 'For that special occasion' and 'Nobody ever got fired for buying a…'. Seasonal sales and the occasional special offers of such products are made on the basis of very modest percentage reductions.

A company's pricing policy should be simple so as to achieve consistency in pricing strategy, tactics and decisions, and to avoid complications that can arise from short-term arbitrary rulings. It should also minimize the amount of executive time spent wrestling with day-to-day pricing problems.

Pricing policy must not violate legal regulations, must treat all customers fairly and equitably, and ensure that the company makes profits in the long run.

Other factors are the product, its distribution, promotion and service. What is not always fully understood is that decisions taken in any of these four primary marketing areas will directly or indirectly affect the price.

4

Secondary factors affected by a company's pricing policy are: production, labour policies, research and development, competitive position, market share, attractiveness to investors, and government and regulatory agencies.

Pricing policy is not usually included in the marketing plan, and in many successful companies a pricing policy or strategy is not even committed to writing. This is not to imply that such companies do not consider pricing important or that they operate without an overall guide. On the contrary, pricing is considered as fundamental in such companies and it frequently occupies the time of a special group.

In *IBM: How the World's Most Successful Corporation is Managed* (Kogan Page, 1987) David Mercer, the former UK manager, states that 'pricing policy has usually been notable in the IBM plans by its absence'. He explains that pricing is so vital to IBM that it is the responsibility of a separate department, and that IBM prices its products very carefully to maximize profitability.

In contrast, another large and highly successful company, Lever Bros, has highly specific pricing policies. Len Hardy, former chairman, describes in his book *Successful Business Strategy* (Kogan Page, 1987) a pricing policy for a dominant market leader, pricing policy for brands sharing market leadership, pricing policy for brands holding a lower level share in the market, and pricing policy for a brand that is a segment leader.

The reason for having a pricing policy is to enable all marketing activities, strategic and tactical, to be co-ordinated towards the attainment of specific objectives. Pricing policy provides reference points for the development of long-term pricing strategy and for easier decision-taking in pricing tactics.

PRICING STRATEGY

For at least the last 20 years, the vogue word in marketing has been 'strategy'. You have to have strategy to be successful. The latest courses and books advertised are for strategic-this and strategic-that.

Strategy is not new in business activities, although the various interpretations made closely follow the usual dictionary definition of tactics: that is, manoeuvring in the presence of the enemy (competitors), or purposeful procedures (with customers).

5

While consulting with a number of companies in the UK, continental Europe and further afield, I have observed that 'strategy' and 'tactics' are often used by business executives as interchangeable: one company's strategy is another's tactics. The words are confused to the extent where pricing strategy and pricing tactics are used synonymously with pricing 'decision' and, occasionally, with 'policy'.

Strategy is an overall plan or campaign; tactics are the techniques and ploys used to carry out the plan. John Harvey-Jones, a not unsuccessful international businessman, says in his book *Making it Happen* that while one must be aware of the strategic significance of what is going on, battles are won tactically, not by strategy.

While policy and strategy do not possess a strict dichotomy of meanings, to explore them would require soaring into the realms of academic discourse and serve little practical purpose.

The Management Brief in *The Economist*, 7–13 October 1989, starts with the opinion of one of the more successful marketing men that most of the academic writing on marketing was unintelligible twaddle. While I do not agree with this generalization, I offer further evidence of this general anathema to figures and difficult concepts by quoting from Stephen Hawking's acknowledgement at the front of his brilliant and necessarily complex *A Brief History of Time*. Hawking was advised that every equation included in the book would halve its sales; he therefore included just one, by Einstein, linking mass and energy.

A book on pricing has to be practical; but you can't have a book on pricing and leave out the numbers despite the fact that most readers find numbers, and worse, statistics, akin to ancient Sanskrit. I have not indulged in twaddle or word artistry and, hopefully, I have not confused readers with obfuscating verbiage; the terms and definitions are kept as simple as possible. The financial and statistical analyses and text have all been kept at the same elementary level.

A simple, three-level approach to pricing policy is adopted – pricing strategy, pricing tactics, pricing objectives. The scheme is illustrated in exhibit 1.1. We move from a broad statement about the pricing strategy to be adopted in the various markets, to the tactics, actions, methods, procedures, ploys etc. to be used to implement the strategy, and the specific objectives expected to be achieved. This suggested treatment accommodates the fact that there is frequently no great distinction between policy and strategy, and that they are widely regarded as the same thing.

Exhibit 1.1 The development of pricing policy

What might be considered new in the book is the use of personal computer spreadsheets for tables, analyses and flow charts.

Trying to get something new in pricing is like the story of the woman who was undecided as to where she and her husband could go for their holidays. She visited the local travel agent, and to each of his many suggestions said that they had been there. With an increasing number of people waiting, and in desperation, he asked her to look at a huge globe of the world that decorated the agency. After dealing with the other customers, he turned to her and asked, 'Well, have you found somewhere that interests you madam?' 'Not yet,' she replied, with a smile, 'but do you have another globe?'

This book is not a new globe for pricing, only new ways of looking at the subject and using PC layouts and actual formulae in clear type ready for the reader to transfer to his or her particular marketing situation.

Management of a company has the responsibility of constructing a workable and profitable pricing strategy and translating this into tactical decisions to deal with day-to-day marketing problems that call for price variations and adjustments. They are confronted with many factors.

A PRICING MODEL

It is difficult to represent price with just one model, because we often have different prices for the same product, in different geographical locations, to different customers and at different times. Furthermore, we cannot consider pricing as a sterile operation divorced from the market. Simply setting a price does not imply a sale: if the price is too high, there will be no sale and no profit.

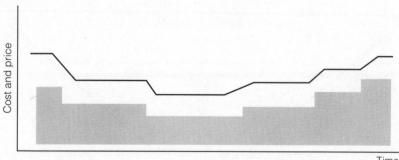

Exhibit 1.2 Cost and price of a product over time

The objective of pricing is to make a sale and a profit; we must therefore assume that price is the amount of money asked, and exchanged for, a product or service. This can be for a single transaction or for several transactions with similar products throughout the market. Several similar transactions in the total market can be represented on a two-dimensional model as in exhibit 1.2. The base represents time and the vertical axis cost and price. With economies of scale and improved manufacturing methods, costs and prices have declined; later, in a period of inflation, they have increased.

If we add a third dimension to represent the geographical extent of the total market, as in exhibit 1.3, we have what looks like a topographical model. The base represents the costs of making and supplying the product to different parts of the market over time; the upper layers represent the added costs and profit which also vary over time and according to specific market conditions.

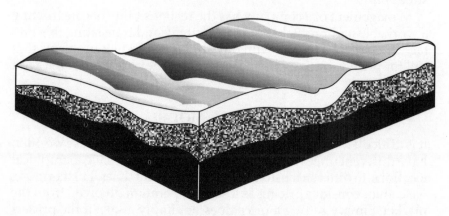

Exhibit 1.3 Three-dimensional model of cost and price

Models are not always exact representations of reality and sometimes, as in this case, provide a conceptual structure against which to test hypotheses, theories and actions. The three-dimensional model in exhibit 1.3 is a 'frozen image' of what is happening over a period of time. However, marketing activities are not static but constantly changing. Strictly, the time element requires the model to be in motion so that the continuous undulations, the price increases and decreases at varying rates in the total market could be appreciated.

Trying to use even a static three-dimensional model that can be printed in a book is difficult enough, let alone a moving one!

COMPONENTS OF PRICE

Price does not make profits; sales make profits, and sales are stimulated by the perceived value compared with the price. Price influences how many we sell and how much profit we make. This underlies the real purpose of marketing, which is to find and satisfy customers; profit measures our success in that quest. Price is a marketing tool that can be used to influence sales and profits. We may have a low, attractive price for a product, but it does not mean we will make a profit; first, we have to make a sale. And to make a sale we have to ensure that the perceived value is greater than the price.

Price consists of three components: the cost of producing; various oncosts, including the cost of getting it to the customer; and profit. This is illustrated in exhibit 1.4, using solid black for basic costs, light shading for oncosts and no shading for profit.

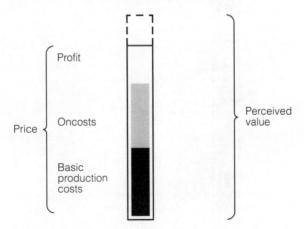

Exhibit 1.4 The three components of price

9

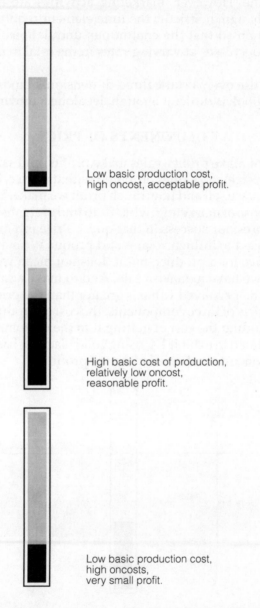

Exhibit 1.5 Components of price for different types of products

Each of the two main categories of costs may be divided into fixed and variable elements. Basic production cost has a fixed part that is incurred irrespective of production level, and costs that vary with output. Similarly, oncosts contain fixed costs, such as amounts levied by management or incurred irrespective of the level of sales, and variable costs that are in proportion to sales.

The oncosts levied on the product are usually those required by company policy such as management charges, contribution to research and development etc. Oncosts that vary with sales are mainly the distribution costs, transportation, warehousing etc., but often a part of these marketing oncosts can be regarded as fixed. The annual cost of the internal sales organization, the field sales force and that part of the advertising that has been booked and cannot be cancelled may be regarded as fixed for the year.

Different types of products and services can be represented by varying the cost and profit components, as in exhibit 1.5.

This concept can be applied to a new or existing product. A new product entering the market is illustrated in exhibit 1.6. Costs have been incurred in setting up the production and marketing activities, and start to be recovered as sales are achieved.

Where considerable investment in capital equipment and research and development is required before the product can be produced, let alone launched on the market, the position is dramatically different. As soon as the product is ready for the market, distribution costs are incurred; also, to stimulate interest in the

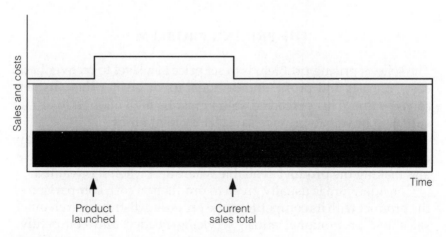

Exhibit 1.6 A new product entering the market

11

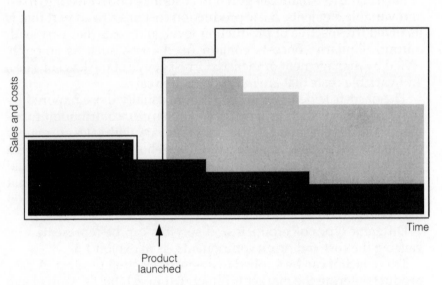

Exhibit 1.7   A new product with heavy pre-launch investment

product, it is offered at a discounted price. Sales eventually generate profit. The position is shown in exhibit 1.7.

Sometimes, a product is developed, manufactured and put on the market at a price that is higher than the market will pay, as illustrated in exhibit 1.8. The solid and shaded areas represent a dead loss to the company.

THE PRICING PROBLEM

The seller's pricing problem is to set price at a level to recover basic costs, oncosts and profit, and be equal to, or greater than, its perceived value. This perceived value must be high enough to attract sufficient buyers to provide satisfactory total profit.

Basic costs contribute to the perceived value in a material way; oncosts contribute by informing and educating potential customers, and making the product available where and when it is wanted.

Consideration is usually given to production cost, comparison of the product with its competitors, the proposed distribution channel, sales and promotional effort, servicing needed and competitive prices.

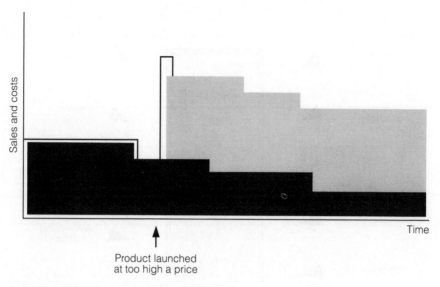

Exhibit 1.8 A loss-making new product

All these could be described as passive reflections. They do not assess and exploit the specific aspects the seller could develop in basic production costs, specific oncosts, or the profit component, to create a competitive advantage in total price.

The three components of price, illustrated in exhibit 1.4, are multifaceted and subject to many influences. The impact of some of these, such as suppliers of raw materials, product formulation and local rates and taxes, is mainly restricted to one of the price components. Others can have an impact on different aspects of the three components.

Some are internal and may be controlled, but the majority are external and the seller can only influence them to intensify or moderate their impact. The total competitive environment in which a price for a product or service has to be set is illustrated in exhibit 1.9. The various conflicts and pressures that affect the pricing activity are discussed below.

PRODUCT POLICY

Decisions on products, especially on product formulation and production methods to be used, should not be made without some

13

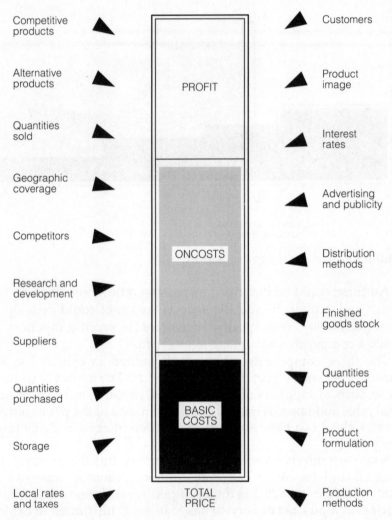

Exhibit 1.9 The competitive environment

consideration of price. While this does not mean that every product must immediately yield a profit, the long-run profitability of a company is directly related to the ability of its management to price wisely.

Improvements in modern production methods concurrent with the opening up of markets have created many more opportunities, and perhaps a greater need, for securing a competitive advantage at the production stage.

Technology has escalated exponentially, productive capacity increased, labour content declined (although its costs are a higher proportion of total costs), import barriers have been eroded, and markets, such as the European Common Market, have united to form large, powerful buying and selling alliances.

The specific price set for a product should establish its quality in the minds of customers and contribute to its position in the market.

A price that is high, because of the high added value in its production, usually enables a company to differentiate the product from competitive offers. It should follow that the greater the added value of a product, the less that price is important. If so, the significance of price would be inversely proportional to its distance from being a primary product. This implies that the nearer a product is to its basic raw material, the more crucial is price in the buying decision; conversely, the further it is removed from that basic raw material, the more the added value, the greater the potential product differentiation, and price is less important in the buying decision.

Such is the rate of technological innovation that new products with ever-increasing sophistication are entering the market more frequently, each outperforming earlier models with dramatic effects.

In such a highly competitive market, with product differentiation having limited consequence, a company may be forced to adopt a low price. In the basic cost component every attribute has to be evaluated in terms of cost to produce and importance to the potential buyer.

Pricing of these products has assumed critical proportions, often dictating the difference between success and failure. The large investments necessary for research and development of new hi-tech products cannot simply be written off; neither can they necessarily be recovered in the price of the resulting products. An overall pricing policy has to be adopted that will provide adequate funds for such development without, at the same time, inviting competition too quickly because of high profits.

THE BASIC COST COMPONENT

The amount of cost in the price often assumes major influence. It is almost too logical to ask: 'What does it cost? What profit should we make? How much do we need to sell it for?' The result is the price. Pricing at levels near to cost is easy; all the costs and expenses are known and an acceptable profit figure can be added.

A much more difficult question to answer is: 'What will the buyer pay for the product?' Yet this approach offers greater advantages to the company *and the customer.* If costs are to influence price, it is more realistic to argue that market price – what the buyer will pay – *less* sales and distribution costs, *less* admin costs, *less* production costs, establishes the profit figure. This strategy stresses profit as the objective and emphasizes that no product will be produced unless the price is equal to total costs and profit.

There is no guarantee that potential buyers will pay what it costs to make a product, and many products cease to be produced or are not marketed at all, because the market sets a value on them lower than their cost of production and distribution. From these comments, it should be clear that costs should not be the overall determinant of price.

SUPPLIERS

While there is usually active competition among suppliers to sell materials and components at attractive prices and terms, the opposite is sometimes experienced. Suppliers are occasionally in a position to wield considerable bargaining power by restricting supplies, raising prices, or offering a lower quality.

Lowering of quality is typical in those industries where the product is secondary to the supplier's main product, or improved supplier processing or manufacturing methods reduce the quality of the secondary product.

Occasionally the cost of switching suppliers is a major factor. An example can be quoted from the chemical industry. A company was using an additive in powder form for one of its products. Over a period of five years the sole supplier of the powder had increased price more than could be reasonably expected from the rate of inflation. The customer company decided to use an alternative product which was in liquid form. This required the installation of new equipment for the addition of the liquid and monitoring the formulation. The cost of switching to the new supplier was greater than the increase in costs from the original supplier.

The power of suppliers is intensified if substitutes are not readily available, second sourcing is difficult, or the supplying industry is in the hands of a few dominant firms.

Another *supplier* that is universal to all companies is the supply of labour which, in general, is relatively immobile. Highly skilled labour, scarce labour and well organized labour can demand premium wages to increase a company's costs. In the UK during the late 1980s the South-East of England approached very nearly full employment. This greatly increased wage and salary levels of all grades of labour with the consequent effect on company costs.

Increases in costs have to be absorbed in manufacturing costs or passed on to the customer. If there is already a high degree of competition in the manufacturers' industry, the cost increases may mean lower profits.

QUANTITIES PURCHASED

In certain industries it is possible to keep costs at a lower level by placing contracts with suppliers, arranging forward orders, generally increasing the quantities placed with one supplier and maintaining stock so as to have fewer deliveries. Against this must be balanced the investment required in the stock and the cost of storing it.

A company's competitive advantage, enabling it to price lower than competitors, is sometimes the result of organizing purchases of materials and components at advantageous prices.

Similarly, producing in larger batches to achieve lower unit costs of manufacture can also give a company a competitive edge to pass some of the savings on to customers in the form of lower prices.

In addition to holding larger stocks of raw materials, a company can sometimes take advantage of the nature of its product and hold larger stocks of finished goods than those of its competitors. Much will depend on the cost of storage, the fashion element of the product and the conditions in which the finished goods are required to be stored.

LOCAL RATES AND TAXES

Local taxes, such as those levied on business premises, are beyond the direct control of companies, and vary with geographic location and the extent and quality of local services provided.

In the 1990s the UK changed from local authority rating assessments to a central government business rating scheme. The consequent reapportionment of local tax was felt most in the South-East of England, despite the fact that its effects were spread over several years. Retail businesses were particularly hard hit with the considerable increase in their basic operating costs; either prices had to be increased, or profits reduced.

RESEARCH AND DEVELOPMENT

Many products are the result of, or are improved by, research and development. Some require such a high level of investment that it is not possible for one company alone to fund it. Companies sometimes combine their resources and share the costs and benefits or reduce their departments to a size sufficient to carry out essential development work and support an appropriate department at a university. Some very costly ventures, such as aircraft manufacture, space exploitation and nuclear projects, can only be developed if countries combine their resources.

Apart from these notable exceptions, many companies conduct their own R&D, but the investment needed to produce some products, particularly pharmaceuticals, is so great that, to include the cost of their research and development in the price would be impracticable. The usual method is for the board to agree an annual budget for the company's R&D, and the oncost component of each product contains a percentage contribution to the budget.

DISTRIBUTION METHODS

The channel used to distribute products will influence price. The nearer a supplier gets to the ultimate user, the greater the control over marketing and selling activities, but the more costly is the method, because the supplier has to carry out more of the intermediate functions.

There are two main ways to get products to users: direct to the user, or through one or more intermediaries. For consumer products, typically, there are two intermediaries: wholesalers and retailers. For industrial products, sales are either direct to the user, or through one intermediary.

Whichever distribution methods are used, the well-established company has the advantage of market coverage and, if aggressive, market penetration.

Distribution costs, unlike production costs, do not decline with increased scale of operations, but tend to be in proportion to the geographical area served.

THE SINGLE EUROPEAN MARKET

With the enlarged single market in Europe, costs of increased distribution facilities for the markets at a greater distance from production points must be taken into consideration during the pricing process. The customer in Birmingham will expect to pay a similar price for a product whether manufactured in Manchester, Madrid or Milan. Greater differential pricing for the same products will undoubtedly develop as a result of the distance of markets from production, but pricing will also reflect how much the frontier controls between Community members are dismantled.

The postponement of signing the Schengen pact by France, West Germany, Belgium, Holland and Luxembourg in December 1989 threw a shadow on an internal market without frontiers. The pact was to have been the first stage in the removal of controls and abolition of frontier barriers. With the unexpected breaching of the Berlin Wall in late 1989, democracy spreading in Eastern Europe and the realization of what a lack of frontier controls would really mean to each of the countries, their representatives agreed to wait.

If the five, with all their experience of co-operation in finance, trade, transportation, legal requirements and law enforcement cannot readily agree, the prospects for a truly single market look bleak, and throw an even greater burden on the pricing executive.

Pricing of products for Europe must take into consideration relative life-styles and therefore attractiveness of a product, prices of similar, locally produced goods and, where appropriate, climate. Price will need to reflect comparative material and labour costs, distribution and marketing costs, distance from manufacturing source and cost of transportation and warehousing, local taxes and not the least, costs of frontier delays.

(In January 1990, according to the Commission's report on barriers to trade, approximately 25 per cent of company profits on shipments are eroded by costs and delays of frontier formalities.)

An aspect of the so-called single market that has direct effect on price, and which might be described as a local tax, is value-added tax. In the early 1990s rates range from a low 12 per cent in Luxembourg and Spain to a high 25 per cent in Ireland, and therefore vary too widely for a single market. Contrary to what was expected, rates will not be equalized in 1992, and finance ministers have agreed to postpone until 1996, at the earliest, a fraud-proof VAT procedure.

One could conjecture that sub-markets of groups with similar VAT rates might develop: Britain, West Germany, Luxembourg and Spain; Belgium, France, Holland and Italy; Ireland and Denmark. This would leave Greece and Portugal to associate with either of the first two groups.

PROMOTIONAL POLICY AND PRICING

The price of a product must include an amount to cover its promotion because, in the long run, all promotional funds must come from sales. With a new product, when entering a new market or one in which competition has a strong hold, funds are usually specially allocated to promote it. This substantially increases the size of the marketing component in unit price.

When constructing promotional policy, a clear distinction should be made between short-run and long-run promotional needs. In the short-run, such needs are likely to be greater than keen pricing would allow. Even with established products, especially in highly competitive situations, it is not always possible to generate sufficient revenue to provide for adequate promotional funding. Thus, the overall pricing policy must be constructed to accommodate products with particular promotional needs.

Whether it is a small company entering a new market, or a large company expanding its operations, a *critical mass* has to be reached before everything starts to work and profits are generated.

Strictly speaking, critical mass refers to a body of fissionable material, such as uranium 235, large enough to sustain a nuclear chain reaction. The analogy, as used in marketing, indicates the level and size of activities that have to be reached before customers buy the product, money starts to come in, and profits begin to be generated. A minimum input of sales and marketing effort, especially advertising and promotion, is required before the messages cross the *perception threshold* of potential customers, gain attention and have impact.

The critical mass is not an absolute measurement but relative to the size of company and the particular operation. With a small outfit, critical mass can often be reached fairly quickly. In a large organization, despite the pressures it can exert with aggressive pricing and promotion, it takes time for decisions, actions and implementation to ripple through its structure before a foothold can be gained in the market. Meanwhile, costs continue to mount and outrun profits, as illustrated in exhibit 1.7. Price is an important factor in the critical mass equation.

MARKET COVERAGE

With some exceptions, notably steel, glass, motor car and furniture manufacture, the market is often related to geographic area. The greater the market coverage, and therefore the larger the geographic area, the larger the total marketing and distribution requirement. It is seldom advisable, even if financially possible, to cover 100 per cent of the market from the word go. Market coverage should be large enough for adequate sales to be generated, and small enough to be manageable by the company. The sales level must be sufficient for the unit marketing component in price not to reduce the profit component to an unacceptable amount.

For the marketing of consumer products, especially frequently purchased goods, it is often necessary to have close to 100 per cent market coverage. In a compact market such as the UK, with many different distribution channels available, cost-effective market coverage is possible; in continental Europe and further afield, distance is an important consideration. France, for example, with a slightly smaller population than the UK, has over two and a half times its land area.

DISTRIBUTION POLICY AND PRICING

Marketing is often simplified to mean getting the right goods, at the right price, in the right place and at the right time.

Provided that your product is not a highly perishable food, customers are unlikely to complain if it is available before they wish to buy it; however, if you are late getting it to the market your sales are liable to be affected. Distribution is vital in marketing; products must be made available at convenient outlets for customers to buy them; if not, sales will be zero.

Customers are not always able to buy products which exactly fit their needs; compromises have to be made for price, size, colour, quality, performance etc. Quality may be acceptable but price more than they wish to pay. Price may be acceptable, but they have to compromise with performance, or colour, or size, or whatever.

If the product is not there, no compromise can be made: there will be no sales. No amount of advertising will overcome the lethargy of inept distributors or inadequate distribution.

Finding and maintaining the services of competent distributors and middlemen, who are able to market aggressively, costs money. Adequate compensation for their labours in holding stocks and distributing the products must be included in the price.

Whereas the costs of product improvements, introductory or special promotional and selling efforts can often be borne by other products, or charged to contingency reserves, distributors expect to receive their earnings immediately. This earnings figure in the distribution component must match the margins and discounts that distributors receive from competitive suppliers; it is a major consideration in the construction of price.

THE ENVIRONMENT

A company is not a closed system, but open to the environment, which contains a multitude of factors that have an impact on prices. Before a price is decided for a product, it should be positioned in the market relative to its main competitors, and considered in the four main aspects of the environment. These are: political, economic, technological and social. This is explored in more detail in chapter 6.

CUSTOMERS

The influence of a product's perceived value on customers is probably the most important factor in the price/sales equation. The ability to satisfy a want – a product's utility – determines this value, and should be considered from the product planning stage. The degree of satisfaction provided by a product can be enhanced in three ways:

- by giving the product more utility;
- by educating the buyer on the value of its utility;

- by adjusting price to fit the product's existing utility.

Utility may be estimated by carrying out market surveys with potential buyers; putting the product on sale in a test market situation; or by making estimates within the company. This third possibility is often responsible for flaws in pricing because subjective judgments are too readily influenced by extraneous points.

The value of technical products can sometimes be determined more objectively by measuring the savings made by a product's use, and then capitalizing these savings at an acceptable rate of interest.

Unfortunately, personal judgment can distort what is otherwise a sound approach to setting a price as the following account typifies. A company with world-wide sales and services has a division that manufactures air-compressors. For their 1989 range, they had developed an improved compressor. Although almost identical to an existing model it provided a considerable increase in air. When the time came to make a final decision on price, the chairman overruled his marketing committee. He asked for the percentage improvement in air delivered. On being told that it was 12½ per cent, he instructed his executives to price it at 12½ per cent higher than the comparable model. From the customer's viewpoint, the new compressor offers no additional benefit whatsoever.

COMPETITORS

If marketing is war these days, competitors are the enemy. Competitors can indirectly influence price by developing improved product formulation or production methods, competing for scarce raw materials and components, by securing strong links with suppliers.

They can directly influence price in two main ways: their own pricing structure, and their marketing activities. Their prices can usually be discovered by normal business activities, and it is possible to determine the amount of money devoted to 'above the line' publicity from published statistics. What is not so readily discovered is the amount spent on 'below the line' promotions.

Assuming your company has four competitors, the position could be as in exhibit 1.10. Competitors *A* and *B* have a lower price, *D*'s price is higher and *C*'s is the same. Obviously, it would be necessary to take into consideration the relative qualities of the products and establish their sales turnovers. In a normally price-sensitive market, turnover figures could be expected to be in proportion to perceived value and price.

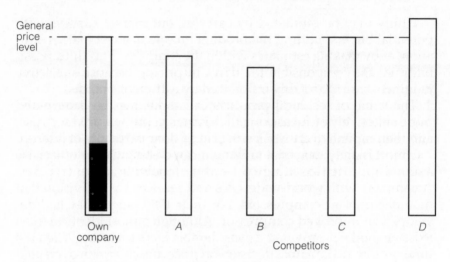

Exhibit 1.10 Competitors with different prices

If your company desires to be more competitive, it is not simply a question of reducing price, but competing on cost, marketing expenses, profit, or volume of sales. Any combination of these might account for a competitor's lower price.

If all are obliged to use a similar production process, then the size of the cost component is likely to be the same for each. If processes can be varied, or economies of scale operate, the cost component may be an important reason for the lower price of *A* and *B*.

An appraisal of competitor marketing and advertising activities, especially the support they provide and receive in the distribution channels, could indicate that less is spent more effectively, or that a particular product image has been developed.

An inspection of annual returns might disclose general profit margins but, with a multi-product company, this line of investigation is unlikely to yield specific information useful for pricing purposes.

If your company were simply to reduce price without an appraisal of competitors it might succeed only in depressing profits. Attention and action may be needed on aspects of the cost or marketing component of price.

A company may stimulate competition by setting a high price, or discourage it with a low one. If the product is difficult to manufacture, or requires special knowledge, skills or equipment to make it, then a low price will not invite competitors to enter the market. If a high price is set, then it may be worthwhile for other manufacturers to produce a competitive product.

COMPETITIVE PRODUCTS

Probably the greatest competition and impact on price is from identical, or similar products. The many different brands of beer, chocolate, cigarettes, computers, motor cars, kitchen furniture, bathroom suites, fork-lift trucks and hydraulic presses are in direct competition with every other member of their particular group.

Often it is difficult for potential buyers to distinguish between one product and another. Where this differentiation is very small, the pressure on price becomes very high.

ALTERNATIVE PRODUCTS

Few products are unique in the sense that they and only they can provide comparable satisfaction. Trains, buses, airplanes and cars are alternative methods of transport over many routes. Where it is necessary to cross water, the alternative products are airplanes, ships, hovercraft and jet-foils.

The impact on price made by alternative products is exerted by the manufacturers or providers of alternative products and services. By the design and function of their products, the investment made in marketing, advertising and selling them, and their price, pressure is applied to the price of alternative products.

This can probably best be appreciated with the prices of consumer foods. If oven-ready chickens are heavily promoted and aggressively priced, this creates a considerable pressure on the price of other meats. If the promotion is sustained over a period of time, it will cause the prices of other meats to fall. It is only the fact that people get hungry and buy food every day that mitigates the alternative product price effect.

If the product is one that is not purchased very often, such as an exotic foreign holiday, a suite of furniture, a motor car, or new machinery for the factory, the prices of alternative products and services will have a much greater pressure on prices.

PRICE AND PROFIT

Price and profit are linked. The higher the price, the greater the profit; the lower the price the lower the profit. This dichotomy confronts those who have to recommend or set a price for a product or service.

A higher price may achieve less sales, but greater unit profit.

A lower price may achieve more sales but smaller unit profit.

The problem to be tackled is the relationship between unit price and the number of units sold. A company stays in business because it makes profits. While unit profit is important in pricing decisions, it is *total profit* that determines whether or not a company stays in existence, not high unit profit. A balance must be sought between the unit price selected and likely sales, as will be discussed in later chapters.

INTEREST RATES

The rate of return on investment in a product should be compared with interest rates in the free market. The greater amount of work involved in manufacturing and marketing products requires that this rate of return is considerably higher than prevailing interest rates.

Despite this proviso, rate of return often exercises undue influence on price and is related to total cost of making and marketing. A company that relies heavily on costs as a basis for setting prices routinely adds a percentage to cover profit. Their starting point is usually *the company's 'normal' rate of return*. Such a method ignores market forces and competition on the components of price.

Occasionally it is necessary for a company to adopt an investment budget for the marketing of a product as indicated in exhibit 1.7. This is particularly appropriate for a new product in hi-tech industries, extending market coverage with an existing product, or when faced with particularly strong competition. Winning new or virgin market share cannot be done on the cheap, and little or no profit may be enjoyed for a period of several years.

THE INFLUENCE OF THE SALES MIX

Although control and considerable flexibility can be exercised over the product mix and costings, what cannot be controlled is the sales mix. You cannot control what the market will buy; you can only influence it.

Exhibit 1.11 Company sales and profits for three years

	Sales (£)	Percentage change in sales	Profit (£)	(%)	Percentage change in profit
1986	1,180,730		113,198	9.6%	
1987	1,226,580	+3.9%	111,665	9.1%	−1.4%
1988	1,274,380	+3.9%	108,794	8.5%	−2.6%

To a certain extent this influence can be exerted by advertising, promotion and general selling pressure, but the greatest influence is pricing. Sales figures must be continuously monitored so that prices can be adjusted when it is necessary or desired to affect sales.

A company in South-West England that had started business in 1981 progressed rapidly in its first five years and gained an impressive share of the market. It then experienced three years of modest growth that failed to keep pace with inflation; but, more seriously, profits began to decline while sales increased. Their profits fell from 12 per cent in 1985 to just over 8 per cent in 1988. The situation for the last three years is shown in exhibit 1.11. Their product range had developed considerably and, by 1986, they listed nearly 500 different types and models.

The cause of the problem was the changing sales mix. However, with such a wide variety of products and complicated production processes, it was difficult to identify and isolate some of the costs. It was necessary to group the products into a number of convenient cost centres to analyse their figures. The analyses for the three years, in which the product groups have been edited for clarity of explanation, are illustrated in exhibits 1.12–1.14.

The company had started life by specializing in the products which form a substantial proportion of the first two product groups and, with a keen pricing strategy, had quickly penetrated the market and gained a good market share. This general pricing policy had not altered over the years, despite changing market trends.

Sales have increased every year, and over the last three years these two main product groups have provided 53, 58 and 64 per cent of total turnover.

For most of the products in these two groups a low-pricing strategy had been maintained, but pricing differentials with competitive products have widened such that the company's products are

Exhibit 1.12 Company sales and profit mix for first year

Product group	Sales (£)	Sales mix	Profit (£)	Profit (%)	Proportion of total profit
A	350,540	30%	17,527	5%	15%
B	275,000	23%	22,000	8%	19%
C	180,120	15%	18,012	10%	16%
D	150,220	13%	18,026	12%	16%
E	80,500	7%	11,270	14%	10%
F	75,650	6%	11,348	15%	10%
G	43,200	4%	8,640	20%	8%
H	25,500	2%	6,375	25%	6%
	1,180,730	100%	113,198	9.6%	100%

Exhibit 1.13 Company sales and profit mix for second year

Product group	Sales (£)	Sales mix	Profit (£)	Profit (%)	Proportion of total profit
A	425,670	35%	21,284	5%	19%
B	285,380	23%	22,830	8%	20%
C	178,000	14%	17,800	10%	16%
D	140,220	11%	16,826	12%	15%
E	68,000	6%	9,520	14%	9%
F	69,300	6%	10,395	15%	9%
G	39,860	3%	7,972	20%	7%
H	20,150	2%	5,038	25%	5%
	1,226,580	100%	111,665	9.1%	100%

Exhibit 1.14 Company sales and profit mix for third year

Product group	Sales (£)	Sales mix	Profit (£)	Profit (%)	Proportion of total profit
A	492,560	39%	24,628	5%	23%
B	314,770	25%	25,182	8%	23%
C	190,440	15%	19,044	10%	18%
D	125,370	10%	15,044	12%	14%
E	62,480	5%	8,747	14%	8%
F	45,630	3%	6,845	15%	6%
G	29,570	2%	5,914	20%	5%
H	13,560	1%	3,390	25%	3%
	1,274,380	100%	108,794	8.5%	100%

now very keenly priced. They have a low profit yield of between 5 per cent and 8 per cent, but management had been content with the fact that the products in the two groups accounted for a large majority of the company's profit and was now nearly a half of the total.

The analysis indicated that the sales mix was being over-influenced by price. It was decided that this influence had to be changed from price to promotion.

Prices for most of the products in the first two groups had to be increased. The problem that then had to be resolved was the degree of sensitivity of the market to an increase in price. The increase had to be sufficient to provide greater profit, but not to affect sales too much. Some of the increase in profit was earmarked for increased advertising and selling effort for the products.

Subsequently the price increases did not greatly affect sales because of the relatively inelastic demand for the products. This aspect of pricing we look at in more detail later in the book.

SERVICE

Service covers before-sales, during-sales and after-sales activities. Whatever organization is involved, good service has to be recovered in the price. This applies to preparation of estimates, tenders and quotations, installing and commissioning of machinery and equipment, delivery, credit and leasing, training middlemen's employees, guarantees, warranties, repairs and maintenance.

Many products have little or no service element in their transactions. Sales of staple products and convenience goods, foodstuffs, everyday items, toiletries etc. require mostly a specialized form of before-sales service: window displays, store layout, island sites, testing facilities. Even so, this service has to be recovered in the price of the product.

The term 'free service' is a misnomer, since someone has to pay for the service carried out, and failure to recover servicing costs by an adequate pricing policy will adversely affect profits.

Over a period of time, costs of servicing will average out, enabling an oncost to be inserted into the price structure, but early in a product's life – especially with complex or hi-tech products – servicing costs are likely to be considerably higher than the long-term average. This higher-than-average cost of servicing must be considered in the overall pricing and servicing policies.

Most companies regard the service aspect in price as two problems: 'Should it be provided *free*?' 'Should a separate scale of charges be levied?' In the former case, the cost is normally recovered in the price of the product. With the latter, the company has to construct a separate pricing policy for servicing, and must decide whether, for marketing purposes, it is better to follow a high-price or low-price policy.

PRICING OBJECTIVES

Once the company's overall pricing policy and general strategy have been formulated, formally or otherwise, attention can be given to the establishment of pricing objectives. If a strategy is established without subsequent clearly defined objectives, only confusion will result, and possibly the development of practices that run counter to the interests of the company.

Objectives should be described in terms of the results to be achieved in a given time period. In addition, they have three essential requirements: they must be understandable, measurable and achievable.

A number of dangers await the unwary in the setting of pricing objectives. They can be too general, liable to conflict with one another, over-ambitious, or ignore competition.

Here is a suggested list of aims that need to be quantified and timed to be acceptable as objectives:

- maximum long-term profits;
- maximum short-term profits;
- increased annual profits;
- company growth;
- consolidation of market share;
- maintenance of price leadership;
- continued support of middlemen;
- avoidance of increased union demands;
- maintenance of company image;
- dissuading new competitors from entering the market.

The first aim, maximum long-term profits, is often seen in company policy statements. When challenged as to what it means, a reply is sometimes received that restates the 'objective' in different words. 'Long-term' is said to be up to about five years or so; 'profits' are those shown in the annual revenue accounts; 'maximum' – 'Well, this is as much as we can get'!

Consider the third aim: increased annual profits. If the company made say, £2 million profit last year, the objective would be achieved if they made £2,000,050 profit this year. Whoever constructed the objective is unlikely to agree. Words such as 'maximum' and 'optimum' are often used unwittingly, and serve only to confuse. Where possible, the actual level of achievement should be quantified.

Objectives will vary from company to company, but they must relate to the company's financial resources, its position in the market and, above all, be realistic.

CARELESS PRICING

Occasionally an anomalous situation develops because company management is guilty of pricing without due care and attention.

During a consultancy session in 1989 with a company that manufactures a range of office machines and equipment, I reviewed their pricing policy. One section stated that they will sell to wholesalers, dealers and users at appropriate prices for the three types of customer. Another section stated that they will grant quantity discounts to any customer.

The price lists are prepared by the sales department and agreed with the appropriate division. In their *User Price List*, a machine is priced at a basic £850. If ten or more units are ordered, unit price is £750; orders for 25 and up are at £700.

On the face of it, this looks reasonable enough. An order for ten units would attract a discount of nearly 12 per cent (£100 off £850). An order for 25 units, just over 17½ per cent (£150 off £850). In practice, the situation is quite different. Consider exhibit 1.15.

To purchase nine machines, a customer pays a total of £7,650; ten machines cost £7,500 – *£150 less!* In effect, this means that a customer who buys nine machines can have another one free, *plus* £150. Similarly, 25 machines cost less than 24 machines. The company had not constructed the price list with this intention, but after this eccentricity was pointed out they used it as an advertising ploy.

This is not an isolated case. Companies are often guilty of constructing price lists that have similarly embarrassing overlaps.

The problem can be avoided by extending the price list at the price change points and estimating the value to the customer of buying an extra one, or unit quantity, to obtain a price advantage.

31

Exhibit 1.15 Careless pricing

No. of machines ordered	Unit price (£)	Total (£)
1	850	850
9	850	7,650
10	750	7,500
.	.	.
.	.	.
.	.	.
24	750	18,000
25	700	17,500

SHORT-TERM PRICING OBJECTIVES

Short-term pricing objectives are the tactical weapons used in specific situations, individual products or product groups, and in unique market segments.

Short-term pricing objectives may relate to volume sales, turnover, profit, market coverage, number of orders, or number of new customers which can be achieved in a relatively short period of time. Again, the term is largely relative and must take into consideration the nature of the product and buying habits.

LONG-TERM PRICING OBJECTIVES

Where the company intends to be in the future pricing league cannot be meaningfully expressed in objective terms. It could extend over many years, and is associated with the company's total marketing efforts. A long-term pricing aim depends on the nature of the product, the industry in which the company is operating, and short-term objectives.

A long-term pricing objective – that is, one couched in specific results – can be a constraint and lead to a situation where pricing efficiency is forfeited by over-pricing to meet goals, or under-pricing when the goal has been achieved. Long-term pricing objectives ignore short-term market responses.

The long-term pricing aim most often quoted is 'maximization of profit', but this fails to supply the pricing executive with a realistic market-related guidance system or an indication of short-term objectives, let alone the tools to structure a price. Any attempt at profit maximization in the short-term attracts competitors into the market, with the inevitable impact on market shares of all.

32

A better long-term pricing aim is the range of percentage returns that would be acceptable. Using the profit percentages achieved for appropriate products over the past three or four years as a guide, a percentage range that represents good performance is set as the general aim. Thus, the goal would be measurable, realistic and attainable, because similar rates have already been attained.

While this aim is more practical than 'maximization of profit', it is not so easy to implement in a multi-product company. Direct costs of production, and many sales, administrative and other expenses, can be accurately apportioned, but general overheads and common costs are usually allocated arbitrarily. This subjective allocation distorts the real figures and leaves the company inadequately prepared for countermeasures against aggressive competitors who use more flexible pricing procedures.

Provided a company has flexible procedures to combat declining sales or a price attack, using percentage rate of return as a basis for pricing is a simple method to implement. What tends to militate against its use is that it ignores the profit that might have been achieved if the resulting price is below what the market would accept. At best, it is a guide and not a determinant of action.

More realistic long-term pricing goals are statements of market positions. The reader may like to consider the following as some that are currently adopted by companies operating in Europe:

* Become the lowest priced supplier of a product.
* Create the widest price range of products.
* Maximize penetration of a named market.
* Create price leadership in the industry.
* Position the company in a specific market segment.
* Obtain a specific share of a market.

PRICING FOR PROFIT

The price level selected has important, often critical, impact on a company's fortunes and future abilities. The situation may be summarized:

To the extent that executives price unwisely, they decrease profits and tend to increase the dissatisfaction of customers.

It is easy to see how unwise pricing can adversely affect profits. If the price is too low, the company makes a low profit and might even incur a loss if unforeseen circumstances arise. If the price is too high, insufficient volume will be purchased to provide adequate profit.

It is easy to see why too high a price can dissatisfy customers, but it may not be so readily apparent why too low a price should cause dissatisfaction. However, the experience of an early entrant into the video-recorder market will illustrate this.

The company had achieved a technical and production advantage over its competitors and was first in the market with the video-recorder. When the executives priced the product which was marketed through appointed stockists, they attempted to penetrate the market fairly quickly with a cost-price approach, and set a low price.

Sales were disappointing and much lower than had been estimated because, at that time, the consumer market was not ready for the VCR. Although the price was very keen, this fact did not stimulate sales.

In the oncost component was an amount to cover the costs of the number of returns thought likely to occur from early faults; this had been estimated at approximately 5 per cent. Subsequently the percentage faults reached nearly 40 per cent, and the amount allowed for repairs and adjustments under the guarantee was woefully inadequate. So inadequate, in fact, that the company was unable to provide a fast enough service; in many areas they were embarrassed by the high numbers of returns and calls for assistance. This poor back-up service was so deficient that a great degree of dissatisfaction for the product was created in the market. This dissatisfaction lingered for some years afterwards, not only for the early VCRs, but for other products of the company. Special efforts were subsequently required to restore the quality and image of their service to its former standing.

The company should have adopted a high price and concentrated on a small market segment for whom the acquisition of a video-recorder would be an important addition to their facilities: this was the education and training market. At that time universities, colleges and business training establishments had ample funds available for such aids. It should be added that this advice was given to the company but they chose to ignore it.

2

Practical pricing theory

THEORY AND PRACTICE

In this chapter we look at some of the theoretical explanations of what is happening in pricing situations and consider how these can be used in a practical way.

There is a tendency to think that theoretical descriptions are different from what happens in practice. Theory and practice are manifestations of the same thing, rather like thunder and lightning, which are the sound and sight of the same electrical discharge – we see it first and hear it later. The reason for having theory is to explain something that happens too quickly, is not easy to demonstrate, is too small to be observed, or is invisible. If it's right in theory, it's right in practice.

If it's 'right' in theory but 'wrong' in practice, it wasn't theory we had, but hypothesis.

THEORY IN PRICING

All the following analyses are at an elementary level but the tables and explanations should be read carefully and certainly not in one sitting. They should be worked through so that the principles are understood.

An understanding of the theoretical explanations will be of assistance to those responsible for setting prices. Pricing theory establishes the underlying framework in which decisions should be made, and will help executives avoid hazards that might not otherwise be apparent.

Price has two main considerations: long-term market price, where the price stays acceptably above the costs of production and marketing; and spot price, the short-term price at which products change hands between supplier and seller. Exhibits 1.2 and 1.3 in chapter 1 illustrated long-term price; exhibits 1.4, 1.5 and 1.9 referred to spot price.

LONG-TERM MARKET PRICE

Long-term price in a free market is based on an analysis of supply and demand. Supply is maintained or increased by suppliers as long as profits are received, and continued until profits decline towards zero. Usually supply is stopped well before zero profits are reached, but at times it is continued even with losses being incurred, because the supplier has reasons other than profit for staying in the market.

Long-term price also assumes that buyers will continue to purchase as long as they obtain satisfaction from the products. They may be using their purchases, incorporating them into other products, or reselling them. When the satisfaction received, or profits made by their use, falls below a certain limit, customers will cease to buy.

Long-term price for products tend to fall towards their cost of production.

SPOT PRICE

Spot price is also 'market price': it is the price paid in the short-term and may be unrelated to the cost of production. Short-run price correlates with the ease and speed with which additional supplies can be made available to buyers. Supply of some products is seasonal, and some, such as agricultural crops, have the additional disadvantage of being subject to adverse climatic conditions.

If the current season's output of, say, cereals, is less than demand for it, price will be well above costs of production. Such a situation might encourage farmers to produce more cereals the following year, and, if similar conditions prevailed, even greater acreage would be put down to cereals in the following years. (All this assumes freedom from restrictions of an imposed agricultural policy.)

Spot price is the particular price paid at any one time for the cereals; long-term market price is established over a period as equilibrium becomes established between supply and demand. Whenever this equilibrium is disturbed, such as in a year with a poor harvest, spot price will vary from long-term market price.

Excess of supply over current demand depresses spot price, and, if the supply is greatly in excess of demand, spot price could be below cost of production. Suppliers experiencing such adverse conditions may decide to reduce production substantially the following season and use the land for other purposes. There would thus be a tendency for equilibrium to be established in the subsequent years as supplies are equated to demand.

As we saw in chapter 1, the purpose of setting a price is to achieve sales and profit. Sales take place at prices that result from the interaction of supply and demand. To understand how this works, we consider the two economic forces, supply and demand.

DEMAND

Demand for a product is realistic only if a price has been explicitly stated, or implied. Demand cannot be estimated in the absence of price. In those meetings where executives sit for hours considering the likely sales of a new product, if no price has been mentioned, their discussions are academic. Without even a provisional price, they cannot talk realistically about a product's demand; *potential demand* perhaps, but not demand.

Demand is the total quantity that will be purchased at a given price level. Consider exhibit 2.1. Estimates have been made of the quantities likely to be sold at two different prices: 800,000 at £6, and 600,000 at £7.

Exhibit 2.1 is a *demand schedule*. Demand schedules are useful when considering likely prices for a new product or price changes for existing products.

Half of this demand schedule might be factual: the company has actually sold 800,000 at £6, and an estimate made that they would sell 600,000 at £7. They might also consider how many they would sell if price were increased to £6.25 or £6.50

Exhibit 2.1 Demand for a product

Price (£)	Quantity demanded (000)
6	800
7	600

DEMAND CURVES

A graph of a demand schedule is a *demand curve*, but before we draw the demand curve of the exhibit 2.1 schedule, let's look at the theoretical extension of our argument. Consider the general condition that, at a price of P_1, quantity Q_1 is purchased.

If price is reduced to P_2 a higher quantity Q_2 is purchased. Conversely, if a company's price is P_2, a price increase to P_1 would change the position from P_2Q_2 to P_1Q_1, as illustrated in exhibit 2.2.

Obviously this is theoretical: you cannot sell the products at one price then take them all back and offer them at a different price to the same people to see how many they would buy!

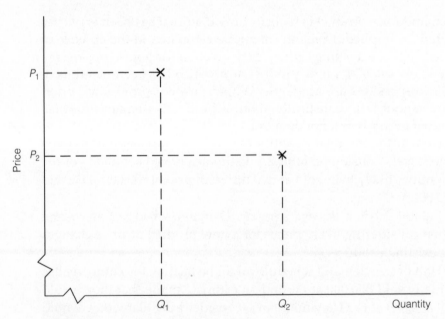

Exhibit 2.2 Demand at different prices

38

To test likely demand in practice, a product is put on sale in different parts of the country at different prices over the same time period. This measures the quantities purchased at different prices but, as the test is conducted in different parts of the country, the conclusions are not wholly reliable.

It is only possible to carry out such a test with certain categories of goods, such as fast moving consumer goods (FMCG) – chocolate bars, soap powders, biscuits etc., because of the high frequency of repeat purchase. It is not so easy with cars, furniture, personal computers, electric drills etc., which are bought infrequently or once only.

The two test market areas must be sufficiently distant from one another to avoid any overlapping of customers, or information about the product's price in one area being known in the other.

When selling more costly products, particularly capital goods, you cannot 'test' the market at different prices; you have one chance to get the price right, or you don't get the order.

The demand curve is also theoretical because we make an assumption. We plot the coordinates P_1Q_1 and P_2Q_2, and join them to obtain a *demand curve*. This indicates the quantities *likely to be sold at all points between the two coordinates*.

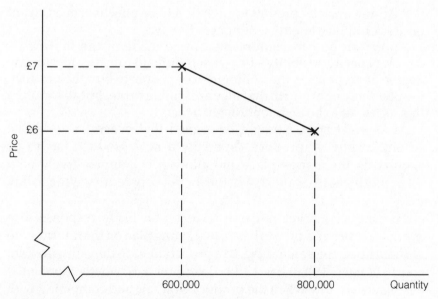

Exhibit 2.3 Demand curve of demand schedule in exhibit 2.1

In exhibit 2.2 a straight line could join the two coordinates; it could well be a curved line. If there were more coordinates, the demand curve might be estimated more 'accurately'. But, apart from actual records of sales at given prices, *all other coordinates are estimates.* Without additional data, to join two coordinates in anything other than a straight line is purely conjectural.

While a demand curve is an acceptable explanation of what can happen in the market-place, there are practical difficulties in observing it. In effect, it illustrates graphically all the different sales of a product *at different prices to the same group of customers at the same time!*

Exhibit 2.3 has the coordinates of the exhibit 2.1 demand schedule joined to indicate the quantities that might be sold at prices between £6 and £7.

EFFECTIVE DEMAND

For effective demand to take place, three requirements are necessary:

- a need, want, or desire for the product by potential customers;
- the ability to buy the product, i.e. by possessing sufficient money or access to funds or credit;
- a willingness to buy.

All three must be present for demand to be effective: need (want or desire), ability to pay, willingness to buy.

Appraisals and measurements can be made of the first two – degree of need and ability – but what is difficult to estimate with any degree of accuracy is the willingness of people to buy the product. Responders might affirm that they are willing to buy but all too often this turns out to be an intention not a fact.

At *the right price*, it might be argued that everyone would be willing to buy. A product, especially a new product, has to be exposed in the market-place and allowed to compete freely with other products, to establish whether or not people are willing to buy it.

To conduct market research to ascertain likely response to a product's price and then to base a marketing plan on the information without applying some subjective probabilities to the estimates is to court disaster. What has to be determined is whether potential customers *will* buy when the product is on sale and competing with every other product.

One possibility is *test marketing* – putting the product on sale in a restricted geographical area for a short period. However, the weights of the various factors of marketing must be kept in proportion to size of the area; in particular, distribution and promotion must not be exaggerated. It is sometimes difficult to restrain the enthusiasm of executives keen to test a product's acceptability. If the test is distorted by, say, a special introductory price offer, heavier-than-normal advertising, or distinctive promotion, any marketing plans based on the results are speculative.

SUPPLY CURVES

A supply schedule is constructed in a similar manner to a demand schedule. It indicates the quantities of a product that suppliers are prepared to offer for sale at different market prices. Consider the supply schedule in exhibit 2.4.

Exhibit 2.4   Supply schedule

Price (£)	Supplies available (000)
6	550
7	750

The quantities that suppliers are prepared to offer at particular prices are, understandably, greater than the quantities that buyers are prepared to buy. Compare exhibits 2.1 and 2.4: at a price of £6, buyers are prepared to buy 800,000 units, whereas suppliers are willing to supply 550,000. At a price of £7, buyers are prepared to buy only 600,000, but suppliers are willing to supply 750,000.

In exhibit 2.5, the two coordinates for supply are inserted on the graph of the demand curve and joined by a straight line. Where the supply and demand curves intersect is the equilibrium point; it represents the quantity that suppliers are prepared to supply and buyers are prepared to buy, *at that price*. As you can see, it is about £6.50 and, at this price, approximately 700,000 will be purchased.

WHAT DETERMINES DEMAND?

The demand curves in exhibits 2.2 and 2.3 focus on the price of the product and how sales rise or fall with price variations. As price

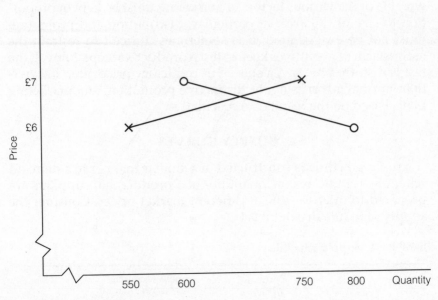

Exhibit 2.5 Supply and demand curves

increases or decreases, so the quantity demanded extends or contracts *along the demand curve*.

Demand for a product is determined by price, a major determinant, but there are other factors. The number of potential buyers will
affect demand: a small geographic area will have less potential
demand than a large one. The incomes and wealth of potential
buyers influence demand; availability of substitute products influence demand; an increase or decrease in promotion also affects
sales.

All the factors are called *determinants of demand*, but those other
than price are termed *conditions of demand*.

A change in price causes movement along the demand curve –
upwards or downwards.

A change in anything other than price, that is, a change in any of
the *conditions of demand*, creates another demand curve to the right
or left of the original one.

If the company's area of operations is expanded, and the number
of potential customers thereby increased, this will create a new
demand curve to the right. If market coverage is reduced, with the

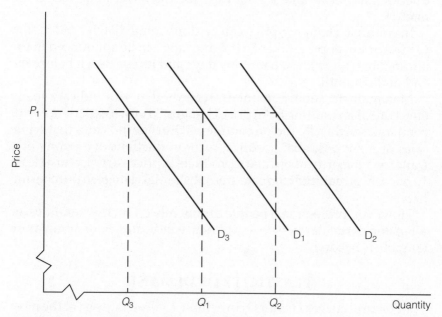

Exhibit 2.6 Changes in conditions of demand

subsequent reduction in potential customers, another demand curve to the left of the original will apply.

With price constant, a change in any of the conditions of demand will create an increase or decrease in demand, with new curves D_2 or D_3 to the right and left respectively of the original demand curve, D_1. This is illustrated in exhibit 2.6.

HOW DRASTIC IS THE CHANGE?

The size and type of change will affect sales. Sometimes a small change will have substantial impact on sales and profits; other times, a large change has very little impact.

Of the determinants of demand, the company can control price, product quality, advertising, promotion, size of served market, distribution, service etc.

Other determinants, such as wealth and income of buyers, prices of substitute products, availability of substitutes, taxation and currency rates, are beyond the company's power to alter.

Changing anything other than price, that is, any of the conditions of demand – promotion, advertising, distribution methods, or product quality – can take a long time for the effect to be felt in the market.

In contrast, changing price can be done immediately. A decision to raise or lower price taken in the morning can be announced in the afternoon, widely known in a few days and its effects felt before the end of the month.

Management should maintain records that will indicate likely effect on sales resulting from price changes. My own experience with companies in the UK and on continental Europe indicates that while sales of many essential products turn on fractions of a penny or a franc for a majority of ordinary products, a price variation of at least 10 per cent is required to create any substantial change in purchasing habits.

However, professional people cannot rely on such generalities, or what one particular person's experience indicates. Something more tangible is needed.

ELASTICITY OF DEMAND

The demand curves D_1 and D_2 in exhibit 2.7 illustrate one of the most important and useful characteristics in pricing.

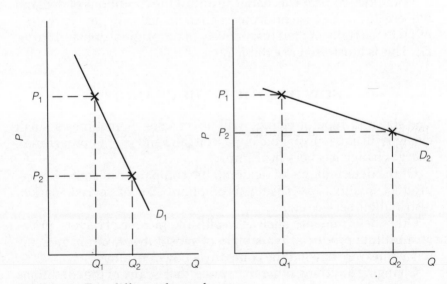

Exhibit 2.7 Two different demand curves

44

Assuming the scales to be the same for the two diagrams, in the left-hand diagram, the interval between P_1 and P_2 is greater than the interval between Q_1 and Q_2: the change in quantity demanded at the two prices is smaller than the change in price. This means that a substantial price change has caused a comparatively small change in sales.

If the slope of the demand curve D_1 were much steeper, perhaps nearly vertical, the change in sales as a result of a price change would be almost negligible, no matter how much the price was changed. This relatively unresponsive change in demand as a consequence of a price change is described as *inelastic*.

In the right-hand diagram, the response of demand to price change is the opposite. The change between P_1 and P_2 is much smaller than the change between Q_1 and Q_2. For only a small price change there is a greater effect on sales.

The diagrams in exhibit 2.7 illustrate *elasticity of demand*. The left-hand diagram, *inelastic demand*; the right-hand, *elastic demand*.

To avoid confusion over scales used in such diagrams, percentage, or proportionate changes of quantity and price are used. Elasticity of demand is determined by the relationship between the *proportionate change* in quantity demanded and the *proportionate change* in price.

Common, everyday purchases such as razor blades, potatoes, flour, soap, writing paper, garden seeds etc. have an inelastic demand: apart from the occasional promotional price offers, changes in price will not affect the volume purchased. Other goods, such as strawberries, new potatoes, cigarettes, have an elastic demand: their sales are highly responsive to small price changes.

We must distinguish between groups of products and the individual products that make up those groups. A typical example is meat. As a group product, meat has an inelastic demand; consumers tend to buy similar quantities of meat each week. But individual meats – beef, lamb, pork, veal – have an elastic demand. If the price of lamb increases, people buy less of it or buy beef, pork or a substitute product such as chicken.

Not only is elasticity of demand important in pricing, but the degree of elasticity is sometimes crucial in deciding by how much to change a price. If it is proposed to change price of a repeat purchase product by, say, 15 per cent, with no records to refer to we cannot be sure how much sales are likely to be affected. They might change by more or less than 15 per cent; they might not change at all. Yet the magnitude of the likely response could be the deciding factor whether or not to change price.

A greater problem is setting a price for capital equipment or service where there is only one chance to get it 'right'. The price-setter has to use whatever tools are available to determine the degree of responsiveness to price.

If a price has to be set for, say, a machine valued at around £200,000, the degree of responsiveness to price variations is vital. For example, £1 is unlikely to have any impact; perhaps not £100. It is conceivable that a price of £200,500 or £201,000 would create the same degree of responsiveness in the potential buyer as a price of £200,000. The difference is between a quarter and a half of one per cent.

The degree of elasticity of demand can be decisive when setting and changing prices.

COEFFICIENT OF ELASTICITY

With simple arithmetic, we can determine the degree of elasticity, the *coefficient of elasticity* (COE), with the following formula:

$$\frac{\text{proportionate (or percentage) change in quantity}}{\text{proportionate (or percentage) change in price}}$$

If the coefficient of elasticity is greater than 1.0, the situation is elastic; if it is less than 1.0, it is inelastic. If it is unity, it is neither elastic nor inelastic.

Thus, if a 10 per cent change in price causes a 5 per cent change in sales, the coefficient of elasticity is 5/10 = 0.5. If a 3 per cent price increase causes sales to fall by, say, 8 per cent, the coefficient is 8/3, or 2.67.

The more responsive are sales to price changes, the greater the degree of elasticity and the greater the coefficient. Coefficients over 4.0 indicate a high elasticity of demand.

With the same formula, the less responsive sales are to price changes, the smaller the degree of elasticity, the smaller the coefficient; in fact, less than 1.0.

INCREASING OR LOWERING THE PRICE

Exhibit 2.8 sets out sales of a product, 60 at £7 and 75 at £5. If the current price is £5 and this has been increased by £2 to £7, the percentage increase is £2/£5 = 40 per cent. Sales at this increased

Exhibit 2.8 Demand schedule for a product

Price (£)	Quantity
7	60
5	75

price fall from 75 to 60 – a 20 per cent decrease. That is, increasing price by 40 per cent causes a 20 per cent fall in sales. The coefficient of elasticity is 20/40 = 0.5.

Now consider price movement in the opposite direction. Lowering the price from £7 to £5 is also £2, but the percentage change is £2/£7 = 28.6 per cent. Sales rise from 60 to 75 – an increase of 25 per cent. The COE is 25/28.6 = 0.87.

Thus, depending whether an increase or a decrease in price is being considered, the same price and quantity changes result in different COEs being calculated. To overcome this apparent inconsistency, *point elasticity* is calculated.

POINT ELASTICITY

The COE is calculated using the mid-point between prices and the mid-point between the sales at those prices: this is point elasticity of demand.

The mid-point between £5 and £7 is £6; between 60 and 75 the mid-point is 67.5. The proportionate change in quantity is 15/67.5 = 22 per cent; the proportionate change in price is 2/6 = 33.3 per cent. The point COE is therefore, 22/33.3 = 0.66. It is 0.66 irrespective of whether a price decrease or increase is being considered.

However, in each of the three calculations, the COE is less than unity, and the situation is inelastic. The importance of these small variations in the COE is considered in chapter 3.

ELASTICITY, TURNOVER AND PROFITS

By reducing price from £7 to £5, sales have increased from 60 to 75. This is expanded in exhibit 2.9 to show that, despite the increased sales, turnover has fallen by £45!

The purpose of price is to make sales and profits, so it is interesting to see the effect of this price change on profits.

Exhibit 2.9 Sales turnover of exhibit 2.8

Price (£)	Sales	Turnover (£)
7	60	420
5	75	375

Exhibit 2.10 Profits calculated from exhibit 2.9

Price (£)	Sales	Turnover (£)	Fixed cost (£)	Variable cost (£)	Total cost (£)	Profit (£)
7	60	420	200	120	320	100
5	75	375	200	150	350	25

Let us assume that the figures in exhibits 2.8 and 2.9 relate to a week's proposed sales. Each product has a variable cost of £2 for materials and labour, and each week a fixed expense of £200 is incurred. Exhibit 2.10 shows the result.

Lowering price has increased sales volume, but the total revenue is lower; more seriously, profit is lower – down from £100 to £25. In percentage terms it sounds even worse: a 25 per cent increase in sales results in a 75 per cent fall in profit!

These figures are not contrived. The principle applies to all pricing situations and can be stated thus:

> If a product has an inelastic demand and price is reduced, total turnover and probably total profit will be lower.

To maintain the same sales volume of 420 at the lower price of £5 it would be necessary to sell 420/5 = 84. But we are still in trouble because the variable cost rises to £168 (84 × £2) and, with the fixed cost of £200, the profit would only be £52 (£420 – £368).

If your company is selling inelastic products, say, rolls of thermal paper for a fax machine, sheet glass, computer floppy disks, men's industrial boots, stationery supplies, even rubber bands, and you are under pressure to reduce price because of competition, you should appreciate the dangers. Reducing price of an inelastic pro-

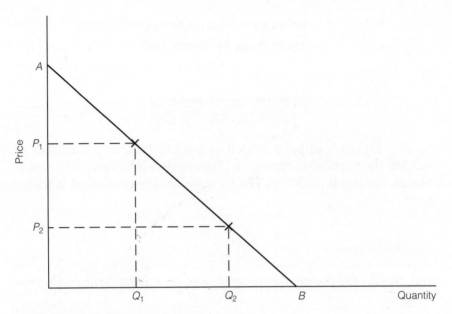

Exhibit 2.11 Elasticity along the demand curve

duct will probably increase sales but have an adverse effect on turnover and profit.

ELASTICITY ALONG THE DEMAND CURVE

Only two coordinates have been used to illustrate the relationship between price and sales because of the theoretical construction of the demand curve. It represents sales at each price level to the same people, at the same time.

To increase the number of coordinates beyond two would be to extend the argument further into the theoretical arena. In practice, trying to obtain even two coordinates is difficult enough; there is little point in trying to measure more. Despite this, extending the demand curve in each direction to cut price and quantity axes provides additional help to our pricing activity.

Consider exhibit 2.11: two coordinates have been inserted and the demand curve connecting them has been extended to cut the price axis at *A* and the quantity axis at *B*.

The coefficient of elasticity is:

$$\frac{\text{proportionate change in } Q}{\text{proportionate change in } P}$$

or,

$$\frac{\text{percentage change in } Q}{\text{percentage change in } P}$$

To simplify, the symbol Δ, which means *a little change in*, is used, so that the proportionate change in Q becomes $\Delta Q/Q$, and the proportionate change in P, $\Delta P/P$. The formula for the coefficient is therefore:

$$\frac{\Delta Q}{Q} \div \frac{\Delta P}{P}$$

and, by turning the denominator upside down and multiplying, we have:

$$\frac{\Delta Q}{Q} \times \frac{P}{\Delta P}$$

Rearranging, this becomes:

$$\frac{\Delta Q}{\Delta P} \times \frac{P}{Q}$$

As the demand curve in this illustration is a straight line, the slope $\Delta Q/\Delta P$ is constant, but the fraction P/Q changes at all points along the demand curve.

Because the left-hand fraction is constant, it follows that the COE depends on where we are on the demand curve, that is, with any particular P and its corresponding Q.

Where the extended demand curve cuts the quantity axis OQ at B the value of P is zero and thus P/Q is also zero. The coefficient is therefore the constant multiplied by zero. Zero multiplied by anything equals zero, which means that the elasticity of demand at B is zero.

More realistically, if we consider the position on the demand curve before it intersects OQ, P will be extremely small – say, 0.001 – and 0.001/Q will also be extremely small, making the coefficient a

50

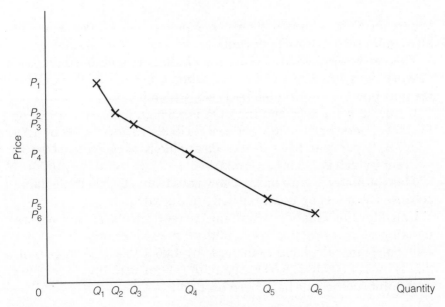

Exhibit 2.12 Demand curve connecting many coordinates

tiny fraction. In general, as we move along this straight demand curve towards the OQ axis, elasticity of demand becomes smaller and smaller, that is, very inelastic.

At the other end, as we get nearer to A, where the curve cuts the price axis OP, Q becomes smaller and smaller and subtends to zero. P/Q is thus P divided by a very small number, which gives a very large number. The coefficient of elasticity of demand near to A is therefore extremely high.

What this discussion has shown is that along the straight-line demand curve, elasticity of demand changes: it is low in the low price ranges, high in the high price ranges.

A more 'accurate' demand curve might be drawn if we had more coordinates, as in exhibit 2.12, but this would merely be increasing the theoretical content, not the practicality. It is not possible to obtain more than one coordinate, representing sales at a price, without changing one or more of the other factors: geographical area, time, packaging, customers.

Because of the difficulty of constructing practical demand curves it is better to investigate price/demand movements and base forecasts on straight-line demand curves.

SIMPLE APPLICATIONS

Where the COE is known, then a change in price of C per cent, will affect sales by (COE × C) per cent.

This can be applied to exhibit 2.1 with the zeros removed for ease of working: when $P = 6$, $Q = 8$; and when $P = 7$, $Q = 6$. The COE at the mid-point is 2/7 divided by 1/6.5, which is 1.86.

If current price is £6 and the COE is 1.86, an increase in price of £1 (that is one-sixth, or 16.7 per cent) is likely to affect sales by 1.86 × 16.7 = 31 per cent. Sales of 800,000 are likely to be reduced by 31 per cent (which is 248,000) to 552,000.

This estimated figure of 552,000 varies from 600,000 in the table because we are using point elasticity in the calculations.

Consider the situation where the current price is £7 and we are thinking of lowering it to £6 – a mid-point price change of 15.4 per cent. Sales are calculated to increase by 1.86 × 15.4 = 28.6 per cent, that is by 171,600 to 771,600. Again, the slight variation is because mid-point coefficients have been used.

DANGERS OF ELASTICITY

Practical applications of analytical demand estimation are investigated further in the next chapter. The main danger is using a little knowledge of demand behaviour to develop pricing strategy beyond a limit that can be supported by theoretical argument. While we may be reasonably sure of a COE at two most recent price levels, it should be used only as a guide when estimating impact on sales of increasing or decreasing price much beyond our immediate experience.

Exhibit 2.11 showed that elasticity of demand is not necessarily the same all along the demand curve. It can vary from extremely small in the low price region to extremely high in the high price region.

Another possibility is illustrated in exhibit 2.13. At every point on the curve, the coefficient of elasticity is 1.0. The table is set out in exhibit 2.14.

Elasticity of demand reflects buyer behaviour. If an elastic demand for a product has been established, it is unlikely that demand is going to change to inelastic if the price is raised or lowered.

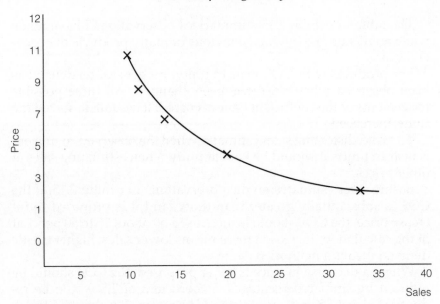

Exhibit 2.13 Demand curve with unity elasticity

Exhibit 2.14 Unity elasticity calculations

P	Q	Change in price	Change in sales	Coefficient of elasticity
11	9			
9	11	20%	20%	20/20 = 1
7	14	25%	24%	24/25 = 0.96
5	20	33%	35%	35/33 = 1.06
3	33	50%	49%	49/50 = 0.98

	Elastic demand	Inelastic demand
Price increased	Coefficient likely to be greater	Coefficient likely to stay the same
Price decreased	Coefficient likely to be smaller	Coefficient likely to stay the same

Exhibit 2.15 Tendency of elasticity coefficient changes

The table in exhibit 2.15 summarizes observations I have made when analysing the buying behaviour of many products over several years.

For products with COE near to unity, no general tendency has been observed when price has been changed. All three possible movements of the coefficient have occurred: it has fallen, stayed the same, increased.

To avoid distorting sales estimates when the observed coefficient is near to unity, it should be kept at unity when estimating sales at other prices.

Basing sales estimates on the observations in exhibit 2.15, if the COE is substantially greater than unity, and it is proposed to increase price, the COE should be increased by about 25 to 50 per cent in the calculation. Increased price means lower sales; higher elastic demand means a magnified decrease.

Where a decrease in price is being proposed, the COE should be reduced by similar percentages: a coefficient of 2.5 would be reduced to about 1.8 and, say, 4.0 would be reduced to about 2.5 to 3.0. Decrease in price means increase in sales, but a lower elastic demand means a less dramatic increase.

AN EMPIRICAL DATABASE

If accurate records are kept of prices and sales of products over time periods of, say, months or quarters, a practical database can be developed. This can be used to estimate future sales at possible price changes.

A large hypermarket in Belgium with many thousands of items has developed such a database and maintains a separate record for each major product. Sales and price details are inserted regularly in the top part of the form, which is large enough for a year, and the COE calculated.

The lower portion is used when it is required to estimate sales of the product at proposed price changes. Part of the form is reproduced in exhibit 2.16. It is emphasized that the lower portion is used for estimating, and contains figures that were inserted before the actual sales were known and subsequently recorded in the database in the top portion.

In September 1989 it was proposed to reduce the price of an electric domestic appliance for which the COE was 2.0. In the sales estimate in the lower portion of the form a COE of 1.5 was used.

Exhibit 2.16 Form for database and sales estimating

Sales and price data of product

Period	Price	Sales	COE
. . .			
. . .			
Aug			
Sep	1,525.00	243	2.0
Oct	1,335.00	285	1.4*
Nov			
Dec			

* COE is percentage change in sales divided by percentage change in price

Sales estimate with new price and assumed COE

Period	Price	COE	Sales
Sep	1,525.00		243
Oct	1,335.00	1.5	288*

* Estimated sales = previous sales × [1 + (COE × percentage price change)]

Price was reduced from BFrs 1,525 to BFr 1,335, that is, by 12½ per cent. Sales were estimated to increase by 1.5 × 12.5 per cent = 18.75 per cent, i.e. from 243 to 288.

In fact they were 285, an increase of 17½ per cent, which indicates a COE of 17.5/12.5 = 1.4, and justified the reduction of the original COE of 2.0 to 1.5.

In October they used their database to estimate sales for a number of their products. One, a fast moving consumer product with a COE of around 3.0, was considered if price were reduced by 10 per cent for the early December period.

They reduced the COE from 3.0 to 2.5 in their calculations and estimated that sales would increase by 2.5 × 10 = 25 per cent.

The lower portion of the form is reproduced in exhibit 2.17. Sales were actually 13,750, which was just over 90 per cent of their estimate.

Obviously, a lot of calculations are required and, even if a calculator is used, they are tedious. In chapter 5, which introduces the use

Exhibit 2.17 Estimated Christmas sales

Sales estimate with new price and assumed COE

Period	Price	COE	Sales
Sep	55.00	3.0	
Oct	55.00	3.0	12,060
Nov			
Dec	49.50	2.5	15,075[*]

[*] Estimated sales = previous sales × [1 + (COE × percentage price change)]

of a personal computer to such tasks, the actual computer layouts of exhibits 2.16 and 2.17 are given in exhibits 5.30 and 5.31, together with the formulae to use.

3

Methods of pricing

COST-PLUS

The choice of pricing method is usually based on the prevailing conditions in the particular industry. Obviously, methods used for capital goods differ from those for fast moving consumer goods. Where consumers make their choice of a product every week, suppliers have much wider scope for pricing flexibility and experimenting in different locations.

One of the most common pricing methods is cost-plus; its popularity is its simplicity. The cost of making or buying-in a product is calculated and then percentages added for other activities and profit; the result is the price.

In retailing, items are subject to a single standard oncost to establish selling price. To obtain the retail selling price a set percentage is added to the bought-in price, plus an appropriate percentage for value added tax. The standard oncost includes the profit margin.

The percentage added to the bought-in price reflects the normal speed of sales of the product. The slower the stock movement, the greater the percentage mark-up. Retail mark-up on such things as greengrocery, fish, soap etc. is low; in contrast, furniture, which is purchased infrequently, has a high mark-up – of the order of 45 or 50 per cent.

Products sold by direct marketing methods – mail order and catalogue selling – also carry a high mark-up because each sale is a separate transaction.

Pricing industrial products can be crude, with only one or two percentages added to arrive at a net-of-tax price, or highly developed, with the total purchasing and manufacturing activities broken down and a full analysis made of costs.

DEVELOPMENT OF A STANDARD MARK-UP

A plastics products company in the English Midlands used to have a fairly simple pricing procedure when its range of products was limited. As the company prospered and broadened its activities the old system became inadequate.

They had started business with one injection moulding machine but soon obtained a second. Their plant and equipment grew and diversified; machines of widely varying usage and capital value were acquired.

For the first year, after they had analysed all their costs and standing charges, they applied a mark-up of 61 per cent to the cost of raw materials and direct labour to get the price. The 61 per cent was sufficient for all other costs and profit. A product that contained £8 worth of raw materials and £3 of direct labour was priced at £11 plus 61 per cent, to make a price of £17.71.

This was a simple and speedy method of setting a price, and, while their production facilities were fully occupied, they saw no reason to change the procedure until it became evident that competitors were increasingly beating them on price. They persisted with the method but frequently reduced the percentage oncost figure to arrive at a price that was more competitive. Obviously, product profits varied from the norm achieved with a 61 per cent oncost to considerably less depending on how much they reduced price to get the order.

Towards the end of the second year, they realized that they had to have a more accurate means of pricing, not only to keep a check on costs and profit, but to be able to price more keenly against competition. They decided that it would be sensible to keep their basic cost-plus method, but to break down the percentage oncost and get at the true costs for their increasingly varied manufacturing processes. Although at that time their product range was still limited, they designed a comprehensive pricing procedure.

Exhibit 3.1 Pricing sheet of an industrial products company

Costing sheet for pricing			
Product	_____	Date	_____
Prepared by	_____	Last Updated	_____

	£	£
	___	___
Raw materials		
Components/bought-ins	_____	
Inward transport		
Warehousing		
Internal handling	_____	
Direct labour		
Servicing labour		
Finishing		
Finished goods warehouse	_____	
G & A		
Management		
HQ		
Advertising		
Contingencies	_____	
		_____
Oncost 20%		_____
		_____
Transfer price		======

Exhibit 3.2 Completed pricing sheet

Costing sheet for pricing

Product	'G' Clamp	Date	11 Jun 89
Prepared by	JB	Last Updated	

	£	£
Raw materials	8.50	
Components/bought-ins	2.38	
		10.88
Inward transport	0.16	
Warehousing	0.30	
Internal handling	0.20	
		0.66
Direct labour	1.75	
Servicing labour	0.18	
Finishing		
Finished goods warehouse	0.33	
		2.26
G & A	0.49	
Management	0.33	
HQ	0.08	
Advertising	0.16	
Contingencies	0.54	
		1.60
		15.40
Oncost 20%		3.08
		18.48
Transfer price		18.50

A costing sheet, illustrated in exhibit 3.1, was used for each product; the various percentage oncosts were calculated by an analysis of the company's figures for the previous two years. A number of modifications such as 'contingencies' and 'inwards transport' were included. The company used its own transport to obtain some of its supplies and the owner insisted on an oncost for inward transport in the form. A completed form is shown in exhibit 3.2.

This pricing form and procedure has persisted to this day. Every six months – earlier if there is more than 2.5 per cent variation in any major cost, or new equipment is installed – management reviews all percentage oncosts in the light of actual costs and modifies them – mostly upward, but on rare occasions downward.

This general cost-plus approach is widely used in different types of company: attributable costs are identified and included in the pricing form. Fixed overheads and other costs are analysed, and the way in which they are to be spread over the current product range decided. These are then inserted as percentage oncosts in the costing sheet to achieve a recovery of overheads at an agreed level of capacity.

FAILINGS OF COST-PLUS

The simplicity of the cost-plus method of pricing persuades many companies to adopt it. It is acceptable for companies with straightforward value-added activities; if more complex operations are involved, a regular procedure should be adopted for updating percentage oncosts.

Once a company's manufacturing or value-added activities develop beyond the rudimentary, an analytical approach to pricing is essential. However, a standard mark-up procedure with no periodic appraisal of market and economic conditions offers no stimulus to efficiency. It is easy to become accustomed to a standard, or worse, a fixed mark-up: costs that might otherwise be challenged and investigated are accepted because it is assumed that the pricing procedure is sufficient to cover them.

Any deficiencies in a standard mark-up process will be concealed as long as other companies follow similar procedures. However, vigorous competitors are quick to spot opportunities for differential pricing strategies in an industry accustomed to standard mark-up methods.

A more serious objection to the use of a standard mark-up is its almost exclusive concern with the supply side of the demand–supply function, and a failure to take into consideration the perceived value of a product or service. Pricing is to make sales and profits, both of which arise from demand. If the demand side is ignored and price based mainly on supply factors, profit will be adversely affected. Either insufficient profit will be made, or so much included in the price that sales and profits will be low.

Companies who use a cost-plus pricing method exclusively are ignoring opportunities for profit that would come from a strategy based also on demand considerations. Nevertheless, cost-plus pricing is widely used by middlemen, and the manufacturers whose products they handle, assume the task of determining and recommending the final price.

VALUE-PRICING

Value-pricing is also known as *skimming the market*. A high price is set for a small segment of the market which is *creamed off*. Price is maintained at the high level so that new customers have to upgrade themselves into the segment of the market that is prepared to pay the high price for the product.

Such a strategy may be observed in the pricing of certain wristwatches. They are manufactured to a very high standard of finish and performance, several in gold or platinum and some decorated with diamonds. It is possible to purchase a timepiece just as accurate for about one-tenth of 1 per cent of their price. The company value-prices the range and is selling status symbols rather than watches. They continue to skim the market; customers have to move up into the segment.

FOLLOWING THE DEMAND CURVE

The practical use of the demand curve in pricing is explored later in this chapter. As a strategy it is similar to value-pricing, but instead of price being maintained at a high level and persuading customers to upgrade themselves, it is scaled down at a controlled rate. The product can be given minor improvements and changes to differentiate it – appearance, advertising, packaging, perhaps a different distribution channel. The price is held at each lower level long enough to attract all available demand. As sales start to decline at a level it is time to consider a price reduction.

Consumer electric blankets were marketed in this way. A high price was set to start with and after demand had been largely satisfied at the high price level, it was lowered stage by stage. With modification of the product, repackaging and to the accompaniment of bursts of advertising, demand was stimulated at successively lower price levels.

Electronic calculators were also marketed with this strategy. One of the first offered in the UK was a mains electric model made by Sharp which cost £200. It would add and subtract, one calculation at a time, giving the result by pressing the white key; multiplication and division calculations were obtained by pressing the red key. Subsequent models by Sharp, Casio and many others were priced successively lower as the demand for calculators extended.

One of the first quartz watches which incorporated a calculator was on sale at Harrods in London for around £2,000. The keys of the calculator were tiny and had to be operated with a ball-point. In 1987 a similar watch could be obtained free with the purchase of a 5-litre can of motor oil! Scaling down price is, by necessity, often fast in hi-tech industries.

PENETRATION PRICING

Penetration pricing strategy is big company strategy. It is to price at around total cost, enter a market and expand quickly to gain high market share and secure cost advantage from the large volume production. Such a strategy is suitable for products manufactured under conditions where increasing returns operate, and also, with a heavy investment budget, to fight a strongly entrenched competitor. Exhibit 3.3, based on the model introduced in chapter 1, illustrates the strategy. The product is launched on the market at little profit and when high sales are achieved unit basic cost increases unit profit.

In the USA the running-shoe market has been led in turn by Keds, Converse and Nike. Then in 1983 Reeboks International, with previous sales in the region of $13 million, added a fashion element to their functional running-shoes and penetrated the market, achiev-

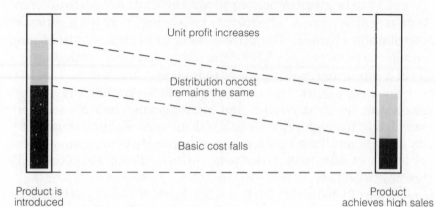

Exhibit 3.3 Penetration pricing strategy

ing a turnover of $1.4 billion. The product is mainly for the teenage market but each successive generation looks for a 'new' image. Reebok's initial success was with women's fashionable aerobic shoes enabling wearers to slim elegantly to music. Although Nike started a counterattack in 1988, price is still a major factor: Nikes sell for £50 to £60 and Reeboks for around £30.

Sony sought to penetrate the watch market in 1988 with a throw-away fashion accessory: a watch called Gotta Watch. This is a small liquid-crystal digital display showing time and date on a plastic-coated strip of card which serves as watch face and strap. It was launched in Japan in time for Christmas 1988 for 500 yen (about £2) and subsequently in the USA for around $3.50. The market segment was the under-twenties, and, with straps printed in pop-art and fanciful designs, it was estimated that at least two-thirds of the market would spend about £5–£10 on the product.

Provided that large-scale production is available, penetration pricing is an aggressive strategy to expand into the fad and fashion-conscious segment as quickly as possible.

PRE-EMPTIVE PRICING

Pre-emptive pricing is also for the big company. It is similar to penetration pricing but used for a different policy, namely to 'burn' off competition or to dissuade possible competitors from entering the market. Price is set as near as possible to cost so that profits are low and only attractive when sufficient volume is reached.

BREAK-EVEN ANALYSIS

In setting a price, a company may wish to relate supply with demand forces; supply, over which there is some control, and demand, over which there is far less control, only influence. Of help here is the technique of *break-even analysis*. Properly used, it enables the executive to establish relationships between total revenue and total costs at various price levels. The 'best' price is where profits are maximized; this is where total revenue exceeds total cost by the largest amount.

Two types of costs have to be identified: *fixed* or *rigid costs* and *variable costs*. Fixed costs are incurred irrespective of the volume of output, and in the short-term are unrelated to changes in production. In the long-term, increased output that requires new machinery and possibly new buildings will increase fixed costs.

Costs that may be considered as fixed include rent, taxes, insurance, salaries and wages that cannot be readily varied, and advertising costs that cannot be cancelled.

Variable costs are related directly to output: raw materials, bought-in items, sales commissions and other items that rise or fall in proportion to the level of output.

Semi-variable costs are a form of variable cost, and are related to output but not directly. They include such items as heating, lighting, power, some production wages, transportation, warehousing, and perhaps advertising if it can be varied slightly.

The total revenue line   The total revenue line is inserted on a graph, as illustrated in exhibit 3.4, with costs and revenues as the vertical axis and output as the horizontal axis. Maximum production of 8,000 has been multiplied by the price of £6 to obtain £48,000. The coordinates 8,000 and £48,000 give the point to be joined to the point of origin (zero): this produces the total revenue line.

The fixed cost line   The fixed cost line is drawn parallel to the base at £7,500.

The total costs line   The unit variable cost, £4.50, is multiplied by total production of 8,000 to obtain total variable costs of £36,000. The coordinates are £36,000 above the £7,500 line (£43,500) and 8,000. This point is joined to the intersection of the fixed cost line and the vertical axis.

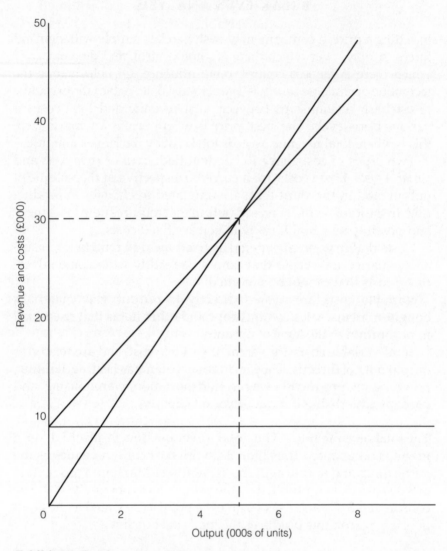

Exhibit 3.4 Break-even analysis

BREAK-EVEN POINT

At the intersection of the total cost and revenue lines, total costs equal total revenue. This is the break-even point, indicated as an output and a revenue figure.

The break-even point may also be calculated arithmetically. From the price, deduct the variable cost; divide the result into the total fixed costs.

In this example, price is £6, variable cost is £4.50; the difference is £1.50. Total fixed costs are £7,500, therefore 7,500/1.50 = 5,000. The break-even sales volume is 5,000; the break-even revenue is £30,000.

Raising the price increases the slope of the total revenue line and lowers break-even point. Lowering the price decreases the slope and increases the break-even figure.

A useful variation is shown in exhibit 3.5, where the output axis has been replaced by a time axis. The month when break-even occurs is clearly seen, but three points must be stressed.

DON'T BE BEGUILED BY BREAK-EVEN

First, break-even analysis is an aid to pricing and not a graphic representation of what will occur. Straight lines depict regular sales and production throughout the year – a highly unlikely possibility.

Consider the situation where the bulk of the cost of a year's production has to be committed at the start of the year, such as with viniculture, and sales are highly seasonal, perhaps most of them achieved towards the end of the year. The graph would be as exhibit 3.6.

Secondly, break-even should not be considered as a major objective; it is a signpost on the road to profitability. The first major objective is an agreed profit ratio.

Thirdly, and the most important point, is the level of production capacity achieved. These break-even calculations and graphs have been based on 100 per cent capacity: maximum output, maximum sales, maximum revenue. All figures should be recalculated at an operating level of, say, 80 per cent.

When calculating break-even figures, use levels of production and sales operations consistent with previous achievements. The figures should then be modified by the sales estimate for the following period. Allowances should be made for possible disturbances such as plant breakdowns, delivery failures, labour and industry disputes, power failures, transportation problems. The activity level at which it is planned that overheads will be recovered should have the support of management and those responsible for results.

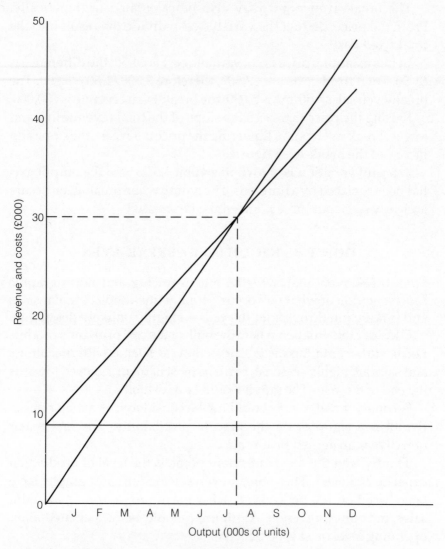

Exhibit 3.5 Break-even analysis over time

STRAIGHT CURVES?

Bearing in mind the limitations of using a straight-line demand curve discussed in chapter 2, such a line can be calculated if the results of a couple of sales periods are known. The basis for this is illustrated in the graph in exhibit 3.7, where a straight line is extended to cut one of the axes. The vertical axis *OP* is price, and the

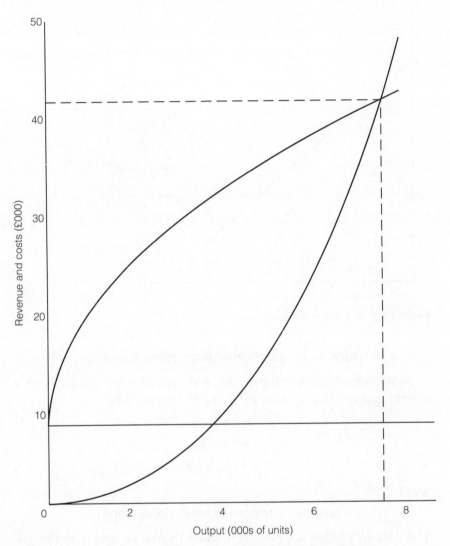

Exhibit 3.6 Break-even analysis with varying sales and production rates

horizontal axis *OQ* is quantity. The demand curve is extended to cut *OP* at *a*.

The general formula for a straight line is $y = a + bx$, from which y may be found for any particular x, provided that the intersection, a, and slope, b, are known. We use p for price instead of y, and q for quantity instead of x, so that the equation is:

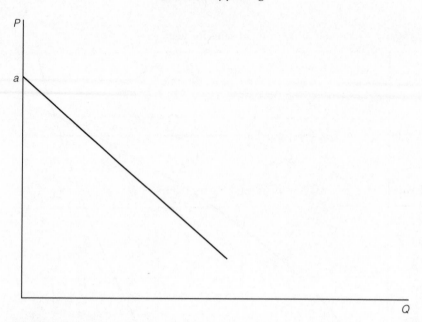

Exhibit 3.7 Extended demand curve

price = intersection + (slope times quantity)

As we wish to determine quantity at a given price, the formula is rearranged to make quantity the dependent variable:

$$p = a + bq \quad \dots \dots \dots \dots \dots \text{[1]}$$
$$p - a = bq$$
$$q = (p - a)/b \quad \dots \dots \dots \dots \dots \text{[2]}$$

that is:

quantity = (price – intersection)/slope

The data in exhibit 3.8, has been taken from a company in the UK selling industrial equipment at two prices during one year. The information is used to position the demand curve and its slope.

Zeros are suppressed and only significant digits used. The two coordinates P_1Q_1 and P_2Q_2 are (8, 24) and (9, 19), which are joined and extended to intersect OP at a.

To find the intersection a and slope b we insert the data (8, 24) and (9, 19) into exhibit 3.9, complete the calculations, and substitute the totals for the letters r, s, t, u, v and n in the formulae for intersection

70

Exhibit 3.8 Industrial equipment sales for year

	Price (£)	Sales (000)
	80	2,400
	90	1,900

Exhibit 3.9 Calculation of straight line for exhibit 3.8

	q	p	q^2	p^2	pq
	24	8	576	64	192
	19	9	361	81	171
Totals	43	17	937	145	363
	r	s	t	u	v

the intersection a is $\dfrac{st - rv}{nt - r^2}$ . . . .[3]

the slope b is $\dfrac{nv - rs}{nt - r^2}$ . . . .[4]

Substituting in equation [3] for the intersection:

$$a = \frac{(17 \times 937) - (43 \times 363)}{(2 \times 937) - (43 \times 43)} = 12.8$$

and, [4] for the slope:

$$b = \frac{(2 \times 363) - (43 \times 17)}{(2 \times 937) - (43 \times 43)} = -0.2$$

Therefore, using the formula [2] above,

$$q = (p - a)/b \quad . . . .[2]$$
$$q = (p - 12.8)/-0.2$$

and slope, which are standard statistical formulae. n is the number of coordinates; in this example $n = 2$.

The demand curve would cut the price axis at 12.8, and have a downward slope of –0.2.

Suppose we are considering increasing price to £10, we can insert this in the equation to obtain estimated sales:

quantity = (10 − 12.8)/−0.2

quantity = −2.8/−0.2

= 14

Lowering the price to £7, will indicate sales of:

quantity = (7 − 12.8)/−0.2

= 29

CURRENT PRODUCT PRICING

Setting prices for products currently in a company's range, or being added to the range, calls for a different procedure from pricing a new product: this is the subject of chapter 10.

As discussed in chapter 2, if sales records are available, pricing products already in the company's range can be helped by considering elasticity of demand.

While from the purely statistical viewpoint it is more reliable to base analyses on as many data as possible, the records used to analyse elasticity of demand should cover as small a period as relevant to the product's average frequency of purchase.

The composition of the market is always changing: customers move away, use different suppliers, go out of business; new customers and suppliers enter the market; methods and procedures change. All these and more make the current market different from what it was a year ago. The change is mostly imperceptible, but it is continuous.

ANALYTICAL ESTIMATION OF DEMAND

The *law of demand* indicates that customers usually purchase more units at a low price than at a high price. The *price elasticity of demand* defines the sensitivity of buyers to price changes in terms of quantities likely to be purchased.

How COE is calculated – by pencil and paper, with a calculator, or by computer, which is discussed in more detail in chapter 5 – will determine the degree of accuracy achieved. However, accuracy is not a crucial factor. Inelasticities are indicated by coefficients of less than 1.0, therefore fractions or decimal places are used. This can create a false impression of accuracy. COEs are merely convenient numbers used to compare changes in demand with price changes.

SIGNIFICANT COEFFICIENTS

The coefficients 0.65, 0.54 and 0.02 are examples of increasing inelasticity. Similarly, 1.8, 2.25 and 3.4 indicate increasing degrees of elasticity. Because demand analysis is not an exact science it should be categorized broadly – inelastic, unresponsive, or elastic.

Thus, coefficients of 0.02, 0.35, 0.54 are considered as inelastic. Coefficients around unity: 0.8, 0.9, 1.05 and 1.1 do not indicate a strong responsiveness one way or the other; products with such COEs might subsequently develop an inelastic, or elastic, demand. Coefficients considered as significantly elastic are usually greater than 2.0; depending on the price bracket, these are of the order of 3, 3.5, 4.75 and so on.

Although more of a product tends to be purchased at lower prices, actual results occasionally indicate the contrary; price is lowered and, instead of sales increasing, they fall. This is because other factors are influencing demand. Competitors might have lowered their prices even more; a new product could have been launched without its being known; a competitor might have increased advertising, given greater discounts, offered the sales force higher commissions. The possibilities are endless but effective enough to distort elasticity calculations.

A POSITIVE MISTAKE

All coefficient calculations should be double-checked and the deductions drawn from the analyses appraised for validity. If the arguments used to support recommended price changes were based on a miscalculation or simple error, the method itself becomes suspect. Even otherwise well-written material suffers from the occasional oversight. The following has been taken from a well-known textbook on marketing:

...price elasticity is computed by dividing the percentage change in quantity demanded by the percentage change in price charged...

Methods of pricing

The textbook then gives the following formula:

$$\frac{(Quantity\ 1 - Quantity\ 2)/(Quantity\ 1 + Quantity\ 2)}{(Price\ 1 - Price\ 2)/(Price\ 1 + Price\ 2)}$$

Taking values of Price 1 = £6, Quantity 1 = 16; Price 2 = £7, Quantity 2 = 11 and applying the formula we obtain:

$$\frac{(16 - 11)/(16 + 11)}{(6 - 7)/(6 + 7)}$$

This resolves to 0.185/–0.077, which gives a *negative* coefficient of –2.4, indicating that *as price is increased, sales increase*, which is not the case. Price is increased to £7 and sales follow the law of demand and decrease from 16 to 11.

The formula should be:

$$\frac{(\textit{difference} \text{ in quantity})/(Quantity\ 1 + Quantity\ 2)}{(\textit{difference} \text{ in price})/(Price\ 1 + Price\ 2)}$$

Using the same figures, we have:

$$\frac{5/(16 + 11)}{1/(6 + 7)}$$

This resolves to 0.185/0.077, which gives a positive coefficient of 2.4.

This should alert you to the inconsistencies that can creep into calculations and give wrong figures.

The importance of being able to calculate coefficients of demand elasticity accurately cannot be overstressed. You can present your pricing proposals to management and colleagues more confidently when your recommendations are based on market responsiveness of likely demand. Challenges can be more professionally dealt with and, as battles in the market-place have first to be won in the 'boardroom', you must be sure of your ground.

ELASTICITY OR DEMAND CURVE EXTENSION?

We have considered two techniques for estimating sales at price changes, but are they compatible? Is it better to use COEs or an extension of the demand curve?

When considering a price outside the range previously used for a product the problem should be tackled cautiously. Quantitative analysis will indicate whether or not the recommendations are based on sound argument.

74

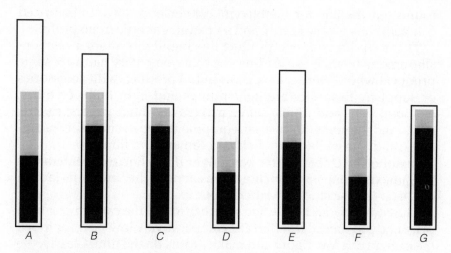

Exhibit 3.10 Product-line pricing

Straight-line demand curves over a wide range of prices exist only in textbooks; they do not occur in business. If only a small price change is being considered, say, around 5 per cent, either method of estimating likely demand could be considered. However, if the product has a highly elastic demand, demand curve extension gives distorted results. This is explored in more detail in chapter 5.

PRODUCT-LINE PRICING

Product-line pricing is setting prices for individual products in a group. As far as manufacture is concerned, the products may be made from different materials and processes, and even come from different factories. The group is purchased as a related product line by the market. Different levels of demand may exist for individual products, and a company may have a marked competitive advantage for some of them. This is illustrated in exhibit 3.10 where products A, B, D and E provide the majority of profit from sales of the total line.

While there is a natural tendency for a company to concentrate its marketing activities on these high-profit products, generally the market wants a full line to be offered. In such circumstances the company has considerable flexibility in pricing the products for which a competitive advantage is held, while the other products that round out the line for the buyers' convenience have to be priced competitively – very keenly and sometimes at little or no profit.

This rounding out of a product line highlights another relationship among members of the line: the complementary nature of some products where there is a main, or initial product, with accessories or supplies. Examples are light fittings and light bulbs or tubes; ballpoint pens and refills; coffee makers and filter papers; electric drills and fitments; industrial equipment and technical consumables; and, the well-known Polaroid camera and film.

Invented by Dr Land after World War II, the Polaroid camera was the subject of intensive pricing discussions at the time of its launch and later in case studies written about it.

The company had to decide whether to sell the camera at a high price and the special fast film at a comparatively low price, or to sell the camera at a low figure and make profits on the film. Clearly, the sales of film are not related to the sale of cameras, but to the number of cameras owned and in use.

Initially, in the USA, Polaroid priced the camera on the low side – remarkable when their then restricted output and vast market potential is considered. On launching the product in Europe, however, a high-price strategy was adopted both for the camera and the film.

A long-range outlook for pricing strategy in such situations is essential and will be effective only as long as no competitor is able to capture a substantial portion of the market by a low-price policy or, if the product is protected legally, by circumventing the patent.

Polaroid was fully patented but Eastman-Kodak launched its competitive Instamatic camera; as far as the public was concerned, it was an identical system of instant pictures. The resulting battle in the market-place was eventually transferred to the courts, where Polaroid forced Eastman-Kodak out of the instant film business. In 1988, after a long legal wrangle, Eastman-Kodak reached a compensation settlement with the 16.5 million holders of its unusable instant camera.

Developing and pricing a full line is also a matter of great concern for companies whose product lines contain items that are competitive or can be readily substituted for each other. If the market is segmented by, say, disposable income, such as for motor cars, the manufacturer who possesses a limited range, as was the case with the early Volkswagen 'Beetle', will appeal only to a small part of the market. By carefully differentiating several models with variations such as shape, styling, engine specification, accessories, price etc. a manufacturer can appeal to a much wider market than is possible if there were a concentration on one model.

Pricing in such circumstances will rely heavily on the strength of the demand elasticity at different price levels. As we have seen in the previous chapter, demand at higher price levels tends to be more elastic than at lower levels. Therefore, low-priced models need to be priced similarly to competitive models; the high-priced models may be priced to achieve a higher percentage profit margin.

A further consideration is that the total price is often much less important than the method of payment. If payment is spread over a period, the relevant factors are the amount of the initial down payment, interest rate, size of repayments and period over which they can be spread.

The particular influence of the product line on the price of an individual product depends on the nature of the relationships that exist among the products. Product-line pricing should take consideration of the relative acceptance and demand for each of its members, and then price them as members of the line and not as individual products. The aim is to achieve a total revenue for the product line that maximizes profit. When the product line consists of a product mix that comes from the same factory or even the same plant and equipment, pricing is likely to be over-influenced by an arbitrary allocation of joint processing and manufacturing costs to the line members.

PRICE PLATEAUX

For many products, particularly convenience goods, a price plateau or bracket has been established by custom. Such products are priced within fairly well-defined upper and lower limits; the range between the limits generally relates to the frequency of purchase. A product with a high frequency of purchase will tend to have a smaller price bracket than a product that is bought less frequently.

Such products are normally readily available in many outlets and are purchased with little time and effort. Price is not a great influencing factor in their purchase, and producers have to use other marketing tools to maintain their market share. New products introduced into such markets with established price plateaux must be designed, produced and marketed within the limits set by market forces.

FOLLOW-MY-LEADER PRICING

In some industries, mainly basic ones where demand is largely inelastic, a majority of companies elect to maintain their individual prices which are similar or near to the price set by the company with the largest market share. The type of market has an important influence on this tendency. A growing market does not usually witness 'follow-my-leader' pricing methods, but a fairly stable market, even a declining one, often exhibits them.

Competition in such conditions is still keen but is generally non-price competition focused on product improvement, promotion, distribution, service and what little product differentiation is possible.

PSYCHOLOGICAL PRICING

While man (and woman) is often claimed to be a reasoning animal, able to make economic choices from scarce resources, he (or she) is really an emotional one, frequently conditioned by appropriate stimuli.

Psychological pricing exploits illusions. A retailer is likely to sell more of an impulse good priced at 97p than at £1, because it's 'under a pound'. A product priced at £2,200 will be described as a little over £2,000. A wife, arriving home with a new dress, will tell her husband that it cost under a hundred pounds, even though it was ninety-eight fifty: it seems to lighten the blow!

The lower the actual price, the smaller the deduction should be for the psychological price. A product that could sell at, say, £2 may be offered at £1.99; a product that normally sells at, say, £10 may be priced at £9.95; one at £50 may be priced at £49.50.

One American experience indicated that the most popular prices for goods selling under $5 should be priced ending in 9 ($2.99, $3.99 etc.) and those up to $20 should be priced ending in 95 ($10.95, $14.95 etc.)

We buy in price plateaux, therefore such plateaux should be identified for each product and price rounded up or down to comply with these psychological illusions. Even in the professional arena of industrial marketing, emotion plays an important part in pricing decisions.

The Steel Company of South Wales used to purchase phenolic-formaldehyde and fabric bonded bearings for the roll necks of their cogging and blooming mills. These were supplied by a subsidiary company of Vickers Ltd, whose products ranged, at that time, from hospital rubber sheeting to warships.

A competitor supplied, at no cost, a similar set of plastic bearings for the steel company to use when the bearings were automatically changed on their periodic maintenance shutdown. While they were supplied as free samples, their price, if the steel company was interested, was about half the price of the Vickers' product.

The mill engineer at Newport, Gwent declined to use the 'inferior' bearings because, at half the price, he thought that they could not be the same quality as those from the well-known company. Furthermore, to instal them and find that they would last for perhaps only half the time of the 'regular' bearings would be expensive in downtime costs and embarrassing for the engineer. The sample bearings stayed in his office. That is, they stayed there until one day delivery of the usual bearings was delayed.

Every minute a mill is shut down, not working, is costly. Despite the engineer's frantic telephone conversations with the factory in Scotland it was clear that there was no way that a set of their regular bearings was going to be delivered to Newport in time. He did what any desperate engineer would do in the same predicament: authorized the installation of the 'cheap' bearings.

Despite their much lower cost, to the amazement of the engineer and his colleagues, they lasted longer than those from the original supplier. The reason was that the competitor supplied a moulded bearing, with a better surface and longer-wearing characteristics than the machined bearings. They had invested in moulds and hot-pressed the bearings rather than manufacture them from solid blocks of expensive material. The savings in materials, labour and time enabled them to price very competitively and also amortize the cost of the moulds over a relatively short period. The price had been a psychological barrier that had prevented the engineer and his staff from accepting them under normal circumstances.

HIGH-PRICE POLICIES

All of these strategies may be described as a *high-price* or a *low-price* strategy. A high-price strategy has merit and should be considered:

- where the product is unique, is heavily advertised, or is well-protected legally;
- if considerable educational effort is required for customers to use the product;
- if the ultimate size of the market is expected to be restricted and too small to be attractive to competitors;
- if there is evidence that customers are willing to pay a high price for the product and demand would not be affected by a reduction in the proposed price;
- where the company has limited financial resources and additional funds costly to obtain;
- if technical problems restrict the development of a similar product or expansion of output.

LOW-PRICE POLICIES

The conditions which favour a low-price policy are the opposite of these. Note the phrase describing such strategies: *has merit and should be considered*. This does not mean that any of them is particularly recommended, or that the conditions indicate such a strategy should be followed.

For example, if a company has limited financial resources this should persuade management to consider a high-price strategy. A low-price strategy might not provide them with sufficient profit margin to generate funds for expansion. On the other hand, a high-price strategy might also attract competition, and the company still loses. A lot will depend on how they enter the market with the high-priced product, whether it is a repeat sale, or an item normally only purchased once; whether any servicing is required; whether they can keep a sufficiently low profile not to be noticed by competition; and so on.

4

Consumer goods pricing

CONSUMER PRODUCTS AND SERVICES

Consumer products and services are highly diverse over a vast range of offers – from everyday bread and butter to a luxury yacht; from a quick snack, a while-you-wait repair at a heel bar, a modest shampoo and haircut, to an architect's design for a ten-bedroom house, with tennis court and swimming pool.

Such products may be classified into three main groups: durable goods, non-durable goods and services.

Consumer durable goods are to consumers what capital goods are to industrial buyers. They are purchased infrequently, are usually the result of considerable search, inspection and comparison, and normally involve substantial sums of money. They include motor cars, furniture, boats, personal computers, caravans, central heating, fitted kitchens, television sets, lounge suits and similar substantial purchases.

Consumer non-durable products are purchased more frequently and usually bought when convenient, on impulse, or during the weekend shopping expeditions. They include foodstuffs, toiletries, small items of clothes, matches, newspapers, ball-point pens, chocolate and confectionery, ice cream, books, torch batteries etc.

Consumer services are similar to industrial services and include such things as life insurance, banking, cleaning, travel arrangements, hospital schemes and personal services, hairdressing, manicure, beauty treatment, shoe repairs, health care etc.

Many products that depend on the nature of their appeal to a section of the market may be classified in more than one category. For this reason, when pricing a consumer item it should be classified in relation to the potential buyer and not as a separate, detached object.

All purchases – professional, industrial and consumer – have an emotional content. However, emotion plays a much stronger role in consumer purchasing, and price is but one of many factors in the transaction. The price of a consumer product cannot be managed in isolation; it is part of an integrated package of appeals, designed to win the patronage of customers.

The composition of the package will depend on the type of consumer product being marketed. Obviously, a different set of appeals is appropriate when selling motor cars compared with those required to sell a washing powder. In marketing terms, the package is the *marketing mix*. Reduced to its most simple combination, it has five components: the product, price, place (distribution methods), promotion (including personal selling and advertising) and service. They are widely known as the 4Ps plus S. Consideration of these five components in turn provides a useful guide to the preparation of a marketing plan.

NEEDS, WANTS, DESIRES

All consumers have wants, but, beyond the basic necessities which will be obtained despite the price, few are essential to life. A few items are regarded as almost essentials for modern life, and such needs are always near or at the top of consumers' shopping lists.

Lower down the list are the true wants; these are things that are not necessary but are acquired when conditions permit, or when a special effort is made to buy them. Sometimes they are an exceptional purchase such as a birthday or Christmas gift. Items such as a new suit, washing-up machine, computer, electric coffee maker, juice extractor, air-conditioning, short-wave radio, garden furniture, which may be classified as wants, indicate their wide and differing degrees of appeal to consumers.

Still further down the list are desires. These are products that will only be purchased when all other needs and wants have been, or are being satisfied. Even more than 'wants', desire products are very diverse and reflect the individual aspirations and tastes of consumers.

Beyond basic essentials, the list of wants is entirely subjective: what one person classifies as a want, another will see as a need. The particular classification that a consumer makes of a product does not confer any special connotation on it; it merely reflects the degree of satisfaction to be realized by the consumer in acquiring the product. In the late 1930s television was considered by most people in the UK to be a desire product. From the 1950s it moved to a want. By the 1980s it could be classified almost as a need.

Before pricing a consumer product it should be categorized as a need, want, or desire for the target market it is being aimed at to get a better idea of its perceived value. Before we can do this we need to consider target markets.

MARKETS AND SUBMARKETS

In attempting to define 'the market' for a particular product, an estimate is first made of the total market. Everyone who could possibly, and *sensibly*, buy the product should be included in the 'total' market.

The qualification of 'sensible' is obvious with a product such as a motor car tyre. Clearly, every person in the country over sixteen might be included in those who *could* buy car tyres, but it would be more sensible to restrict the total market to those people who have cars.

To define the total consumer market for some products such as portable typewriters, central heating, or small electric cookers is not easy because the groups to be included or excluded cannot be readily identified.

Once the total market has been estimated as accurately as possible, a decision has to be taken whether the whole market, or a segment of it, is the product's target market.

The potential buyers in the target market must be identifiable and be able to be reached through appropriate media with the description of the product or service and its price.

DISTRIBUTION METHODS

A market consists of potential buyers, with needs, wants, or desires, to be satisfied, and the means of funding their purchase. Thus, in any total market, the potential buyers are geographically dispersed, either profusely or sparsely. For consumer products in general, the buyers will be distributed more or less densely throughout the country.

A product or service can be supplied to a consumer as the user, in three main ways:

- direct from the producer to the user;
- to one middleman (commonly, retailers), who sells it to consumers;
- through two middlemen (wholesalers and retailers), and then to the consumer.

All three distribution systems and the prevailing methods should be considered when preparing the pricing structure and its management.

If the producer decides to sell direct to the consumer, the activities of both wholesaler and retailer have to be carried out and financed. The price must therefore include a margin for the two operations, and the profits normally made by the middlemen are retained by the producer. But the producer must be as efficient as the middlemen who usually carry out the two functions, otherwise sales and profits will be affected.

The producer who sells direct to consumers does not necessarily have to share with them the profits acquired by carrying out the services normally undertaken by wholesaler and retailer. The main advantage of selling direct is that the producer can exercise greater control over the selling activity.

Any subsequent change of channels involves considerable expenditure, but if the producer has a competitive advantage in any of the price components then changing channel could eventually lead to greater profits, from a larger profit component, greater sales volume, or both.

In exhibit 4.1 product *A* may have a competitive advantage in basic cost and, if it is currently being sold direct and the large oncost is mainly marketing expenses, it could be a candidate for marketing through middlemen. There is sufficient margin in the oncost and profit to finance middlemen's margins.

Product *B* may have a competitive advantage with its high profit margin. If it is currently being marketed direct to consumers, the marketing oncost component could be increased and the channel changed to sell through middlemen.

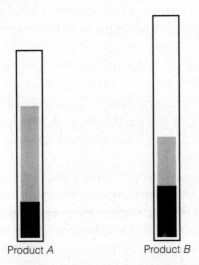

Product *A* Product *B*

Exhibit 4.1 Possible candidates for changing channels

Price composition and the level of sales are not the only factors to be assessed, but, irrespective of the type of channel change being contemplated for a product, an analysis of its price components is the first step. This should reveal the extent and type of any competitive advantage it has, and how this could be used by the company to achieve greater sales and profits by changing channels.

Three main policies may be adopted to market products and services:

- undifferentiated;
- differentiated;
- concentrated.

UNDIFFERENTIATED MARKETING

The whole market is the product's target market. It may be tackled with one marketing mix: one type or range of products, one price structure, one distribution method, one promotional policy, one type of servicing system. The product, its packaging, price, advertising message and the way it is distributed will be the same throughout the country: this is an undifferentiated marketing strategy.

85

DIFFERENTIATED MARKETING

A number of distinct sub-markets may have been identified. Different needs may have been associated with consumers in some areas, and therefore not all potential buyers can be appealed to and reached with the same advertising message and distribution scheme. Competitors may have a strong hold on some areas, be firmly entrenched in the distribution channels, and enjoy a large market share; middlemen may be weak in some areas and provide inadequate service.

Differentiated marketing requires the company to define these market segments and prepare a separate marketing mix for each one. The product and its packaging may be modified for particular segments; advertising could also be focused on individual groups if this is possible; distribution channels and methods may need to be specially developed for some segments.

Pricing will need special consideration because each market segment, by virtue of its definition, has special features and characteristics that distinguish it from other segments.

CONCENTRATED MARKETING

Both undifferentiated and differentiated marketing strategies imply that the whole market is being tackled; either with one marketing mix or several, each one for an identified sub-market. A concentrated marketing strategy aims at one market segment.

The complete market, especially for a new entrant in the field, is sometimes too large to cope with all at once. The reasons for this are varied. The current output may be insufficient to cope with demand from the total market; the company may not have sufficient resources or staff to handle enquiries and sales from the total market; the finance necessary to fund activities on a country-wide scale may be too great in the initial stages. In such a situation the company can adopt a concentrated marketing strategy and focus all activities on one particular segment of the market.

Where a company does not have the financial clout to adopt an undifferentiated marketing strategy and compete in the total market, it is often possible to match competition in one segment with a concentrated strategy. This has implications for pricing, because large competitors, with their greater production experience, usually enjoy larger unit profit. By trimming the profit component, the new entrant can meet these competitors, if not on equal terms, certainly better equipped to fight in the one segment.

PUSH-PULL OPERATIONS

In the marketing of consumer products through middlemen, the ultimate battlefield is the restricted space in retail outlets. There are two main ways to get products into the hands of the customer: the products can be pushed through the channel, that is, sold aggressively into the wholesaler, retailer, or stockist; or the customer can be stimulated by advertising into asking for the product, that is, pulling it through the channel.

Both methods have their advantages and limitations. In general, where a high market share is sought, a pull strategy is preferred because the producer has control over the advertising content and can build the appropriate product image.

PUSH STRATEGY

To push goods through the channel they are first sold into the middlemen – the wholesalers and retailers in the particular distribution channel. The producer provides regular product information, adequate technical and backup service where appropriate, and maintains constant sales pressure to stimulate sales to the trade and encourage them to push the products to the customers.

Pricing plays an important part in push strategy. Middlemen are interested in profit, especially the size of profit but, as sales make profit, they are mainly interested in resaleability of the product. A product carrying a very high margin for the middlemen is of little attraction if it doesn't sell very often. Therefore a push strategy calls for a price with a sufficiently large distribution component and a carefully structured price to make handling the product attractive to the trade.

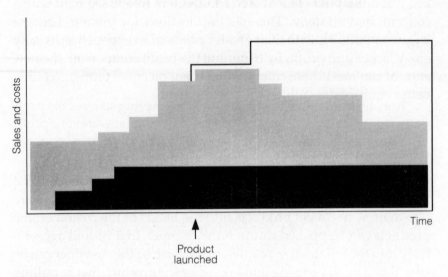

Exhibit 4.2 Product with heavy pre-launch investment

PULL STRATEGY

With a pull strategy, the producer, by advertising and promotion, persuades consumers to ask for the product at retail outlets, and retailers to ask for supplies from wholesalers. The products are thus pulled through the channel in large volume.

A consideration of price composition and the likely behaviour of basics costs, especially a possible decline in unit production cost, will influence marketing and financial strategy. If unit cost declines markedly with volume, the product has a built-in advantage and the situation is similar to the conditions that favour penetration pricing described in chapter 3.

If, however, the percentages of price components remain much the same irrespective of volume, it is the sales volume that determines total profit. A heavy investment in promotion and distribution costs is needed before adequate volume is achieved. Frequently the oncost has to be committed before the product is launched, as in exhibit 4.2.

Sustained advertising to consumers is necessary to force stockists in the distribution channel to hold stocks. The distribution element in the oncost is a significant item, as it must also include the margin for the middleman.

SHORT-TERM AND LONG-TERM PLOYS

A push or pull strategy may be employed in the short or long term.

Long-term push, in general, requires a steady growth of good relations with the trade channel and therefore the oncost component must be adequate to implement this strategy.

Short-term push can be effected by pre-empting some of the profit component, or by an injection of funds from total company profit. The aim, of course, is to stimulate sufficient sales to pay for the short-term promotion to the trade.

Short-term pull can be achieved in a similar manner to short-term push tactics. Either some of the unit profit component can be used, or separate funds applied to stimulate sales. Typically, it is used to stimulate sales at certain times during the year and it is also advisable to have a degree of short-term push in trade channels.

Long-term pull is the most costly method of marketing and requires sustained expenditure on publicity in the oncost component, especially if the product is branded. The aim is to built a sound and attractive image of the product in the minds of the consumer. This normally compels the oncost component to be a high percentage of price compared with the percentages of basic cost and profit components.

SELLING PUSH PRODUCTS

Unit price is generally high. Sales are achieved through personal contact between the consumer and the stockist by means of sales presentations, demonstrations etc.

Stockists are able to contribute to the image of the product or brand, and have a strong influence on the ultimate choice of product. Where appropriate they are responsible for transporting the product to the consumer and its installation, financing credit to the consumers, terms and after-sales service.

Push products usually require considerable store space, and stockists need to have trained sales personnel and demonstrators. Because of the time required by consumers to decide, stockists must possess the resources to afford the time, money and manpower to sell the products. Such products have to *sold* by the stockists, and they expect adequate reward in the price.

Stockists are normally required to make a substantial investment to sell push products, because turnover of invested capital is relatively low. While a certain level of publicity is expected of the manufacturer, especially below-the-line promotion, the chief weapon used to persuade them to sell the product is price. The price structure must be sufficiently attractive for the stockist to have a good margin, and know that resaleability is not adversely affected.

SELLING PULL PRODUCTS

Unit price of pull products is generally low. Selling is by impersonal contact between the manufacturer and the consumer through advertising, sales literature, promotion, contests, display and packaging.

Stockists have little or no influence on the brand or product image and choice of product. As transportation and installation are not usually involved, stockists have little subsequent contact with the consumer. After-sales service is usually carried out by the manufacturer or specifically appointed service agents.

Pull products occupy little individual space in retail outlets, and retailers do not need sales people highly trained in product capabilities or, if appropriate, great ability to demonstrate them. Pull products are *bought* by the consumers.

To enter a pull product business the stockist needs a relatively modest investment because turnover of invested capital is relatively high. Because of the low price and unit profit, stockists cannot afford to spend time, money and manpower to sell such products and depend largely on the consumer advertising efforts of the manufacturer.

A crude but accurate distinction may be observed between a push and a pull product: if it has to stand on the floor, push it; if it can sit on a shelf, pull it.

Washing machines, refrigerators and furniture are typical push products; washing powder, foodstuffs, floor polish, chocolate bars and cigarettes are pull products. Pull products are repeat purchased, therefore the profit component in price is small; push products are bought infrequently and possess a relatively high profit component.

BEST VALUE AND BEST BUY

When customers are searching for products to satisfy their needs, wants and desires, they are looking for the best value they can find.

Exhibit 4.3 Best value deep freeze

Cubic capacity (ft³)	Price (£)	Price per cubic foot (£/ft³)
12.5	150	12
15	190	12.70
20	225	11.25
50	300	6

However, 'best value' needs defining. If the best value concept were valid, then customers would always purchase the largest pack of the product that offers the lowest unit price because that would be the best value. Exhibit 4.3 illustrates the best value in deep freezes by dividing the price by the cubic capacity.

Clearly, the 50 cubic foot model at only £6 per cubic foot is the best value. It is not necessarily the best buy from the consumer's viewpoint because it may be much larger than the family needs, it may not fit in the customer's kitchen, and some space may have to be foregone by acquiring it. Because of these considerations, and where the deep freeze will be located in the house, the best value is often not the best buy.

Similarly, instead of buying household supplies in ones and twos, housewives should, to obtain the best value, buy in tens, dozens and greater packs. But in general they don't, unless they are shopping in 'cash and carry' stores which sell only bulk packs.

Best value will be found in large packs of products, usually in plain packaging, and which are typical of what is sold to 'the trade'. Toilet paper in minimum printed outer packs of ten, dozen, or larger offer the best value. The best value in wood screws is in packs of 500; the price per screw is considerably lower than when purchased in half-dozens. The best value in toothpaste, or hair shampoo, is in gross packs; the best value in potatoes is in 100 kilo lots, or even better, by the tonne.

If 'best value' were related solely to price, many more large packs of consumer products would be sold. What customers look for is the best buy, which, for them, constitutes the best perceived value. Value is not an objective attribute related solely to price and quality, but subjective to each purchaser and *specific to each purchase*. Over a period of time, by their repeat purchases, consumers usually demonstrate sound judgement of what constitutes best value.

Consumers judge which product offers the best value by the similarity of its price to the company's previous price, and the price of competitive products. If the product is a member of a product line, the differentials among the prices of related products will also affect the consumer's judgement. Above all, the perceived value of the item in the life-style of the consumer is a major factor in the best buy equation.

While perceived value is a subjective judgement, the elements that blend in different combinations to achieve the 'best buy' at any one time include such things as the shape and colour of pack, the slogan on the product, where it is usually purchased, its advertising message, the personalities associated with it, and a host of other points as well as its price. In a similar manner to the way that the marketing mix can be reduced to its most simple form with the 4Ps + S, so the main elements of what constitutes best buy can be reduced to another 4Ps + S:

- Purpose
- Performance
- Presentation
- Price
- Synergy

PURPOSE

No one buys a product for itself alone, but for the service or satisfaction it provides. This service, or satisfaction, is the purpose of the product. Consumers in general, and housewives in particular, are very much aware of the purpose for which products are bought. As millions of housewives make their weekly choice of breakfast cereals, washing powder, bakery products, toilet paper, cleaners and numerous other supermarket items, they know what the product will do, how it will be received by the family, the extent to which it will satiate hunger or slake thirst, or whether it whitens, softens, deodorizes and cleans.

Not only must the product contribute to its value by meeting the purpose required, this must be readily understood by the consumer from its presentation and price.

PERFORMANCE

A product's value is increased to the extent that its performance meets its purpose. A product for cleaning silverware may perform adequately provided that sufficient 'elbow grease' is used. A competitive product that cleans silverware equally well by simply wiping it over the surface of the article outperforms the first product. Many products have the same purpose but widely differing levels of performance. Often, improved performance reflects the technical skill of the manufacturer in making the product or the cost of the ingredients used in its formulation.

In the 'best buy' equation, the most important performance rating is the one given to the product by the particular consumer. Obviously, this will not be the same for all consumers, and certainly not the same as that accorded to the product by company personnel.

Some ingredients may possess improved technical characteristics which, however, are not readily observed by the consumer. An example is an ingredient in a lubricant which greatly reduces the incidence of rusting. The performance of the lubricant will only be seen over a period of time and the subsequent performance appreciation of the product by the consumer may be unaffected. To have any impact at all, the performance has to be explained and presented to the potential buyer; otherwise, if the improved performance is only communicated by the price difference, the impact will be nil.

Performance is an amalgam of product attributes which are customer benefits, and might better be described as perceived performance. Doing what it is supposed to do to achieve the purpose is but one attribute. The colour and shape of the product and its pack, its size and 'feel', the ease with which it can be stored or packed away: these and many other qualities and attributes, including price, make up a product's performance.

PERFORMANCE TESTS

To test the perceived performance of a washing powder in the UK, a company arranged for samples of it to be delivered door-to-door to a randomly selected number of housewives in the Midlands. Each housewife who agreed to participate in the test was given three packs of washing powder, all similarly printed but in three different colours – blue, green and red.

They were asked to use the three packets in their normal washing during the following three weeks, but to use a different colour pack each week. They were told that they would be visited a month later and asked which powder they had found best. As a reward for their participation, they would receive three month's supply of the powder they preferred. The powders varied in the three packets, and could only be identified by the manufacturer.

In due course the researchers returned, noted the colour of pack that housewives nominated best for their wash and arranged for the supply of the product. As one might expect, opinion of the performance of the three powders varied, but one was a clear leader.

The object of the exercise was not to test the performance of the powder, because it was identical in all three packs. It was to test the overall performance, particularly the colour of the pack. The manufacturer knows that 'performance' includes more than just the washing capabilities of the powder: the name of a product, its price, packaging and general presentation are also part of performance.

In an attempt to qualify the test, all the housewives received three month's supply of a coloured pack they had *not* chosen. It was reasoned that if there were sufficient complaints that the 'wrong' powder had been supplied, it might give an indication of the strength of conviction held of the powder's performance. In the event, nearly 50 per cent complained of having received a different powder from the one chosen.

In an attempt to evaluate the performance of a range of graphite pencils, a similar test was conducted in a large drawing office just north of London. For three months the draughtsmen were offered an adequate supply of pencils that included all the grades from 7H to 7B. Except for these normal grades, they were told that the only difference in the pencils was the way in which the graphite had been formulated and inserted in the wood. Different coloured exterior enamels, blue, green, red and yellow, indicated the different methods of manufacture known only to the manufacturer.

The draughtsmen were asked which of the pencils they preferred and the reasons for the preference. For their participation, the drawing office would be supplied for the pencils of their choice for a year.

There was fairly unanimous opinion that the green enamelled pencils broke most easily and the red enamelled pencils were the hardest, whichever grade was used. The yellow enamelled ones received the majority vote.

The pencils were all manufactured in the same way, the only difference, apart from the grade of graphite, was the final coat of enamel on the outside. This indicates the degree of influence that colour has on perceived performance. There was a factor in this test that was absent from the washing powder test – the influence of group thinking on the individual. Undoubtedly there would have been ample opportunity for the exchange of views and this would have had considerable influence on the individual decision.

Where consumers are repeat buying and using products frequently, provided that the products perform to the expected standard, they become able but conditioned judges of product performance. This equates to the strength of the product or brand loyalty and tends to obstruct their trying a new or improved product.

PRESENTATION

In the context of best buy, presentation includes all the means by which the manufacturer offers, or presents, the product to the potential customer. This includes its name, shape, colour, packaging, appearance in the outlets, style of letters used in printing name and other data, how the price is shown, the ambience of the product, and all forms of advertising and publicity used.

The presentation has two main aims: to get the consumer to try the product, and to develop the product or brand image.

Presentation is obviously related to performance. The higher the performance and greater the advantage over competitive products, the stronger can be the presentation. With a significant product advance, the presentation may include a visual demonstration which is a very powerful way of getting consumers to try the product. However, strong presentation alone is insufficient to persuade consumers to try the product; its price must be related to the promised benefits.

Once having tried a product, a consumer will not be persuaded by presentation to repeat the purchase if the performance and price are not in accord, or are higher than the consumer requires.

The creation of a product image is often vital for success in a highly competitive market. If several consumer brands with the same purpose and performance are available at similar prices, the brand with the image, the personality, will become the best buy.

PRICE

Price is the one element that, with sales, is responsible for profit. The purpose of a product and its performance will be dictated by the research conducted prior to its marketing and the value of its manufacturing or formulation. The more complex the manufacture, the more valuable the ingredients of formulation, the more costly is the product. The greater the investment in presentation – the packaging, sales literature, advertising – the more costly the product.

Not only is price the one element that provides revenue and profit, it is also the most flexible of the elements in the 'best buy' equation. To alter the purpose, improve the performance, or change the presentation of a product not only costs money, but takes time; price can be altered immediately.

This immediacy of price change also has its disadvantage. One company's price change can be very quickly copied by all competitors. If it is an attempt to influence the 'best buy' opinion, and is a price reduction, competitors are likely to follow the move. The result would be unchanged market shares but lower revenues for all.

In the consumer market, price is a powerful weapon. More than any other element, price is responsible for market segmentation. Customers buy in price brackets or price plateaux. A man who is looking for a camera of a certain performance will look at those in the appropriate price range, say, between £150 and £200; he is not interested in cameras outside this price bracket.

The family planning their summer vacation will undoubtedly look in the price range that suits them. Exotic holidays, the other side of the world, or modest camping holidays within a couple of hundred kilometres of their home will be of no interest to them if the price of either is above or below what they are looking for.

SYNERGY

Synergy, or synergism, is the working together of components to produce an effect greater than the sum of the individual effects. In the 'best buy' concept, the constituent parts – purpose, performance, presentation and price – will have a greater effect if the right combination is achieved.

A product with modest performance and high price is unlikely to succeed, whereas one with a high performance but low price is a formula for obtaining sales. High sales do not necessarily mean high profits unless the profit component is substantial, or the company has the cost advantages of volume.

Adequate consideration should be given to a product's purpose and performance, its price and presentation in the quest for best value so that each will enhance the others. The purpose of the product will be related to the particular needs of the market segment selected. The performance will be adequate for its purpose and carry an appropriate price tag; that is, performance and price must be balanced. The price must be right for the market segment, and right when compared with competition. With these combinations achieved, the product must be properly presented: a high-class product needs a high-class presentation; an inexpensive product needs a moderate presentation.

By getting the interactions between the components balanced for overall effect, synergism will be achieved and a strong, acceptable personality created for the product.

BEST BUY IN CAMERAS

When Japanese cameras entered the UK market in the 1960s, consumers were slow to buy them because their price was low compared with the German quality cameras. Consumers apparently considered that a quality camera could not be sold so cheaply, so they were not regarded either by the trade or consumers as a best buy. Chemist shops traditionally sold photographic products, and one in High Holborn, London, had a notice in its window warning potential customers of the dangers of buying 'inferior' cameras with plastic components.

It took three or four years of sustained marketing effort for the Japanese manufacturers to change their previous image as imitators, for the cameras to be accepted, and a further period for them to be widely acknowledged as a best buy.

BEST BUY WASHING POWDER

Selling washing powders is a highly competitive consumer business. In the UK, Persil, the product of Lever Bros, has been the most successful brand since 1970. While its presentation, particularly its advertising, has contributed to its success, it was the continual updating of its 'best buy' image that maintained its market dominance.

It responded to repeated attacks from competitors with powerful messages about Persil washing whiter and cleaner; the pack had a slightly greater weight of powder to give consumers a subtle price advantage; it was reformulated for use with the automatic, front-loading, high-speed machines that tended to fill up kitchens with foam if ordinary washing powder were used.

By maintaining the right combinations of performance, price and presentation, the company has kept the product firmly in consumers' minds as the standard by which to judge all other powders.

In India, Lever Bros were also the market leader in detergents in the 1970s, dominating the market with Surf. Mr Karsanbhai Patel decided that Surf, although a high-quality product was also a high-priced product, and that a latent potential market existed for a low-priced product. He decided to market a competitive product and adopt a penetration price policy.

In view of the inevitable counterattacks he would be subject to, he had to ensure that his manufacturing and distribution costs were sufficiently low to combat these. He eschewed modern manufacturing methods and constructed his manufacturing methods to Indian conditions. He started a chain of workshops in which people mixed the ingredients by hand – not using any electric power. His low-priced Nirma brand is reported to have outsold the Lever product by about three to one. In 1987 his turnover exceeded £150 million and his intention was to double that within four years.

His labour costs are estimated to be about one-fifth of Hindustan Lever's costs and his work-force is non-unionized. His overheads are low, with about 200 supervisors looking after a work-force of some 10,000.

BEST BUY PRICE

If price for a consumer product is skilfully set, carefully monitored and managed, it will become the 'best buy' price and play an important role in the product's long-term profitability. It can also help to develop a growth product into a market leader. On the other hand, a carelessly set or poorly managed price will erode profits and offer profitable opportunities to competitors with the added reward of assuming dominance in a market.

Price plays an obvious and vital part in marketing tactics; it is also an important factor in long-term strategy. A product should cover its cost of production and distribution, contribute to the general cost of running the company, and provide profit to keep the company in business. The success, or otherwise, of a product therefore depends on the margin it can generate. This margin is the profit component of price and is the difference between the product's basic cost and oncost, and its net selling price.

All costs that can be directly attributed to a product are established; the total of these deducted from the net selling price is the margin. Costs and overheads that are general to all products and cannot be readily and equitably allocated to individual products are lumped together as fixed costs or general overheads. The general treatment of costs and margins is very important and treated separately in a later chapter.

PRICING PRODUCTS

The following notes summarize the main differences between push and pull products for the components of the market mix and show how each is related to the pricing strategy.

Push products

Product Demonstrable features. Service worthwhile carrying out. Packing is only functional. Innovation is important. To improve market coverage and penetration more than one brand and pricing structure might be useful.

Place Direct contact between the manufacturer and the stockist is essential. Dealer training must be offered; price structure must include training costs. A limited number of national accounts and key dealers should be developed.

Promotion   Image building is more important than product advertising. Sales promotion can be a great stimulus and it is essential to maintain a regular flow of product information and news. The sales organization must be capable of educating and training stockists and generally help them to sell out. There should be adequate margins in price structure to allow for sufficient below-the-line activity.

Service   A complete backup service to the stockists, with parts, components, replacements, modular exchanges and general servicing information must be maintained. Warranty and guarantee obligations must be accounted for in the price, but servicing should be priced so as to provide its own profit margin.

Price   Discounts usually have an important influence on market share. Price should enable the product to be attractive and provide good profit to the stockist. Price of a major consumer product is not so important as the initial payment and hire purchase terms.

Pull products

Product   High performance, quality and reliability, more important than low price. Frequent product innovation and modification is desirable. Use 'plus features' in publicity. Claims made in all publicity, promotion and advertising must be believable and presented in terms of product benefits. Self-service packing, display, instruction books. Packaging should sell the product. Strong branding style necessary; possibly some distributor brands necessary. Pricing structure must allow for multi-channel marketing, and respect the margins in each.

Place   No need for any contact between manufacturer and stockist; advertising does the pre-selling. Number of middlemen or wholesalers should be kept to a minimum consistent with the maximum number of retailers. Need to consider exclusive, selective or intensive distribution. Wholesalers encouraged to buy in container loads based on annual purchases. Computer-guided weekly supplies based on actual sell-out. Reduce fixed cost investment in transportation and warehousing where possible by using third parties. Concentrate on limited number of big customers; reduce number of direct accounts to minimum possible. Aim for:

- low number of orders and invoices;
- high value per order/invoice;
- minimum transport/handling costs;
- low stocks by supplying direct from factory;
- maximum selling expenses of, say, 10 per cent.

Promotion Strong product advertising above the line essential. Pre-test and post-test all copy. Some below the line activities. Sales promotion important for sales organization and stockists to stock and display more. Oncost component should be adequate to include allowance for these activities.

Service Centralized or decentralized service centres is a major policy decision that should be guided by the volume of likely servicing and potential profit. Over-the-counter replacement is desirable, reducing high labour content servicing to minimum. Oncost component must allow for amount of 'free' service likely.

Price Degree of price elasticity of demand is important in highly competitive field. Discounts have a variable influence on market share. 'Resaleability' is more important than price.

COMPETITORS' VIEWS

Consumers' opinions on price changes may be reflected in their purchasing; equally important is how competitors might act. There is little sense in reducing the price of a consumer product if all competitors follow. A price reduction may be seen by competitors as a signal that:

- the quality has been lowered and the price is much the same;
- the product isn't selling well;
- a new product is about to be launched;
- the product is at the end of its life or season;
- the company needs cash.

They may take the view that a price increase means that:

- the product is in short supply;
- the price will soon be increased again;
- the product is very popular;
- the product offers good value and the company is making hay.

Between the manufacturer and the consumer are the middlemen – the trade. How they see price changes is also important. However, whether or not a price change is perceived and, if perceived, how it is interpreted and assessed by the trade, your customers and competition should be evaluated before the price change decision is implemented. Suppose you are thinking of reducing the price of product by 15 per cent, the following assessments might be made:

Perception

Customers   80 per cent will perceive this within one month; only 90 per cent of those who notice it will perceive it accurately.

Competitors   Major rivals and the majority of competitors will perceive the reduction before it is known to customers.

Trade   80 per cent will perceive it accurately as a promotional device; 20 per cent will fail to understand it.

Interpretation

Customers   Of the 80 per cent who perceive it, perhaps a half will assume that a new product is about to be launched on the market. The others will either place no interpretation on the change or assume that the product is in some way inferior.

Competitors   Depending on the relative market shares held, competitors will see it as an attack on their markets or an attempt to increase your cash flow, or is a preliminary to a new model being introduced.

Trade   75 per cent might see it as a means to move the product through the channel more quickly into the hands of consumers; the rest may see it as a ploy to increase their stock holdings.

Assessment

Customers   The 80 per cent who perceive it correctly may fall into four groups: 20 per cent will favourably assess the change and be prepared to buy; 20 per cent will regard it favourably but wait for further reduction; 20 per cent will feel aggrieved at having paid a higher price previously; 20 per cent will not assess the change.

Competitors   Those with a similar market share to the company will react with an increase in promotional activities, or make a similar, or deeper, price cut.

Trade   Those who see it as a promotional device will co-operate, assessing it as a means to increase their own turnover. A small number will resent the lower trade margin resulting from the price reduction.

PRICING FMCG

The proficient management of prices of fast moving consumer goods (FMCG) can make a significant difference to the long-term profitability of a product. Such goods tend to be repeat purchased frequently, and there is more scope for the manufacturer to use a flexible pricing strategy. Setting prices without discretion or, worse still, pricing products indifferently, will present competitors with opportunities to exploit one's markets.

Sound pricing policy requires a manufacturer to have an agreed strategy, such as to maintain the lowest price in the market comparable with quality, to maintain price leadership by setting as high a price as the market will bear, or to use price as a dynamic marketing tool and offer varying discounts from list price.

For fast moving consumer goods, price plays two particularly important roles: it determines the unit profit margin and it greatly influences the sales volume

PRICING WITH A LOW MARKET SHARE

The company with a competitive product that has a low market share has to be guided by the market leader for price. Any ploy that might be construed as a price attack will quickly invite retaliation. This retaliation from a market leader can be sufficient to see off the marauder because of the usually wide variation in direct and indirect costs. Furthermore, if the market leader is a multi-product organization, it is possible for a strong counterattack to be launched by the leader offering substantial discounts, any losses being absorbed by other products.

Market leaders are well known; their products are usually heavily advertised and promoted. Middlemen are normally willing to accept a lower unit profit margin for such products because they make up in volume turnover what they lack in unit margin. Thus, the company with the low market share will have to offer similar products at a lower price to the trade so that a higher unit margin is obtained.

Earlier we discussed three different type of marketing policy – undifferentiated, differentiated and concentrated.

A concentrated marketing policy is of interest to the company that has a low market share and wishes to adopt a sensible pricing strategy that may not unduly disturb other competitors in the market. The company's attention is focused on one segment and an appropriate marketing mix devised for it. This may mean slight changes in the product or packaging; advertising and promotion must be restricted to that segment; the distribution channel used may be different from their other activities; the pricing structure can be more flexible when operating in a corner of the total market. What is important is to segment the market adequately; it must be:

- measurable;
- accessible;
- different enough to be distinguishable;
- substantial;
- durable.

Here are some of the characteristics that can be used to segment a market for a product:

- product usage;
- perceived customer benefits;
- volume and frequency of purchases;
- previous purchasing behaviour;

- method of purchase;
- geographic location;
- responsiveness to marketing variables;
- SIC industry group;
- size of middleman organization;
- servicing requirements;
- profit margin.

Sometimes a special case exists where a large organization continues with a low-profit product that has a low market share. If the product rounds out a line, such as product G in exhibit 3.10 in chapter 3, then the pricing of the other products in the line will be more important. If the low-share product is being used by the manufacturer to prevent the price leader from increasing prices, this may be affecting the leader's profit and cash flow.

A different situation exists where a low market share product is in a rapidly growing market. There is a strong temptation to go for growth, increase market share and turn the product into a star performer.

The reasons supporting this strategy are sound enough: the market is growing; increased sales are available. Staying where it is until the market stabilizes results in the product being 'frozen in' with a low market share in a declining market situation.

The problem of going for growth is the cost of obtaining an increased market share. Opposition from the high market share products can be so great that the additional expenditure required to increase market share outweighs the additional profits received from the increase.

PRICING WHERE THERE IS NO DOMINANT LEADER

Where a number of products hold similar market shares and there is no dominant market leader, a state of equilibrium in price and performance exists, and sales reflect the perceived value of each product. This equilibrium will persist unless or until one of the competitors achieves a competitive advantage. Each product retains its loyal customers, but loses and gains customers who switch their purchases.

		Product purchased this time	
		A	*B*
Product purchased previous time	*A*	0.7	0.3
	B	0.4	0.6

Exhibit 4.4 Transition matrix

		Product purchased this time		
		A	*B*	*NP*
Product purchased previous time	*A*	0.68	0.28	0.04
	B	0.35	0.60	0.05

Exhibit 4.5 Transition matrix with a 'no purchase' decision

The situation concerning fast moving consumer goods can be represented in a *transition matrix* as in exhibit 4.4. Two products are depicted, each with its propensity to retain its customers, and each having a proportion of 'switchers' – customers who switch to a different brand or product from time to time.

This particular matrix indicates that if a customer bought brand *A* last time, the chances are 70 per cent that brand *A* will be purchased again, and 30 per cent that brand *B* will purchased. Similarly, for a customer who purchased brand *B* last time, the chances are 60 per cent that *B* will be purchased this time, and 40 per cent for a switch to product *A*.

It is not a cross probability matrix; it is read across the rows, each of which adds to unity because it is assumed that a decision will be made to buy one of the products.

Product purchased this time

		A	B	C	D	E
	A	0.85	0.03	0.02	0.04	0.06
Product purchased last time	B	0.02	0.88	0.01	0.04	0.05
	C	0.04	0.03	0.82	0.05	0.06
	D	0.04	0.08	0.05	0.78	0.05
	E	0.07	0.02	0.06	0.05	0.80

Exhibit 4.6 Transition matrix for five products

If a 'no purchase' decision by the customer is to be included, this would be shown as a 'no purchase' brand, *NP*, as in exhibit 4.5.

In a market where there are many more than two competitors, the transition matrix becomes more complicated. To obtain sufficient information for a transition matrix to be used means that extensive and expensive market surveys are required.

A sufficiently large enough number of customers is interviewed to find out the brand that has currently been bought and the brand previously purchased. From a survey of, say, 500 people, it would be possible to extrapolate for the whole market and devise a table of brand-switching tendencies.

For this analysis to be of any value, continuous market surveys, such as the retail audits conducted by some market research organizations, are necessary to determine any changes in product loyalty, and if there are, the percentage probability of switching to another product.

In the matrix in exhibit 4.6, *A* is shown to have 85 per cent loyal customers; 15 per cent (0.03 + 0.02 + 0.04 + 0.06) tend to switch to another product. The situation becomes complex with FMCG because eventually some of *A*'s customers who switch from *A* will also switch back to *A*. Obviously, this tendency will be replicated by all the other products.

The modelling technique used to analyse brand switching is Markov analysis, after the Russian mathematician Andrei Markov (1856–1922). He observed the apparent random movement of gas particles in a sealed chamber and found that if he knew where a particle had been in the immediately previous time period he could predict with accuracy where it would be in the immediately following period. Knowledge of the previous two periods enabled him to predict the next two periods; three previous periods, three forward periods, and so on.

The figures in italics in exhibit 4.6, show the amount of brand loyalty or repeat purchase rate. All other figures are the switching rates.

These are percentage probabilities to remain loyal or switch, and do not indicate the actual market shares held. If product, price, performance and presentation are relatively stable, or any changes by one competitor are matched by the others, the situation approaches an equilibrium state: the actual market shares of competitors become stable.

A further property when no one competitor gains a competitive advantage is that, irrespective of the initial market shares, they will stabilize at the same equilibrium for a given set of transition probabilities.

During a period of stability, and assuming that they all have approximately the same level of operating efficiency, unit margins will remain much the same for all competitors, and all will achieve a reasonable level of profitability.

Cutting price in such circumstances would be folly. But, should a competitor develop a significant competitive advantage in product performance, this will eventually affect the pricing strategies of all competitors in the market. The improved product may be introduced without a price change to reflect its improvement. This would be a form of price reduction because customers will be getting a better product at the same price. If the product improvement has necessitated extra costs, the manufacturer's profit will suffer unless the improved product can generate sufficient additional sales for the extra profit to offset the increased cost.

If extra sales are achieved and competitors cannot match the product improvement, their retaliation must be mainly on price;

they would have little to publicize with a product of inferior performance.

If the improved product is introduced at a higher price to reflect the significantly better performance, its degree of price elasticity and the level of brand loyalty for it will be crucial in determining sales. If presentation is also strengthened to emphasize the improved product, unless competitors can equal the product's better performance they are likely to use price as a counter-attack weapon. Depending on the nature of the market, this could also take the form of indirect price incentives such as free gifts, coupons etc.

Any manufacturer contemplating the introduction of an improved product should be aware of the observations that have been made of the importance of price and performance. Where product performance is significantly better than before, irrespective of the price, success is usually reported.

Failures are experienced in about 80 per cent of the cases where performance is not perceived by the consumer to be different, or is actually worse; again, this is irrespective of price.

PRICING FOR THE MARKET LEADER

The dominant market leader, because of the relatively greater sales and volume of production, should have the advantage of lower unit cost and therefore, higher unit profit. Higher market share allied to higher unit profit means much greater power in dictating price strategy.

This can be seen in exhibit 4.7, where the product has achieved a high market share relative to its competitors, and its basic cost component has been reduced. The increased profit component gives the producer substantial advantage in pricing tactics.

The market leader should be able to supply customers with the best value and, no matter how high the performance level set, should be able to supply at a lower unit cost and therefore lower price than any competitor. This assumes that the leader is an efficient and effective operator.

In such a situation the market leader has to monitor the market diligently and develop a responsible pricing strategy, because any actions the leader takes will have repercussions throughout the market. If the market leader reduces price, all competitors are likely

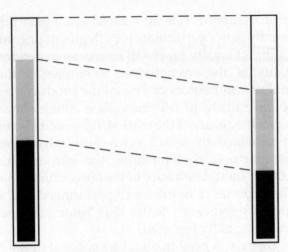

Market share of product is increased from average to
relatively high with accompanying advantage in basic cost

Exhibit 4.7 Product having achieved high market share

to have to follow. Because of the difference in unit profit, competitors who are forced to follow the price reduction will have their margins squeezed. This will cause them to redouble their efforts to obtain a competitive advantage.

Should the market leader continue to operate with a high unit profit margin, the whole market is provided with a price umbrella or shield. This releases funds for competitive product improvement, search for competitive advantage, increased investment in presentation, and development of product or brand image.

Therefore, the market leader's pricing strategy, particularly the level of profit component set for a product, is of fundamental significance to the marketing efforts of all competitors. The stage reached in the product's life cycle and the penetration of the market generally will also influence the market leader's decisions.

If the market is still growing, the leader should maintain a low-price strategy so as to obtain a major share of the additional sales, restrict the activities of the current competitors, and dissuade new ones from entering the market. As growth continues, unit costs should decline. Sooner or later the leader is faced with the decision whether or not to reduce price, and, if so, by how much.

The decision to lower price should be taken when the leader is sure that increased volume and increased total profit are in harmony with decreased unit costs. Leaving the decision too late might persuade a vigorous competitor to gain a competitive advantage with an improved product, or to build a new plant which might provide the competitor with much lower unit costs.

When the product is in its maturity and the market has possibly slowed to a stable situation, the leader has a different situation but certainly is unable to ignore possible competitor moves.

CHAPTER

5

Speeding up investigations

EXPLORING PRICING POSSIBILITIES

To explore the possibilities of pricing and use price as a dynamic marketing tool will often require extensive calculations. The possession of a personal computer is not a prerequisite for using any of the suggestions in this book; all the analyses and tables can be prepared with pencil and paper, or with the aid of a simple calculator, but this is time-consuming. The use of a personal computer (PC) and a spreadsheet program such as Symphony, Lotus 1-2-3, Quattro, Excel or SuperCalc simplifies procedures. Basic layouts and tables with interlinked formulae can be prepared, and innumerable 'what if' situations evaluated.

The basic formats for pricing alternatives, demand schedules, elasticity tendencies, cash flow budgets and their effects on turnover and profit can be set up in a spreadsheet and used with different inputs. In this chapter we start with a simple elasticity problem adapted to the PC, and then explore various pricing situations. The computerized version of the empirical database introduced as exhibit 2.16 in chapter 2 is given at the end of the chapter, exhibit 5.30.

IMPORTANCE OF COMPUTER 'ERRORS'

All the tables and exhibits illustrated in this and the following chapters have been taken directly from spreadsheet files, therefore you may find occasional discrepancies. In most spreadsheet programs, figures are calculated to many places of decimals and carried forward in the calculations. The errors that occur in the final figure in some of the totals are due to rounding figures to a smaller number of decimal places. This is very important because, if your company has sales of products running into scores of thousands, all prices, costings and calculations must be taken to the third decimal place. A variance of only one in the second decimal place amounts to £1,000 in a total of 100,000.

SIMPLE ELASTICITY LAYOUT

Instead of reproducing the computer screen to the size of a page, which makes it too small to be read easily, all layouts are set in normal type. The labels for columns and rows appear in square brackets, [A], [B], [C] ... [1], [2], [3] ... etc., and are as they appear on the screen of the spreadsheet file; these letters and numbers are not typed into the files. All the formulae in the book have been prepared using Symphony, but are easily adapted for any similar spreadsheet program.

Exhibit 5.1 is a layout for determining the coefficient of elasticity between two prices.

	[A]	[B]	[C]	[D]
[1]	ELASTIC1			
[2]				
[3]	Price	Quantity	Revenue	COE
[4]	£37.50	90,000	£3,375,000	
[5]				2.09
[6]	£36.00	98,000	£3,528,000	

Exhibit 5.1 Simple elasticity on a spreadsheet

Before looking at the formulae for the spreadsheet, the COE can be calculated arithmetically by the percentage change method:

$$\frac{\text{percentage change in quantity}}{\text{percentage change in price}}$$

$$8.9/4 = 2.22$$

If point elasticity is calculated, it will be found to be:

$$8.5/4.1 = 2.08$$

The spreadsheet formula is useful because it uses point elasticity and therefore the COE may be used in estimating sales when lowering or increasing price.

In cell [A1] insert the name of the file, for example, ELASTIC1.

```
[A1] ELASTIC1
```

When you are using a number of different spreadsheet files with similar layouts, such as ELASTIC2, ELASTIC3, CASH1, CASH2 etc., having the name at the top of the file will remind you which one you are using.

Leave row [2] blank to improve the appearance of the layout.

In row [3] set columns [A] and [B] each to be 9 units wide; set [C] and [D] each to be 13 units wide.

Label the columns by entering text into the following four cells:

```
[A3] Price
[B3] Quantity
[C3] Revenue
[D3] COE
```

Format column [A] (Price) for currency with two decimal places.

Format column [B] for commas to indicate thousands, but no decimal places.

Format column [C] (Revenue) for currency with no decimal places.

Format column [D] (COE) for two places of decimals.

Formulae are now entered for the automatic calculation of revenues and coefficient of elasticity:

```
[C4] +A4*B4
```

Copy the contents of cell [C4] to [C6], where it will appear as +A6*B6.

```
[D5] ((B4-B6)/(B4+B6))/((A6-A4)/(A4+A6))
```

(Pay particular attention to the number of brackets in all formulae.)

Data are now entered. For this example we use some of the figures from the case later in the chapter. The first entry is the price, £37.50 which is inserted in cell [A4].

114

[A4] 37.50

The second data entry is current sales in cell [B4].

[B4] 90000

(Note that the comma is not typed, but '90,000' appears in the cell if you have correctly formatted column [B].)

Revenue, £3,375,000, should automatically appear with its commas in [C4] if the column has been formatted for currency.

The third data entry is the lower price of £36 in [A6].

[A6] 36

We assume sales of 98,000 at this price.

[B6] 98000

(98,000 appears in the cell.)

The revenue of £3,528,000 will automatically appear in [C6] and the coefficient of elasticity of 2.09 in [D5].

This is a simple layout with just four items being inserted, two prices and two quantities, to obtain the coefficient. Nevertheless, it is an improvement on having to calculate the coefficients every time. You can now experiment with different prices and estimated sales at those prices to see the effect on the coefficient.

For example, in [A6] change the price of £36 to £35.50, but leave the amount of sales at 98,000. The coefficient changes from 2.09 to 1.55 (see exhibit 5.2).

	[A]	[B]	[C]	[D]
[1]	ELASTIC1			
[2]				
[3]	Price	Quantity	Revenue	COE
[4]	£37.50	90,000	£3,375,000	
[5]				1.55
[6]	£35.50	98,000	£3,479,000	

Exhibit 5.2 New price changed

What happens if the price of £35.50 is changed back to £36 and the quantity, 90,000, is the same at both prices? In [A6] insert 36 and in [B6] insert 90000. Exhibit 5.3 shows that the coefficient changes to zero.

	[A]	[B]	[C]	[D]
[1]	ELASTIC1			
[2]				
[3]	Price	Quantity	Revenue	COE
[4]	£37.50	90,000	£3,375,000	
[5]				0.00
[6]	£36.00	90,000	£3,240,000	

Exhibit 5.3 Original prices, both quantities 90,000

	[A]	[B]	[C]	[D]
[1]	ELASTIC1			
[2]				
[3]	Price	Quantity	Revenue	COE
[4]	£37.50	90,000	£3,375,000	
[5]				2.58
[6]	£36.00	100,000	£3,600,000	

Exhibit 5.4 Original prices, new quantity increased

	[A]	[B]	[C]	[D]
[1]	ELASTIC1			
[2]				
[3]	Price	Quantity	Revenue	COE
[4]	£37.50	90,000	£3,375,000	
[5]				1.32
[6]	£36.00	95,000	£3,420,000	

Exhibit 5.5 Original prices, new quantity 95,000

Change the sales in [B6] from 90,000 to 100,000 and notice that the coefficient becomes 2.58 (exhibit 5.4).

From the discussions in chapters 2 and 3 you will recall that at higher price ranges elasticity of demand tends to be greater, that is, the coefficient is larger; at lower prices, the coefficient is smaller.

Thus, if price is lowered to £36, with other things such as promotion and selling effort remaining the same, we would expect a sales figure that would give a coefficient less than the original, 2.09, in exhibit 5.1. 100,000 gives a coefficient of 2.58; we need to try sales of below 100,000.

Exhibit 5.5 has 95,000 inserted in [B6] and gives a coefficient of 1.32. This may be a little too low and indicates that sales would be above 95,000 but below 100,000.

	[A]	[B]	[C]	[D]
[1]	ELASTIC1			
[2]				
[3]	Price	Quantity	Revenue	COE
[4]	£37.50	90,000	£3,375,000	
[5]				1.15
[6]	£32.00	108,000	£3,456,000	

Exhibit 5.6 New price £32, new quantity 108,000

	[A]	[B]	[C]	[D]
[1]	ELASTIC1			
[2]				
[3]	Price	Quantity	Revenue	COE
[4]	£37.50	90,000	£3,375,000	
[5]				1.00
[6]	£32.00	105,500	£3,376,000	

Exhibit 5.7 New price £32, new quantity 105,500

	[A]	[B]	[C]	[D]
[1]	ELASTIC1			
[2]				
[3]	Price	Quantity	Revenue	COE
[4]	£37.50	90,000	£3,375,000	
[5]				2.00
[6]	£32.00	123,800	£3,961,600	

Exhibit 5.8 New price £32, new quantity 123,800

Various combinations can be tried by inserting different prices in [A6] and sales in [B6] to see the effect on the coefficient.

In exhibit 5.6 the original price of £37.50 has been reduced by 15 per cent to £32, and sales of 108,000 have been entered to achieve a coefficient of just over unity.

Exhibit 5.7 explores this further to achieve unity. By successively entering different sales figures it is found that sales of 105,500 will give a coefficient of 1.0.

One of the advantages of having a file in a spreadsheet on a PC is the degree of flexibility possible in the deliberations without worrying if mistakes are made. For example if instead of inserting

117

Exhibit 5.9 Various coefficients

Price	Quantity	Coefficient
36.00	98,000	2.09
33.75	100,000	1.00
33.75	105,000	1.46
33.75	110,000	1.90
33.75	125,000	3.09
31.00	125,000	1.72
32.00	125,000	2.06
41.25	125,000	(3.42)

105,000 you inserted 10,500, the COE shows '(10.00)'. The wrong figure is quickly changed.

Exhibit 5.8 shows what sales quantity has to be entered to achieve a coefficient of 2.00; it is 123,800.

You can experiment with 'what if' suggestions; different prices, different quantities, and their effect on the elasticity coefficient. Exhibit 5.9 lists some for you to check with your settings.

By changing price and the estimated sales at that price, and keeping the COE between, say, 1.5 and 2.5 will provide a range of prices which you can gradually narrow down to make a choice. Prices and quantities can be inserted that result in coefficients well outside this suggested range, but, unless you have recent evidence from sales records of high or low elasticity, you should avoid using a coefficient that varies too much from the original.

The coefficient is not a statistical measure but an indication of the likely responsiveness of buyers to a price change *over a relatively small price range*. Move out of that price range, or base your investigation on records too old to be relevant, and you will obtain distorted and unrelated degrees of responsiveness of little use to your current pricing task.

INCREASING SALES, DECLINING PROFIT

A division of a large multinational organization had accepted from a multiple retail chain a large order at a special price for one of its products. Sales had exceeded estimates and the multiple had re-ordered.

However, although the division's sales of the product were increasing, their profits were declining. The price of the special deal with the retail multiple had been agreed without considering the possible effect on the future sales mix, and the division was suffering from the earlier enthusiasm to obtain the order. Divisions had no written pricing policy but all divisional directors are expected to employ pricing procedures that maximize profits without eroding their market share.

The case which follows arose from consultancy with the company concerned, and has been written to highlight different problems that can ensue when several people with insufficient knowledge of pricing are involved. The underlying principles are the same for any company, and can have considerable impact on sales and marketing results. Names and figures in the case are close to the actual facts but have been altered to preserve the anonymity of the company.

DOMESTIC PRODUCTS DIVISION

George Mann had recently been appointed divisional director of Domestic Products Division (DPD), whose main product has a list price of £50 less a standard discount of 25 per cent. In the previous year, with sales of 90,000 – just over half its total capacity of 160,000 units – the division lost over £150,000. The revenue account is shown in exhibit 5.10. Mr Mann was given the responsibility of putting the company into a profitable position.

He discussed the situation with four people: Tom Salman, the sales manager; Michael Advent, the advertising manager; David Marcus, the marketing services manager; Sarah Proctor, the product manager. They had different viewpoints, and some of their recommendations were in conflict.

Sales manager's opinion

Tom Salman, the sales manager, is a comparative newcomer. Previously he was with a competitor but was made redundant when they were taken over. He recommends a price cut of 10 per cent from list, which, he contends, would result in the company selling the whole capacity of 160,000.

Exhibit 5.10   DPD revenue account for the year

DPD revenue account for year ended 31 Dec 19xx			
	£	£	£
Sales 90,000 units @ £37.50			3,375,000
Cost of sales			
Direct materials		1,350,000	
Direct labour		450,000	
Production overheads			
Fixed	590,000		
Variable	270,000		
		860,000	
			2,660,000
			715,000
Selling, distribution costs			
Fixed			
Salaries and wages	297,000		
Advertising	40,000		
Variable			
Commission*	168,750		
Distribution	50,625		
		556,375	
Administration			
Fixed	300,000		
Variable	16,875		
		316,875	
			873,250
	Net profit		£(158,250)

* Sales commission is 5 per cent of sales. All other variable expenses vary directly
with units sold, and production is maintained at a level in line with sales.

Advertising manager's opinion

The advertising manager, Michael Advent, believes that a more vigorous promotion campaign is necessary. He points out that the present weight of publicity is light compared with competitive advertising, and suggests that it should be increased by £125,000. He also considers that the price is on the low side and should be increased by 10 per cent. To achieve this, he recommends that the price structure should be altered so that the product is priced at £55 but carries a 25 per cent discount.

As a further stimulus to sales, he recommends that sales commission is raised from 5 per cent to 10 per cent. He is confident that, with these two amendments to the marketing campaign, increased publicity and increased commission, the company would sell a minimum of 125,000 units.

Marketing services view

David Marcus, the marketing services manager, is adamant that the price of £50 should not be altered, but considers that the company should adjust its strategy for the product, and aim for a sales turnover of about 80 per cent capacity of the factory.

'I agree with Mike; we are not spending enough on advertising,' he said, and added, 'It would be interesting to know what extra has to be spent on promotion to obtain say, 130,000 sales at a net profit of 5 per cent.'

Product manager's problem

Sarah Proctor, the product manager, is negotiating with a well-known direct-marketing organization. She explains that they wish to place an order for 50,000 units ex-factory (that is, no distribution costs would be involved), but they are asking for £12,500 towards the cost of promotion, and £10 per 100 packaging cost.

No commission would be paid as it is a head office transaction. It is clear from the discussions that she has been having with the potential customer that the existing market of 90,000 units at the current price would not be affected. 'But,' she emphasized, 'it has to be at the right price.'

Exhibit 5.11 DPD unit costs

Variable cost	Cost of 90,000 (£)	Cost per unit (£)
Raw materials	1,350,000	15
Direct labour	450,000	5
Production overhead	270,000	3
Distribution	50,625	0.5625
Administration	16,875	0.1875
	Unit variable cost	£23.75

Exhibit 5.12 DPD fixed costs

	Fixed costs (£)
Production	590,000
Salaries and wages	297,000
Advertising	40,000
Administration	300,000
Total	1,227,000

The executives have considerable differences of opinion as to what price to quote the company. Mann compared the results of adopting each of the suggested proposals, and considered the price that Sarah Proctor should quote the direct marketing company.

UNIT COST

With most pricing problems, it is advisable to start by determining the various unit costs. In this case, the figures have been edited to avoid too many decimal places being used, but the principles are the same for all similar situations.

Using the figures in the revenue account (exhibit 5.10) we obtain exhibit 5.11. Commission is payable at 5 per cent of price and there are the fixed costs shown in exhibit 5.12.

BREAK-EVEN

Ignoring commission and any other costs related to price for the moment, the number of units that have to be sold for turnover to equal fixed costs, that is, break-even point is calculated thus:

$$\frac{\text{total fixed costs}}{\text{unit net price less unit variable cost}}$$

With commission at 5 per cent of £37.50, this is £1.875, making a net price of £35.625.

Net price £35.625 less £23.75 = £11.875, so break-even point is therefore 1,227,000/11.875 = 103,327 units.

It is always advisable to check results. If 103,327 products must be sold to break even, and the division sold only 90,000, this is a shortfall of 103,327 − 90,000 = 13,327.

13,327 × £11.875 = £158,258, which is approximately the loss for the year incurred by the division.

The evaluations of the executives' recommendations are set out in exhibits 5.13–5.16. Minor variations occur in items such as distribution and administration, depending whether unit cost, which relates to sales volume, or unit percentage cost, which relates to turnover, are used.

The price quoted for the 50,000 will depend on the open market price, and whether this remains as previously, is increased, or reduced. To make about 9 per cent on the order, £36 should be quoted. If the 90,000 units are sold at the previous price, the transactions can be combined as in exhibit 5.17.

THE DPD PRICING TASK

Michael Advent proposes a price of £55 less 25 per cent, £41.25, and estimates that 125,000 products would be sold. Exhibit 5.14 shows that this would achieve a profit of £312,843.

This needs to be appraised, so first we look at likely elasticity of demand because increased sales resulting from an increased price indicates a negative coefficient. Inserting the data in our spreadsheet file gives a negative coefficient -3.42, as it was in the list in exhibit 5.9.

Exhibit 5.13 Sales manager's suggestion

Tom Salman's recommendation Price of £50 less 10 per cent less 25 per cent.

	£	£	£
Sales 160,000 units @ £33.75			5,400,000
Cost of sales			
Direct materials (£15)		2,400,000	
Direct labour (£5)		800,000	
Production overheads			
Fixed	590,000		
Variable (£3)	480,000		
		1,070,000	
			4,270,000
			1,130,000
Selling, distribution costs			
Fixed			
Salaries and wages	297,000		
Advertising	40,000		
Variable			
Commission (5%)	270,000		
Distribution (1½%)	81,000		
		688,000	
Administration			
Fixed	300,000		
Variable (£0.1875)	30,000		
		330,000	
			1,018,000
		Net profit	£112,000

Exhibit 5.14 Advertising manager's suggestion

Michael Advent's recommendation Price increased by 10 per cent from £37.50 to £41.25; price the product at £55 less 25 per cent = £41.25; advertising at £165,000; sales commission from 5 per cent to 10 per cent.

	£	£	£
Sales 125,000 units @ £41.25			5,156,250
Cost of sales			
Direct materials (£15)		1,875,000	
Direct labour (£5)		625,000	
Production overheads			
Fixed	590,000		
Variable (£3)	375,000		
		965,000	
			3,465,000
			1,691,250
Selling, distribution costs			
Fixed			
Salaries and wages	297,000		
Advertising	165,000		
Variable			
Commission (10%)	515,625		
Distribution (1½%)	77,344		
		1,054,969	
Administration			
Fixed	300,000		
Variable (£0.1875)	23,438		
		323,438	
			1,378,407
	Net profit		£312,843

Exhibit 5.15 Marketing services manager's suggestion

David Marcus's recommendation Keep price at £50 less 25 per cent but target for 130,000 units and a net profit of 5 per cent.

	£	£	£
Sales 130,000 units @ £37.50			4,875,000
Targeted profit of 5%			243,750
Cost of sales			
Direct materials (£15)		1,950,000	
Direct labour (£5)		650,000	
Production overheads			
Fixed	590,000		
Variable (£3)	390,000		
		980,000	
			3,580,000
			1,051,250
Selling, distribution costs			
Fixed			
Salaries and wages	297,000		
Advertising	40,000		
Variable			
Commission (5%)	243,750		
Distribution (1½%)	73,125		
		653,875	
Administration			
Fixed	300,000		
Variable (£0.1875)	24,375		
		324,375	
			978,250
Surplus			£73,000

126

Exhibit 5.16   Product manager's suggestion

Sarah Proctor's problem   To quote a price to the direct-marketing organization for 50,000 units, but to provide £12,500 towards promotion, and £10 per 100 units packaging allowance.

Apart from the commitment of £40,000 for advertising, there are three fixed, or rigid, costs to be considered:

Production overhead	£590,000
Salaries and wages	297,000
Administration	300,000
	£1,187,000

This sum is incurred irrespective of the level of sales made by the company.

Full production capacity of the product is 160,000 a year and, at this rate, each unit should contribute £1,187,000/160,000 = £7.42 to fixed costs. The company sold only 90,000 last year, a little over 56 per cent capacity. To recover total fixed costs at this level, would mean that each unit would need to contribute £1,187,000/90,000 = £13.19.

It is sound practice to recover fixed overheads at a level of operations less than 100 per cent of capacity. If the order for 50,000 is obtained, and the company sells a similar 90,000 elsewhere, the total of 140,000 is 87½ per cent of capacity. The price of the product should be based on recovering fixed overheads at, say, 80 per cent capacity; this is 128,000. £1,187,000/128,000 = £9.27 per product towards fixed overheads.

Cost of sales 50,000 × £23 (£15 + £5 + £3)	£1,150,000
Administration 50,000 × £0.1875	9,375
Special promotion allowance	12,500
Packaging allowance	5,000
	1,176,875
Unit cost £1,176,875/50,000	£23.54
Unit contribution to fixed overheads	9.27
	£32.81

If 5 per cent profit is required, this is 5/0.95 = 5.26 per cent on cost.

$$£32.81 \times 1.0526 = £34.53$$

If 10 per cent profit is required, this is 10/0.9 = 11.11 per cent on cost.

$$£32.81 \times 1.1111 = £36.45$$

Exhibit 5.17 DPD combined transactions

	£	£	£
Sales			
90,000 @ £37.50		3,375,000	
50,000 @ £36.00		1,800,000	
			5,175,000
Cost of goods 140,000 @ £23			3,220,000
			1,955,000
Commission 5% on 90,000	168,750		
Distribution 1½% on 90,000	50,625		
Special promotion and packaging	17,500		
Admin. 140,000 @ £0.1875	26,250		
		263,125	
Fixed overheads			
Production	590,000		
Salaries, wages	297,000		
Advertising	40,000		
Administration	300,000		
		1,227,000	
			1,490,125
			£464,875

The remaining capacity of 20,000 units may be sold. As total fixed overheads and advertising of £1,227,000 have been recovered in the above costing, this 20,000 will produce greater profit.

	£	£
Sales 20,000 @, say, £37.50		750,000
Cost of sales @ £23	460,000	
Commission 5%	37,500	
Distribution 1½%	11,250	
Admin. @ £0.1875	3,750	
		512,500
		£237,500

	[A]	[B]	[C]	[D]
[1]	ELASTIC1			
[2]				
[3]	Price	Quantity	Revenue	COE
[4]	£37.50	90,000	£3,375,000	
[5]				1.00
[6]	£41.25	81,800	£3,374,250	

Exhibit 5.18 Advent's price suggestion with coefficient unity

	[A]	[B]	[C]	[D]
[1]	ELASTIC1			
[2]				
[3]	Price	Quantity	Revenue	COE
[4]	£37.50	90,000	£3,375,000	
[5]				2.0
[6]	£41.25	74,350	£3,066,938	

Exhibit 5.19 Advent's price suggestion with coefficient 2.0

It can be argued that changing the price from £37.50 to £41.25, as Advent has suggested, puts the offer into a more elastic area – the coefficient will be greater. We do not know what the coefficient was at the original price but it was not negative; the situation is reassessed with an elasticity of unity.

Consider the table in exhibit 5.18. This is the original layout from exhibit 5.1, with the price £41.25 in cell [A6].

In [B6], quantities are successively tried until the coefficient in [D5] is unity, or as near as possible. 81,000 gives a coefficient of 1.11; 81,800 makes it 1.0.

Thus, at a responsiveness with COE equal to unity, a price of £41.25 indicates sales of 81,800 and lower revenue.

Advent suggests that 125,000 units would be sold at this price if the advertising is increased by £125,000. What he has implied is that the extra sales of 43,200 (125,000 – 81,800) would be achieved with the increased advertising.

In the higher price areas, higher COEs tend to be reflected. A coefficient of unity is probably too low for an increase in price of 10 per cent, and we might have to consider a coefficient of 2.0 or more. By trial and error we find that sales of 74,350 obtains an elasticity coefficient of 2.0, as illustrated in exhibit 5.19.

If elasticity of demand had a coefficient value of 2.0, it means that the extra sales of 50,650 (125,000 – 74,350) would have to be generated by the additional appropriation of £125,000.

The same elasticity layout is used to look at Tom Salman's recommendation. He estimates that the total production of 160,000 would be sold if price is lowered to £33.75. Inserting these data into the spreadsheet produces a very high coefficient of 5.32 (see exhibit 5.20).

At this suggested price of £33.75, if the sales figure is altered until the coefficient is 2.0, we find that 111,200 sales are needed to achieve this (see exhibit 5.21).

	[A]	[B]	[C]	[D]
[1]	ELASTIC1			
[2]				
[3]	Price	Quantity	Revenue	COE
[4]	£37.50	90,000	£3,375,000	
[5]				5.32
[6]	£33.75	160,000	£5,400,000	

Exhibit 5.20 Salman's price and sales suggestions

	[A]	[B]	[C]	[D]
[1]	ELASTIC1			
[2]				
[3]	Price	Quantity	Revenue	COE
[4]	£37.50	90,000	£3,375,000	
[5]				2.0
[6]	£33.75	111,200	£3,753,000	

Exhibit 5.21 Salman's price suggestion with coefficient 2.0

If we assume that the coefficient is more likely to be unity, at Salman's price of £33.75, sales of 100,000 are needed, as will be seen in exhibit 5.22. Sales increase by 10,000, but turnover remains the same; this would, of course, reduce the profit figure.

In the pricing task, the coefficient of elasticity is a useful guide in appraising sales estimates and establishing a base before other factors are considered.

We know we will be in a different time period; we realize that we may be appealing to different customers; the enigma is the effect of advertising and promotion.

Speeding up investigations

	[A]	[B]	[C]	[D]
[1]	ELASTIC1			
[2]				
[3]	Price	Quantity	Revenue	COE
[4]	£37.50	90,000	£3,375,000	
[5]				1.0
[6]	£33.75	100,000	£3,375,000	

Exhibit 5.22 Salman's price suggestion with coefficient unity

Exhibit 5.23 Assessing Marcus's suggestion

Proposed price	Suggested sales	COE
£37.50	130,000	ERR
£37.45	130,000	272.55
£37.40	130,000	136.18
£37.00	130,000	27.09
£36.50	130,000	13.45
£36.00	130,000	8.91
£35.50	130,000	6.64
£35.00	130,000	5.27

Marcus suggests keeping the price the same but budgeting for 130,000 sales. If you insert the price of £37.50 into the elasticity table, 'ERR' appears in the [D5] cell. This is because simple formulae have been used. Without rewriting more complex formulae, we can insert prices just a little below £37.50. Exhibit 5.23 lists some of these.

From exhibit 5.15, we know that a surplus of £73,000 would be generated if 130,000 units were sold at £37.50. However, this indicates an extremely high coefficient out of all proportion to what is feasible. A lot more than £73,000 is likely to be needed to stimulate sales near to the total of 130,000 units at a price of £37.50. Also, for every 50p less than the price of £37.50, the surplus falls by a substantial amount. Exhibit 5.24 shows the situations at £37, £36 and £35.

Faulty pricing is the root of the division's problem. A short cut to considering price is to use the total unit cost and total fixed cost. Total unit cost is £23.75 (plus commission). Total fixed cost, including the current advertising appropriation, is £1,227,000.

Exhibit 5.24 Adopting Marcus's 5 per cent profit target at three prices

	£	£
Sales 130,000 units @ £37	4,810,000	
Targeted profit of 5%	240,500	
	4,569,500	
less All other costs	4,558,250	
Surplus available for advertising at price £37		11,250
Sales 130,000 units @ £36	4,680,000	
Targeted profit of 5%	234,000	
	4,446,000	
less All other costs	4,558,250	
'Surplus' at price £36		(112,250)
No surplus and overall profit at £36 reduced to		128,250
Sales 130,000 units @ £35	4,550,000	
Targeted profit of 5%	227,500	
	4,322,500	
less All other costs	4,558,250	
'Surplus' at price £35		(235,750)
No 'surplus' but overall loss at £35		(8,250)

Let us assume that we aim to recover the fixed costs at 75 per cent of capacity, which is 120,000 units. This means that each unit must contribute £1,227,000/120,000 = £10.23 towards the total of fixed costs. Adding the total unit cost to the fixed cost contribution amounts to £23.75 + 10.23 = £33.98, say, £34. Thus, any price has to start at a minimum of £34 to pay its way with the company operating at 75 per cent capacity.

You could take a more optimistic view and plan to recover fixed costs at, say, 90 per cent capacity. This would be £1,227,000/144,000 = £8.52 per unit, making a minimum price of £23.75 + 8.52 = £32.27.

COMBINING COEFFICIENT AND DEMAND CURVE EXTENSION

In chapter 3 we looked at the use of the COE and demand curve extension for estimating sales at different prices. The two tables can be combined in a spreadsheet file to explore alternative estimates. In exhibit 5.25 columns are set to appropriate widths and the name of the file inserted in a convenient cell; here it is in [A1].

The instructions and formulae for this layout have been extracted directly from the spreadsheet and are given below. The conditional statements in the formulae, starting @IF, are written for Symphony, and have commas between statements. If you use another spreadsheet program you may need semicolons instead of commas.

```
       [A]    [B]      [C]       [D]        [E]     [F]         [G]
 [1]   <File name>
 [2]
 [3]    n     q        p         qxq        pxp     pq          COE
 [4]
 [5]
 [6]
 [7]
 [8]
 [9] Demand curve cuts OP:
[10]               Slope:
[11]
[12] Using the formula q = (p - intersection)slope
[13] new price of:        indicates sales of:
[14]
[15] Percentage change in COE:
[16] Coefficient of demand is now:
[17]
[18] Estimating sales based on the new elasticity of demand:
[19] new price of:        indicates sales of:
```

Exhibit 5.25 Demand curve and coefficient calculations

As above, the cells are given in square brackets. Following some of these cell names there are letters and numbers in parentheses (round brackets), e.g. (P0), (C2) etc. These are the formatted instructions for that cell. (P0) stands for figures, punctuated with commas and no decimal places; (C0) is formatted for currency with no decimal places; (C2) is currency with 2 decimal places, and so on.

```
[A1]  <File name>
```

Row [2] is left blank for appearance. In the following cells the '^' symbol centres the label.

```
[A3]  ^n
[B3]  ^q
[C3]  ^p
[D3]  ^qxq
[E3]  ^pxp
[F3]  ^pq
[G3]  ^COE
```

[A4] is used to insert the number of items in the table, which for the formulae being used is always 2.

```
[A4]  2
[B4]  (P0)
[C4]  (C2)
[D4]  (P0)  +B4*B4
[E4]  (C2)  +C4*C4
[F4]  (C0)  +B4*C4
[B5]  (P0)
[C5]  (C2)
[D5]  (P0)  +B5*B5
[E5]  (C2)  +C5*C5
[F5]  (C0)  +B5*C5
[G5]  (F2)  @IF(B5#AND#C5,((B4-B5)/(B4+B5))/
            ((C5-C4)/(C5+C4)),@NA)
[B6]  (P0)
[C6]  (C2)
[D6]  (P0)  +B6*B6
[E6]  (C2)  +C6*C6
[F6]  (C0)  @IF(C6>0,+B6*C6,0)
[G6]  (F2)  @IF(B6#AND#C6,((B5-B6)/(B5+B6))/
            ((C6-C5)/(C6+C5)),@NA)
```

In the following cells in row [7] it is important to note that only two data are summed – rows [4] and [5]. This is because the equation for the calculation of the intersection and slope of the demand curve is based on two coordinates.

```
[B7]   (P0)  @SUM(B4..B5)
[C7]   (C2)  @SUM(C4..C5)
[D7]   (P0)  @SUM(D4..D5)
[E7]   (C2)  @SUM(E4..E5)
[F7]   (P0)  @SUM(F4..F5)
```

Row [8] is left blank for appearance.

```
[A9] Demand curve cuts OP:
```

[D9] is the intersection.

```
[D9]   (C2)  @IF(D7,((C7*D7)-(B7*F7))/
       ((A4*D7)-(B7*B7)),@NA)
[C10] Slope:
```

[D10] is the slope.

```
[D10]  (F4)  @IF(D9,((A4*F7)-(B7*C7))/
       ((A4*D7)-(B7*B7) ),@NA)
[A12] Using the formula q = (p - intersection)slope
[A13] new price of:
[C13] (C2)
[D13] indicates sales of:
```

[G13] gives an estimate of sales using the formula based on demand curve, as the text in Row [12].

```
[G13]  (P0)  @IF(C13,(C13-D9)/D10,@NA)
```

Row [14] is left blank for appearance.

```
[A15] Percentage increase in COE:
[A16] Coefficient of demand is now:
```

Cell [E15] is used to enter any percentage change required in the coefficient of [G4]. By entering a positive or negative number, or zero, the new COE appears in [E16].

```
[E16]  (F2)  @IF(G5,G5*(1+E15/100),@NA)
```

Row [17] is left blank for appearance.

135

```
[A18] Estimating sales based on the new elasticity
      of demand:
[A19] new price of:
[C19] (C2)
[D19] indicates sales of:
```

For any price you insert in [C19] the new coefficient indicates sales in [G19]. The formula in [G19] is a long conditional statement: pay particular attention to the number of brackets.

```
[G19] (P0) @IF(C19,(@IF(C19>C5,B5-(B5*E16*((C19-C5)/
      (C19+C5))),B5+(B5*E16*((C5-C19)/(C19+C5)))))),0)
```

USING THE SPREADSHEET TABLE

A company based in the North Midlands selling toiletries and gift items experienced two different sales figures for a popular product at two of their outlets where there was only a small difference in price.

With unit price of £7.25, sales were 3,875; at an increase of only 25p, sales were 2,835. A price increase of 3.4 per cent resulted in a sales decrease of 27 per cent.

Enter this information as follows into the spreadsheet table that was just created:

```
[A1] Toilet1
[B4] 3875
[C4] 7.25
[B5] 2835
[C5] 7.5
```

The result is shown as exhibit 5.26. The COE for the prices and quantities inserted in rows [4] and [5] appears in cell [G5]. Save this spreadsheet file under the name TOILET1.

This file is adjusted in a second file TOILET2, which is shown in exhibit 5.27. We know that coefficient of elasticity tends to increase in the higher price ranges, but initially we keep it the same and insert 0 percentage change in [E15]: 9.14 then appears in [E16].

Inserting the price of £7.75 into [C19] to determine likely sales using the coefficient of elasticity at 9.14 indicates sales of 2,410 in [G19].

```
          [A]     [B]      [C]          [D]            [E]         [F]          [G]
[1]       TOILET1
[2]
[3]        n      q        p            qxq            pxp         pq           COE
[4]        2     3,875    £7.25     15,015,625        £52.56      £28,094
[5]              2,835    £7.50      8,037,225        £56.25      £21,263       9.14
[6]                                                                            NA
[7]              6,710   £14.75     23,052,850       £108.81      £49,356
[8]
[9]  Demand curve cuts OP:    £8.18
[10]                 Slope:   -0.0002
[11]
[12] Using the formula q = (p - intersection)slope
[13] new price of:           indicates sales of:
[14]
[15] Percentage change in COE:
[16] Coefficient of demand is now:
[17]
[18] Estimating sales based on the new elasticity of demand:
[19] new price of:           indicates sales of:
```

Exhibit 5.26 TOILET1, based on exhibit 5.25

```
          [A]     [B]      [C]          [D]            [E]         [F]          [G]
[1]       TOILET2
[2]
[3]        n      q        p            qxq            pxp         pq           COE
[4]        2     3,875    £7.25      9,922,500        £52.56      £22,838
[5]              2,835    £7.50      8,037,225        £56.25      £21,263       9.14
[6]              2,410    £7.75      5,808,100        £60.06      £18,678       4.94
[7]              6,710   £14.75     23,052,850       £108.81      £49,356
[8]
[9]  Demand curve cuts OP:    £8.18
[10]                 Slope:   -0.0002
[11]
[12] Using the formula q = (p - intersection)slope
[13] new price of:  £7.75 indicates sales of:                                  1,795
[14]
[15] Percentage change in COE:              0
[16] Coefficient of demand is now:       9.14
[17]
[18] Estimating sales based on the new elasticity of demand:
[19] New price of:  £7.75   indicates sales of:                                2,410
```

Exhibit 5.27 TOILET2 with different sales figures

```
[C19] 7.75
```

This sales figure of 2,410, and price of £7.75 are then inserted into cells [B6] and [C6].

```
[B6] 2410
[C6] 7.75
```

The appropriate cells in Row [6] are automatically computed by the program: in [G6], the coefficient of 4.94 appears.

We now check the estimate of sales using the extension of the original demand curve derived from the data in [B4], [B5], [C4] and [C5] by inserting the price of £7.75 in [C13].

```
[C13] 7.75
```

Considerably lower sales are indicated – 1,795 compared with 2,410 using the coefficient of demand method. The reason for the discrepancy is because the coefficient has fallen from 9.14 to 4.94; it is more likely to be over 10.

The file is modified again to create TOILET3, which is shown in exhibit 5.28. We insert an increase of 20 per cent in [E15] and the coefficient in [E16] changes to 10.97; the sales figure in [G19] becomes 2,325.

This sales figure, 2,325, is inserted into [B6] and the elasticity coefficient in [G6] changes to 6.03.

With price in [C6] kept at £7.75, different sales figures are successively inserted in [B6] until the coefficient in [G6] is 10.97. This occurs with sales at 1,971.

Different sales figure are indicated by the two methods. Based on an extension of *the original demand curve*, sales of 1,795 are indicated; based on the coefficient of elasticity of 10.97, sales of 2,325 are indicated.

Copying the basic table and formulae into a PC spreadsheet enables you to consider the implications of endless 'what if' situations. However, such investigations are based on restricted data because the information on demand curves is largely speculative. It is possible to modify the formulae, especially with regard to extension of the curve. But in the absence of any valid observations in the market-place, such changes might introduce a degree of spurious accuracy into your deliberations. In demand curve analysis, the best

	[A]	[B]	[C]	[D]	[E]	[F]	[G]
[1]	TOILET3						
[2]							
[3]	n	q	p	qxq	pxp	pq	COE
[4]	2	3,875	£7.25	15,015,625	£52.56	£22,838	
[5]		2,835	£7.50	8,037,225	£56.25	£21,263	9.14
[6]		1,971	£7.75	3,884,841	£60.06	£15,275	10.97
[7]		6,710	£14.75	23,052,850	£108.81	£49,356	
[8]							
[9]	Demand curve cuts OP:		£8.18				
[10]			Slope:	-0.0002			
[11]							
[12]	Using the formula q = (p - intersection)slope						
[13]	new price of: £7.75 indicates sales of:						1,795
[14]							
[15]	Percentage change in COE:			20			
[16]	Coefficient of demand is now:			10.97			
[17]							
[18]	Estimating sales based on the new elasticity of demand:						
[19]	New price of: £7.75 indicates sales of:						2,325

Exhibit 5.28 TOILET3 with new figures

method to adopt is to consider small increases and decreases and continually update data with actual market-place experience.

Notice the slight difference in values for the coefficient of demand when obtained with percentages, and when calculating the mid-point elasticity. In exhibit 5.26 above, mid-point coefficient is automatically calculated at 9.14.

Using the percentage changes we get 27%/3.4% = 7.9. The difference is not significant as we are not dealing with an exact science, and the mid-point method gives an acceptable figure for practical pricing tasks.

A COMPUTER-AIDED PRICING FORM

The pricing form used by the Midlands plastics company which was illustrated in chapter 3 (exhibits 3.1 and 3.2) has been modified by the company and is now included in their routine pricing with a

```
                 [A]                   [B]      [C]       [D]
 [1] COSTSHT1
 [2]                   COSTING SHEET FOR PRICING
 [3]
 [4] Product _ Aston block _____         Date:  _ Jan 89 _
 [5]
 [6] Prepared by ___ JB _____      Last updated: _ Aug 88 _
 [7]
 [8]                              £           £         £
 [9] Raw materials                        24.00
[10] Bought-in                             8.50
[11]                                                 32.50
[12] Inward transport         0.49
[13] Warehousing              0.91
[14] Internal handling        0.59
[15] Finished goods store     0.57
[16]                                       2.55
[17] Direct labour            2.50
[18] Servicing labour         0.54
[19] Machine shop 1           1.50
[20] Machine shop 2
[21] Finishing                0.75
[22]                                       5.29
[23]                                                  7.84
[24] G & A                                 1.46
[25] Management                            0.98
[26] HQ                                    2.44
[27] Contingencies                         0.65
[28]                                                  5.53
[29]                                                  ----
[30]                                                 45.86
[31]                                                  ----
[32]                              Oncost:             9.17
[33]                                                 -----
[34] Min. Transfer price                            £55.04
[35]                                                 -----
[36]                              Transferred at:   £55.00
                                                    =====
```

Exhibit 5.29 Costing sheet for pricing

PC. The current form for another product is illustrated in exhibit 5.29. The data for the product for raw materials and items bought in are entered in cells [C9] and [C10]. The costs of direct labour, the two machine shops and product finishing, from other data sources, are inserted in [B17] [B19] [B20] and [B21].

140

The relevant formulae are as follows:

```
[D11]  +C9+C10
[B12]  +$D$11*0.015
[B13]  +$D$11*0.028
[B14]  +$D$11*0.018
[B15]  +$D$11*0.0175
[C16]  @SUM(B12..B15)
[B18]  +$D$11*0.0165
[C22]  @SUM(B17..B21)
[D23]  +C16+C22
[B24]  +$D$11*0.045
[B25]  +$D$11*0.03
[B26]  +$D$11*0.075
[B27]  +$D$11*0.02
[D28]  @SUM(B24..B27)
[D30]  @SUM(D9..D28)
[D32]  +D30*0.2
[D34]  +D30+D32
```

The minimum transfer price is decided by management and not computed from a formula. It is rounded to a convenient figure and entered in [D36], at which price it is on charge to the sales department. For this particular product the rounded price is £55.

The percentage oncosts are considered twice a year and modified in the light of prevailing economic and market conditions.

In chapter 2, the basic information of a Belgian company's empirical database was discussed (exhibits 2.16 and 2.17), and we saw how it is being used to estimate sales at proposed price changes. The relevant parts of the computer layouts are set out in exhibits 5.30 and 5.31.

Percentages are used in determining coefficients of demand. The form is in two parts but, for simplicity, both are included in the same spreadsheet file.

The upper part is used to create an empirical database. The periods [A4], [A5] etc. (however many are required, during which sales are observed), should be the same. The nature of the product and its general sales pattern will indicate the length of the periods in which trends may be observed. The store compares monthly sales.

The price of the product is inserted together with its sales for the period. Immediately the second data are entered, the COE is calculated automatically by the formula and appears in [D5].

	[A]	[B]	[C]	[D]
[1]	*<File Name>*			
[2]	PRODUCT	*<Product>*	Last updated	10-Oct-89
[3]	Period	Price BFrs	Sales	COE
[4]	Sep	1,525.00	243	2.0
[5]	Oct	1,335.00	285	1.4
[6]				NA
[7]				NA
[8]				NA
[9]				
[10]	INSERT NEW PRICE AND ASSUMED COE TO ESTIMATE SALES			
[11]	PRODUCT	*<Product>*		
[12]		Price BFrs	COE	Sales
[13]		1,525.00		243
[14]		1,335.00	1.5	288
[15]				

Exhibit 5.30 Computer layout of exhibit 2.16

	[A]	[B]	[C]	[D]
[10]	INSERT NEW PRICE AND ASSUMED COE TO ESTIMATE SALES			
[11]	PRODUCT	*<Product>*		
[12]		Price BFrs	COE	Sales
[13]		55.00	3.0	12,060
[14]		49.50	2.5	15,075
[15]				

Exhibit 5.31 Computer layout of exhibit 2.17

The details and formulae to be inserted are given below.

```
[A1] File name
[B2] Name of product
[C2] 'Last updated'
[D2] Format cell for 'date' and insert @NOW
[A3] Period (of days, weeks or months)
[B3] Price (insert currency and format column)
[C3] Sales
[D3] COE
[B4] Previous price (1,525.00)
[C4] Previous sales (243)
```

```
[D4]  Previous COE if known
[B5]  New price (1,335.00)
[C5]  New sales (285)
[D5]  @IF(B5#AND#C5,(((@IF(C4>C5,C4-C5,
      C5-C4)/C4)*100)/
      (@IF(B4>B5,B4-B5,B5-B4)/B4)*100)),@NA)
```

Copy this formula to [D6], [D7], [D8] and further if needed.

```
[B13] Previous price (BFrs 1,525)
[D13] Sales at previous price (243)
[B14] Proposed new price (BFrs 1,335)
[C14] Assumed COE (1.5)
[D14] @IF(B14,(D13*(1+(C14*((@IF(B13>B14,B13-B14,
      B14-B13))/B13)))),@NA)
```

The lower and upper parts of the form are not linked and each
may be used separately. As mentioned in chapter 2, in October 1989,
the company used the lower part of the form to estimate sales of a
number of their products, as in exhibit 5.31.

6

Product positioning

THE ENVIRONMENT

A product's 'position' refers to its place in the general environment and its relative place in its particular market. In chapter 1 it was stated that there are four main environmental aspects – political, economic, technological and social. Each needs to be continuously scanned to develop a general overall business picture and specifically for particular products. Exhibits 6.1–6.4 list some of the points that need to be considered in the development of a marketing policy in general and a pricing policy in particular.

PRODUCT IMAGE

The position of a product in the market is the combined image that people have for it and its particular standing and reputation compared with similar or alternative products. While individual opinions will vary slightly, the general appreciation of a product, its performance, presentation and price will be agreed by the majority of people. There is often a widely accepted ranking of products: the 'best' is universally acknowledged as such, followed by the others in a descending order of goodness.

This positioning, or image, may be strong or weakly held. It may be clear or relatively obscure; simple or a complex mix of beliefs. Some products that do much the same thing have obviously differ-

Exhibit 6.1 Environmental scanning – political

1 What is the general government of the country? From a left- or right-wing base?

2 What central government controls exist at present that affect company operations?

3 Are there any local controls and regulations that currently affect company operations?

4 What central or regional legislation and regulations that could affect company operations in general and pricing in particular might occur during the next twelve months?

5 What proportion of total raw materials and components has to be imported from where at present, and how vital are these to the company?

6 What is the current relationship between the countries mentioned in §5 and home country?

7 Are the countries mentioned in §5 stable, politically?

8 Are licences or other permits needed to obtain these raw materials?

9 From what other sources could they be obtained?

10 What change in the political environment is possible or likely during the next year or so? What effect would any change have on the company?

Exhibit 6.2 Environmental scanning – economic

1 What has been the rate of growth of the economy in the last five years in terms of gross national product (GNP)?

2 What is the forecast growth in GNP during the next year?

3 What are the inflation figures for the last five years?

4 What rate of increase/decrease in prices generally is expected during the next twelve months?

5 What rate of increase/decrease in own industry prices is expected during the next twelve months?

6 What has been the trend of interest rates over the past three years or so?

7 What are the likely variations in interest rates during the next twelve months?

8 What is the general opinion as reported in national and other authoritative media for proposed changes in the next budget?

9 Are there economic developments that might occur and would affect the company's business either adversely or to its advantage during the next twelve months?

10 What action might be required now to anticipate such economic developments?

Exhibit 6.3 Environmental scanning – technological

---

1 If the company is currently in a low technological industry, this section is only of interest if it is contemplating moving into a hi-tech market.

2 If the company is in a hi-tech industry, or proposing to be, consider the following matrix and indicate in the appropriate cells where the products are at present:

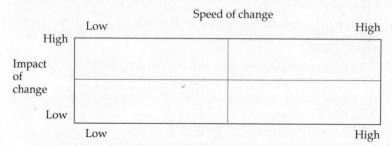

3 Products in the *low speed-high impact* cell are in an erratic and capricious environment and likely to be insidious. The low speed of change can often conceal the impact on price; it is not until a company is faced with a dramatic cut in a competitor's price that the effect of change on price may be realized.

4 Products in the *high speed-low impact* cell are in an aggressive and dynamic marketing environment. Competitors marketing such products often seek to gain quick advantages of price cuts and promotional devices to increase sales and market share.

5 The environment of *high speed-high impact* is chaotic and turbulent. Companies with products in this type of hi-tech market should develop contingency plans to combat sudden product changes and price attacks. The time needed to respond to such assaults should be estimated so that the company will know how long it could be at risk.

6 The *low speed-low impact* environment is relatively stable; products in this cell usually possess fairly constant market shares.

---

ent characteristics: consider for example washing powders and washing liquids, motor cars, perfume, furniture, books, wearing apparel. The reason for selecting one rather than another is an amalgam of preferences, beliefs and feelings, particularly when choosing between products with little visible differences, such as soap, cigarettes, instant coffee and chocolate.

A product's image is closely related to its perceived value and can be enhanced and improved by appropriate use of elements of its oncost.

Exhibit 6.4 Environmental scanning – social

---

1 What is the present rate of unemployment in the country?

2 Is the rate rising, stable, or declining?

3 How many are currently employed in the country, and what has been the trend over the past three years or so?

4 What is the age distribution in the country, and what future trends are forecast?

5 Do the changes in §4 affect demand for any of the company's products to a marked degree?

6 What basic demographic changes have occurred during the last five years or so that have affected the market for the company's products, or for products of the company's customers?

7 What changes are currently taking place in home and overseas markets, such as changed working habits, more leisure time, more women at work etc.?

8 What is the current distribution of wealth and incomes compared with, say, five years ago?

9 Are there any evolving pastimes that might affect the demand for the company's products?

10 Does the company have a price policy and strategy that takes into consideration the changing social environment?

A product's position is therefore determined by the strength of people's perception and preference for it compared with those of competitive products. Perception is relatively stable, changing only slightly with time; preference tends to vary with different conditions, some of which can be influenced by the seller.

Some products hold a position in the market that confounds those who are familiar with them and really know what they will do. The varying opinions held about most products support the view that product differentiation is often a distinction in the buyer's mind and not in the product. Yet such distinctions are crucial to buyers choosing those products and maintaining a loyalty to the product most appropriate to their needs.

While a product's position is a combination of tangibles and intangibles – its quality, performance, size, weight, shape, appearance, where it can be purchased, the type of customer who normally uses it, feelings and attitudes towards it – one attribute is dominant – its price.

Exhibit 6.5 Ranking products

Products	Price (£)
D	56.00
B	40.00
C	38.50
A	35.00
E	29.90

Exhibit 6.6 Ranking and scaling products

Products		Price (£)
D	-	56.00
	-	
	-	
	-	
	-	
	-	
	-	
B	-	40.00
C	-	38.50
A	-	35.00
	-	
E	-	29.90

If price is dominant in reflecting quality, the simplest way to position a product is to list all competitive products in descending order of price. Suppose that we are considering five products, *A*, *B*, *C*, *D* and *E*, they could be listed as in exhibit 6.5.

This is a simple ranking order, with the highest-priced product at the top. The disadvantage is that there is no distinction between

148

products other than rank, and this conceals the magnitude of the gaps. Between the first and second, there is a difference of £16; between the second and third, only £1.50; and so on. An improvement is to insert them on a scale as in exhibit 6.6.

From this it can be seen that a new product could be positioned in the large gap between *D* and *B*. However, a more sophisticated analysis is needed before decisions can be taken on product positioning.

In formal positioning research, extensive use is made of statistical analysis with successive pairs of products being rated by potential buyers for a number of attributes such as performance, convenience, versatility, shape, size, weight, feel etc., as well as cost. The ratings are statistically combined to produce a map that shows the spatial relationships of products.

The essential factor in positioning is that it represents *the opinion of the market* for a product and not necessarily what company executives think about it. With this reservation in mind, an attempt can be made to position the five products using subjective judgements of people in the company.

People are asked to give their opinion of the overall quality and standing of the products. This should be conducted in a way that prevents anyone being able to influence others: circulating a document in the internal mail for people to complete at their leisure is not advisable.

Verbal assessments should not be requested in an open meeting, but a form such as exhibit 6.7 should be used, members being asked to complete it individually there and then. The products are listed in alphabetical order without their current price. A percentage has to be inserted against each product to indicate the responder's estimate of the quality and standing of the product.

With the forms completed, the quality averages for each of the products are calculated and inserted, together with their prices, on another form (see exhibit 6.8).

An index is calculated for each price and each percentage by dividing the figures by the average. Thus, the price index for *A* is $35/39.88 = 0.88$; *A*'s quality index is $70/75 = 0.93$. The results of this example are shown in exhibit 6.9.

In exhibit 6.10 these indexes are plotted on a graph, which has been scaled vertically and horizontally to cover all the results.

Exhibit 6.7 Estimating the image

Product	Estimate of quality and standing
A	_____ %
B	_____ %
C	_____ %
D	_____ %
E	_____ %

Exhibit 6.8 Weighted averages of price and quality

Product	Price (£)	Average estimate of quality and standing
A	35.00	70%
B	40.00	85%
C	38.50	70%
D	56.00	95%
E	29.90	55%
	199.40	
Average	£39.88	75%

Exhibit 6.9 Indexes of price and quality

Product	Index of price	Index of quality
A	0.88	0.93
B	1.00	1.13
C	0.97	0.93
D	1.40	1.27
E	0.75	0.73

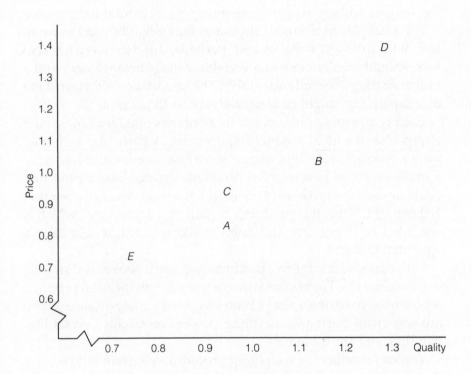

Exhibit 6.10 Spatial positioning of products

We now have a spatial representation for the products based on quality, which has been estimated, and their current price, which is factual.

If the estimates of quality for the five products reasonably reflect their perceived value in the market, they appear to lie in a band; the higher the perceived value, the greater the price. *B* seems to be in a good position, while *C* seems to be overpriced.

ATTRIBUTES ANALYSIS PRICING

This subjective analysis may be used to price consumer and industrial products. The method requires that the desirable key attributes of a product are given weights for importance as customer benefits, the weights adding to a convenient number or to total 100 per cent.

For example, an electrical appliance that might be used in countries with different voltages and, perhaps, different electrical sockets, should ideally possess a variable voltage arrangement and a universal plug to be fully adaptable. The importance of this attribute of 'adaptability' might be weighted, say, at 15 per cent.

Each competitive product has its attributes rated for how well it approaches the ideal product requirement. A particular manufacturer's product of the type of appliance just mentioned might have a multi-socket to take every conceivable voltage, and a plug that could be used everywhere in the world. It would obviously be rated 100 per cent. Thus, this product's benefit of 'adaptability', which is weighted at 15 per cent and rated at 100 per cent, would have a weighted rating of 15.

Let's suppose that the five products *A–E* listed above are domestic suction cleaners. The cleaners are compared with the ideal product, whose quality attributes have been weighted for importance. There are five main attributes: cleaning power, portability, versatility, handling and applications.

You can conduct the weighting procedure yourself, but because the analysis is based on subjective estimates it is improved by having others who are familiar with the products contribute their assessments. If you use other people, sum their individual weights for each product benefit and use the averages.

For each attribute as a customer benefit in a suction cleaner, an estimate is made using percentages which total to 100 per cent as illustrated in exhibit 6.11. This may be done with paper, pencil and calculator, but is much quicker if set up on a PC. The following tables have been processed in the same file on a standard spreadsheet. Column and row numbers are given so that the formulae can be located.

There is just one formula in the section of the spreadsheet shown in exhibit 6.11:

Product positioning

```
            [A]                           [C]
[1]   CLEANER1
[2]   Suction Cleaner          Percentage Importance
[3]      Attribute               as Customer Benefit
[4]   _____
[5]   Cleaning power                    30%
[6]   Portability                       25%
[7]   Versatility                       15%
[8]   Handling                          20%
[9]   Applications                      10%
[10]  <Space left for more
[11]    attributes>
[12]
[13]                                    ____
[14]  Percentage total to be 100%:      100
```

Exhibit 6.11 Attributes of suction cleaners

```
                      [B]      [C]      [D]      [E]       [F]
[16]             PRODUCT ATTRIBUTES RATED AND AVERAGED
[17]  Attribute   Prod A   Prod B   Prod C   Prod D    Prod E
[18]
[19] Cleaning power   70      80       72       75        65
[20] Portability      80      70       78       75        85
[21] Versatility      68      75       75       80        55
[22] Handling         85      90       80       95        75
[23] Applications     65      70       76       85        58
[24]
[25]      <Rows left blank
[26]        for more attributes>
[27]
```

Exhibit 6.12 Products' attributes rated

[C14] (%0) @SUM(D5..D12)

With exhibit 6.11 completed, each product's attributes is then individually rated. When a number of people have rated the attributes, the averages are calculated and inserted into the table. Exhibit 6.12 is a table of the averaged ratings of eight people.

153

	[B]	[C]	[D]	[E]	[F]
[29]		PRODUCTS'	WEIGHTED	RATINGS	
[30] Attribute	Prod A	Prod B	Prod C	Prod D	Prod E
[31]					
[32] Cleaning power	21.00	24.00	21.60	22.50	19.50
[33] Portability	20.00	17.50	19.50	18.75	21.25
[34] Versatility	10.20	11.25	11.25	12.00	8.25
[35] Handling	17.00	18.00	16.00	19.00	15.00
[36] Applications	6.50	7.00	7.60	8.50	5.80
[37] *<for other*	0.00	0.00	0.00	0.00	0.00
[38] *attributes*	0.00	0.00	0.00	0.00	0.00
[39] *if needed>*	0.00	0.00	0.00	0.00	0.00
[40]					
[41] Totals:	74.70	77.75	75.95	80.75	69.80

[44]   Insert total weighted rating of base product in F44 77.75

Exhibit 6.13 Products' weighted ratings

Product *B*'s cleaning power and handling received high ratings. The averages, to the nearest whole number, are 80 and 90 per cent respectively for the two customer benefits. Product *D* was also rated very highly for its handling capabilities, achieving an average of 95 per cent.

The attribute weights in exhibit 6.11 are now multiplied by respective ratings for each of the five products in exhibit 6.12, and set out as in the table in exhibit 6.13.

To illustrate, in exhibit 6.11, cleaning power is weighted 30 per cent. In exhibit 6.12, *A*'s rating for cleaning power is 70 per cent. Therefore, the *weighted rating* for *A*'s cleaning power which has been entered in exhibit 6.13, is $0.3 \times 70 = 21$. For *B* it is $0.3 \times 80 = 24$; *C* is $0.3 \times 72 = 21.6$; and so on. The weighted ratings of the attributes are set out in exhibit 6.13 and totalled.

If this table is being set up in a PC spreadsheet, the formulae for the cells in exhibit 6.13 are:

```
[B32]  (F2)  +B19*$C$5        copy across  [C32]..[F32]
[B33]  (F2)  +B20*$C$6        copy across  [C33]..[F33]
[B34]  (F2)  +B21*$C$7        copy across  [C34]..[F34]
[B35]  (F2)  +B22*$C$8        copy across  [C35]..[F35]
[B36]  (F2)  +B23*$C$9        copy across  [C36]..[F36]
[B37]  (F2)  +B24*$C$10       copy across  [C37]..[F37]
[B38]  (F2)  +B25*$C$11       copy across  [C38]..[F38]
[B39]  (F2)  +B26*$C$12       copy across  [C39]..[F39]
```

	[B] PRODUCTS' Prod A	[C] WEIGHTS Prod B	[D] RELATIVE Prod C	[E] TO BASE Prod D	[F] PRODUCT Prod E
[49] Insert Price:	£35.00	£40.00	£38.50	£56.00	£29.90
[50] Relative weight	96	100	98	104	90

Exhibit 6.14 Products' weights relative to *B* (= 100)

The formulae for the totals in row [41] follow the usual pattern. Up to eight rows of cells are available in the form, but only five are used in this particular example. Obviously, if more than eight attributes were used, the formulae would need to be modified, and extra formulae inserted.

```
[B41]  (F2) @SUM(B32..B39)      copy across [C41]..[F41]
```

The totals will automatically appear as each column is completed.

Assume that *B* is your product: this is made the *base product*. The total weighted rating of the base product is inserted into cell [F44] of the table in exhibit 6.13. The base product is now made to equal 100, and the others are recalculated to be relative.

If another product is chosen to be base product, its weighted rating must be substituted in [F44]. If you are working in a spreadsheet, the changes in each other product's relative index will automatically appear, otherwise the calculations have to be done by hand.

Divide 100 by the weighted rating of the base product, 77.75 taken from cell [F44] in exhibit 6.13, and multiply the result by the weighted ratings of each of the other products, also from exhibit 6.13. With a calculator, the equations for row [50] are:

Product *A*: $(100/77.75) \times 74.7 = 96$.
Product *C*: $(100/77.75) \times 75.95 = 98$.
Product *D*: $(100/77.75) \times 80.75 = 104$.
Product *E*: $(100/77.75) \times 69.8 = 90$.

If you are using more products, multiply each of their weighted ratings by (100/weighted rating of base product).

The spreadsheet formulae for row [50] in the table in exhibit 6.14 are:

```
[B50]  (F0) (B41*100)/$F$44      copy across [C50]..[F50]
```

155

The relative weighted ratings will appear in the computer form. Note that these are rounded to the nearest whole number. To base computations on subjective probabilities and assessments, and calculate to two decimal places, is to create spurious significance.

The table in exhibit 6.14 shows three products, *A*, *C* and *E* with lower prices but lower relative ratings than your product *B*; one product, *D*, has a higher rating and a higher price. Obviously, a product with a *higher rating and lower price* than your product would need investigating.

ASSESSING PRICE IN TWO WAYS

These pricing investigations have been based on actual work with a manufacturer whose product happened to be *B*. To illustrate the method involved it has been assumed that *B* is also your product. However, any of the products could be regarded as yours and used as the base product, provided that the formulae are altered as described above.

The price of *B* may be assessed from the viewpoint of a typical consumer who can judge it in two different ways:

- with competitive products;
- with one particular product.

In the first comparison, the price of *B* is kept as it is, and the prices of the other products recalculated using their respective weightings relative to *B* in exhibit 6.14. The equation for the first assessment, stated in words is:

If product *B* is £*x*, the price of Y may be perceived as $(x/100)$ times the weighted rating of Y, where Y is any other product.

Thus,
the price of product *A* may be perceived as £40/100 × 96 = £38.40;
the price of product *C* may be perceived as £40/100 × 98 = £39.20;
the price of product *D* may be perceived as £40/100 × 104 = £41.60;
the price of product *E* may be perceived as £40/100 × 90 = £36.00.

These calculations have been performed in the same file on the PC and shown in exhibit 6.15. The second decimal place varies from the results obtained by calculator because the weighted ratings of

```
              [A]                        [C]                              [F]
[54]If price of base product is: £40.00 Product A should be: £38.43
[55]                                     Product B should be: £40.00
[56]                                     Product C should be: £39.07
[57]                                     Product D should be: £41.54
[58]                                     Product E should be: £35.91
```

Exhibit 6.15 Perceived prices of competitors relative to base product

the products in exhibit 6.14 have been rounded to whole numbers, but all decimal figures are automatically held in the spreadsheet file.

Product *B* is kept in row [55] so that if you change the base product from *B* the table will still be relevant. If *A* were made base product the price in [C54] would then be the same as in [F54]. If you change the base product from *B* remember to enter the weighted rating for the new base product in [F44] and its price in [C54].

The formulae for the prices in exhibit 6.15 column [F] are as follows (as mentioned in chapter 5, your software may need semi-colons instead of commas in the conditional statements):

```
[F54]  (C2)  @IF($C$54,($C$54/100)*B50,@NA)
[F55]  (C2)  @IF($C$54,($C$54/100)*C50,@NA)
[F56]  (C2)  @IF($C$54,($C$54/100)*D50,@NA)
[F57]  (C2)  @IF($C$54,($C$54/100)*E50,@NA)
[F58]  (C2)  @IF($C$54,($C$54/100)*F50,@NA)
```

Exhibit 6.15 indicates how consumers may judge competitive products with product *B*'s price at £40. Consciously or unconsciously, the respective benefits of products will be compared and rated. The higher the ratings, the higher the expected price. Where the actual price is below the price expected from the perceived judgement, the product is regarded as a good buy. The product with the highest number of 'plus points' would be judged the 'best buy'.

For the second comparison, each of the other products is considered in turn as an individual competitor, and what *B*'s price *ought to be*, compared with the competitor's actual price.

This is illustrated in exhibit 6.16. The *perceived price* of the base product – that is the price it ought to be – is calculated from a comparison with the actual price of the competitor and the competitor's relative weight in exhibit 6.14. The perceived additional advantage or disadvantage of *B* over the competitor is quantified.

From the relative weights in exhibit 6.14 we know that *B* has a disadvantage compared with *A*, *C* and *E*, but a considerable advantage over *D*. Remember, however, that these differences may have been quantified from subjective qualitative data made by company employees, and inserted into the tables; they are not necessarily measurements from the market.

The general formula for the second type of assessment is:

$$\frac{\text{perceived price of } X}{\text{compared with } Y} = \frac{\text{price of } Y}{\text{weighted rating of } Y} \times 100$$

Using the data in exhibit 6.14 we find that:
the perceived price of *B* compared with *A* = £35/96 × 100 = £36.46;
the perceived price of *B* compared with *B* = £40/100 × 100 = £40.00;
the perceived price of *B* compared with *C* = £38.50/98 × 100 = £39.28;
the perceived price of *B* compared with *D* = £56/104 × 100 = £53.84;
the perceived price of *B* compared with *E* = £29.90/90 × 100 = £33.22.

		[B]	[C]	[D]	[E]	[F]
[62]	When base product price :		£40.00			
		Actual	Perceived		Base Product seen	
		List	Price of		with additional	
	Product	Price	Base Product	Advantage	(Disadvantage)	
[68]	Product A	£35.00	£36.43	£ 0.00	£(1.43)	
[69]	Product B	£40.00	£40.00	£ 0.00	£0.00	
[70]	Product C	£38.50	£39.41	£ 0.00	£(0.91)	
[71]	Product D	£56.00	£53.92	£(2.08)	£0.00	
[72]	Product E	£29.90	£33.31	£ 0.00	£(3.41)	

Exhibit 6.16 Product *B*'s perceived advantages and disadvantages

The comparable prices in the table in exhibit 6.16 have been taken from the spreadsheet file. The minor discrepancies between the calculated prices and those automatically computed in the spreadsheet are due to the decimal figures retained in the computer formulae but not used.

The formulae for exhibit 6.16 are:

```
[D62]  (C2)  +C54
[B68]  (C2)  +B49
[C68]  (C2)  @IF(B49,B49/B50*100,@NA)
[E68]  (C2)  @IF(C68<B68,B68-C68,0)copy [E69]..[E72]
[F68]  (C2)  @IF(E68=0,B68-C68,0)copy [F69]..[F72]
[B69]  (C2)  +C49
[C69]  (C2)  @IF(C49,C49/C50*100,@NA)
[B70]  (C2)  +D49
[C70]  (C2)  @IF(D49,D49/D50*100,@NA)
[B71]  (C2)  +E49
[C71]  (C2)  @IF(E49,E49/E50*100,@NA)
[B72]  (C2)  +F49
[C72]  (C2)  @IF(F49,F49/F50*100,@NA)
```

COMPARATIVE ANALYSIS WITH COMPETITORS

So far we have assessed the price of a product by an analysis of its standing compared with its competitors, but rating it only on five attributes seen as customer benefits.

A product's image is its totality in the market. This factor analysis is taken much further by some companies, and a subjective analysis made of subsidiary product characteristics, packaging, sales management, advertising, and many of the marketing functions. Exhibit 6.17 is an edited list of items used for comparative analysis by a manufacturer of consumer electrical products operating throughout Europe.

Forms used for comparative analysis as a basis for pricing decisions are similar to exhibit 6.18, and often run to several pages. The forms, one for each product or product group, and with the competitive products typed in, are circulated to appropriate people in the organization. When completed, they are collated and the scores averaged in a master form.

Exhibit 6.17 Items used for comparison in product positioning

---

Product	Distribution
Quality[*]	% Outlets covered
Range	Geographic coverage
Sizes	Stockturn
Packaging	
Versatility	**Advertising**
	Appropriation
Sales management	Company image
Segment covered	Quality
Size of sales force	Literature
Call frequency	Above as % of below
Field supervision	Creative platform
Selling out	Coverage
New account efforts	Exhibitions
Sales meetings	Promotions
	Press relations
	Direct mail

---

[*] Quality is actually broken down into the relevant attributes and characteristics, but to preserve the anonymity of this manufacturer these are not shown.

Exhibit 6.18 Comparative analysis form for product positioning

---

Rate all products on a scale of 5. Highest is 5, lowest 0.

Product_____Date_____

	Own	Comp 1	Comp 2	Comp 3	Comp 4	Comp 5
Product						
Quality	____	____	____	____	____	____
Range	____	____	____	____	____	____
Sizes	____	____	____	____	____	____
Packaging	____	____	____	____	____	____
Versatility	____	____	____	____	____	____
____	____	____	____	____	____	____
____	____	____	____	____	____	____
____	____	____	____	____	____	____
____	____	____	____	____	____	____
Distribution						
% Outlets	____	____	____	____	____	____
Geog. coverage	____	____	____	____	____	____

Product positioning

[Exhibit 6.18 continued]

Dstrbtr stndng	____	____	____	____	____	____
Local stocks	____	____	____	____	____	____
Warehousing	____	____	____	____	____	____
Stockturn	____	____	____	____	____	____
_____	____	____	____	____	____	____
_____	____	____	____	____	____	____
_____	____	____	____	____	____	____
_____	____	____	____	____	____	____

Management

Segment coverage	____	____	____	____	____	____
Size of force	____	____	____	____	____	____
Call frequency	____	____	____	____	____	____
Field supervision	____	____	____	____	____	____
Selling out	____	____	____	____	____	____
New a/c efforts	____	____	____	____	____	____
Sales meetings	____	____	____	____	____	____
_____	____	____	____	____	____	____
_____	____	____	____	____	____	____

Advertising

Appropriation	____	____	____	____	____	____
Company 'image'	____	____	____	____	____	____
Quality	____	____	____	____	____	____
Literature	____	____	____	____	____	____
Above % of below	____	____	____	____	____	____
Creative platform	____	____	____	____	____	____
Coverage	____	____	____	____	____	____
Exhibitions	____	____	____	____	____	____
Promotions	____	____	____	____	____	____
Press relations	____	____	____	____	____	____
Direct mail	____	____	____	____	____	____
_____	____	____	____	____	____	____
Overall Position	____	____	____	____	____	____

CHAPTER

7

Industrial products pricing

PRICING INDUSTRIAL PRODUCTS

Industrial products vary greatly in size, application and cost. To add to the confusion, many products normally considered to be consumer products are purchased for resale, and such transactions are regarded as industrial transactions.

One of the more common mistakes made in industrial marketing is to treat the market as a single entity and use the same marketing mix irrespective of the characteristics of a specific market. A company manufacturing electric motors, for example, is not selling electric motors to the total market. The motors are sold into different industries for widely differing uses. It is necessary to have a specific marketing strategy for each identifiable sub-market. This is based not on what the product is, but on what the customer uses it for. Thus, it is possible that the same product will have distinctive uses for different customers and should therefore have separate marketing mixes appropriate to each identified marketing segment.

Price is often an important element in distinguishing one marketing segment from another. This can readily be appreciated with airline ticket pricing. The price reflects the importance, flexibility, availability and convenience of the product and the degree of constraint placed on the traveller. Standard-price tickets provide a high degree of flexibility that affect the loading of any particular flight; bargain-price tickets encourage a certain percentage of seats to be taken for any nominated flight. The airline can vary the issue of

162

low-priced tickets for flights to accommodate the demand trend of standard-price ticket travellers. The product is much the same but its use is reflected in the price charged.

Industrial products may be classified as primary materials, materials and components, supplies, capital goods and services. Services are dealt with in a separate chapter devoted to services for all types of customer. For pricing purposes, industrial products may be divided into two broad groups – products that are repeat purchased and one-off products.

Industrial products that are repeat purchased include:

- *primary materials* such as coal, iron ore, rubber;
- *materials* that are incorporated into other products either as bought or changed in some way – insulators, timber, ball-bearings, rubber mechanicals, fabric, wool, silk, leather, sheet metal;
- *supplies*, also known as 'industrial consumables' and 'technical consumables', which are used up or destroyed in the manufacture of other products – lubricating oil, fuel, grinding paste, adhesives, nuts, bolts, washers, screws, nails.

Industrial products that are usually purchased on a one-off basis include:

- *capital* goods – machinery, plant and equipment, jet-engines, fire fighting equipment, boats, rail coaches.

The description 'one-off' is slightly misleading because capital goods are often purchased for a second and third time. Large airplanes are sometimes purchased by airlines in multiple lots; but the purchase of, say, ten new jumbo jets may be regarded as a set of ten. At least, the airlines don't buy such sets very often, and each set could be regarded as a one-off purchase.

Another type of industrial transaction is carried out by the distributor, factor, wholesaler, dealer, or large retail group that buys purely for resale. They are not so much buying industrial products but industrial purchasing. The pricing issues to be met by a supplier negotiating sales with Marks & Spencer in the UK or the Carrefour supermarket chain in France has similar problems to those of a manufacturer selling industrial products to a factory.

The type of product also tends to reflect the degree of consideration given to a proposal before purchase. The siting of a factory, the selection of appropriate plant and equipment will receive much greater consideration in an organization than, say, which suppliers are to provide lubricating oil, rubber, hose-pipe, water softener, wooden pallets and all the other materials and supplies used in manufacture.

INDUSTRIAL BUYERS

The position and authority of the industrial buyer varies greatly, as does the importance of the buying activity in organizations. The buying activity may be little more than a rubber stamp placed on the lowest-priced quotation by a middle manager on a requisition order raised by scientific and technical people. Alternatively, the buying activity may be crucial in the company, with the buyer having a highly qualified staff and exercising considerable power in the assessment of products and prices.

In many companies the buying activity is diffused and involves different groups of people with varying degrees of influence over purchases. Such influences are often spread over many weeks or months, and use of the product is separated from purchase by a lengthy period, such as with a new factory, an oil tanker, a printing press, a training programme, a cathedral or a new motorway.

Many researches have been conducted on the numbers of influences in companies over the purchase of industrial products. Exhibit 7.1 shows an average spread of influences found in nearly 70 medium-to-large companies during the period between 1980 and 1988.

Exhibit 7.1 Buying influence in companies

Number of buying influences	Percentage of companies
6 or more	3%
5	10%
4	18%
3	45%
2	22%
1	2%

THE DECISION-MAKING UNIT

The bulk of all industrial purchases directly involves from two to five people, who may be considered as those formally involved in the buying decision. There are many more who are indirectly involved or influence purchases in one way or another. All comprise the *decision-making unit*. This is a formal or informal group of people in a company who influence where orders are placed. This buying situation is illustrated in exhibit 7.2. Behind the seller is the producer, manufacturer or assembler; surrounding the buyer are the influencers and users.

Between the seller and the buyer (together with the various buying influencers) is the marketing mix: the product, price, place, promotion and service. If the construction of a marketing mix is appropriate for the seller, it must be applicable to the buyer.

The task that confronts the pricing executive is to construct a price schedule relevant to the other mix components, and directed to the total buying influences in the customer's organization, not just to the industrial buyer.

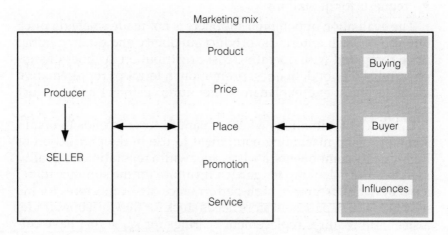

Exhibit 7.2 The industrial purchasing situation

SOURCES OF INTELLIGENCE

If the pricing activity is to be conducted professionally, with the aim of making good profits, it must not be regarded as the sole arbiter of which supplier gets the order. An understanding of modern purchasing techniques will help executives in the price-setting task.

The increasing awareness generated by the 'green' movement throughout the world of the need for resource conservation, has stimulated the rise of 'materials management' and 'facilities planning and management' in organizations.

One activity, more than any other, epitomizes the industrial buying process – the selection and evaluation of sources of supply. All buying behaviour and activities eventually focus on the final, vital decision as to who is to supply the product and services. Apart from previous suppliers, here are the main sources of intelligence for industrial buyers:

- experience;
- associates;
- interviews with representatives of suppliers;
- catalogues;
- trade directories;
- trade and publications;
- exhibitions;
- requests for quotations.

The evaluation of potential suppliers is not made solely on price but also on such criteria as: product suitability and quality; initial price compared with operating costs; distribution facilities of supplier; reliability of deliveries; promotion in terms of representative visits, technical and explanatory literature; customer and product servicing.

Consider the situations where a manufacturer intends to obtain some precision machining equipment to use in the production of high-quality components: a wholesaler with a reputation for quality merchandise is looking for garden furniture for the summer trade; a motor manufacturer of high-performance cars wants tyres for his new model; a department store needs stock for the Christmas trade; a steel mill requires replacement bearings for some that have collapsed unexpectedly.

How important is price in these situations? Important of course; but not all-important. Your company's product may have the lowest price on the market, but if the quality is not high enough for the customer, you will not get the order.

You may have a product of adequate quality and lowest price, but if your delivery is likely to be protracted, the customer may not be prepared to wait; the order is placed with a competitor at a higher price. You can only compete in such a situation if your price is low enough for the customer to 'trade off' longer delivery against lower price.

When setting price you should take into consideration all the other points that customers find important in the buying situation.

VENDOR PERFORMANCE EVALUATION

Three methods are currently used by professional buyers to appraise potential suppliers. Price is playing an increasingly important part in such evaluations and is always related to variations in the other criteria.

Categorical method   The least precise evaluation technique. Subjective ratings are assigned by buying staff to various factors considered important for assessing suppliers' activities. No particular weighting or relevant importance is accorded to the activities, but the buying staff usually discuss the ratings at periodic meetings.

Cost-ratio method   All identifiable buying and receiving costs are related to the value of deliveries from the respective suppliers. The usual categories – quality, price, transportation – are used to identify costs. Quality costs would include visits necessary to supplier, attending demonstrations and benchmarks, approval of samples, incoming goods inspection, reworking necessary for defective supplies, handling and unpacking difficulties. Costs for each major category are calculated as a ratio of value of monthly or quarterly purchases – the higher the ratio, the lower the rating for the supplier.

Weighted points method   Criteria relevant to the purchasing organization, and appropriate to all possible supply situations, are quantified by being weighted for importance. Current and potential suppliers are rated individually on their performance of the evaluation criteria. The ratings are multiplied by the relevant weights, and totalled to provide a composite performance figure for the supplier. The criteria include such things as: quality, delivery, reliability of delivery, service, accuracy of deliveries and invoices, need for checking, frequency of cost-savings made, amount of product usage data.

THE MOST COMMONLY USED EVALUATION METHOD

The most widely used is a weighted points method. From pricing consultancy I have carried out, the following eight criteria are the most widely used by buyers, and are ranked in order of importance as considered by buyers:

- price;
- delivery;
- quality;
- reliability;
- service;
- availability of emergency supplies;
- accessibility of representatives when needed;
- uniqueness, or specific characteristics of product.

Vendor performance evaluation forms used by some large organizations, particularly government departments, run to many pages, with the criteria subdivided into minor categories, all with varying weights and having to be assessed for different circumstances. Price is always a key factor to which all other criteria are related.

Price, delivery and quality are generally considered to be the most important criteria in the selection of sources, but some companies vary their ranking of the three according to the product or service being obtained or the purchasing situation.

The initial selection is commonly based on price because this categorizes the product being offered, and price can usually be quickly established. The quality of a product cannot always be readily determined and may take some time, especially if tests have to be carried out. Delivery cannot be evaluated until the product has actually been delivered.

The eight criteria have been ranked in the general order of importance considered by buyers, but this common ranking conceals the *relative importance* of each criterion compared with the others. Companies use widely differing measurements of relative importance.

The degree of importance of the individual criteria is reflected in the weighting given to them. As you might expect, price, delivery and quality are often given weights very close to one another.

Weights are often decided by a committee or by references to appropriate department heads.

The weights are applicable to all suppliers; ratings are applied to individual suppliers and potential suppliers.

The criteria ratings for an individual supplier are multiplied by the relevant weight of the criteria to give weighted ratings. The sum of these weighted ratings provides an overall performance figure. Suppliers with ratings above a level determined by the buying department are invited to quote for the supply of products. From this survey of supplier performance evaluation it can be appreciated why some companies vary the criteria weightings for different products.

Where quality of a product is of paramount importance, the evaluation forms for that product will have a very high weight for quality. If the company buys certain products 'on price' then price and delivery are relatively highly rated.

The pricing executive can make use of this technique by requesting the sales organization to find out the evaluation procedures of some of the company's more important customers. If they could obtain sample forms from customers showing weights this would indicate the customers' opinions on the relative importance of price.

If it were possible to obtain customers' evaluations of the company, showing not only the weight for price but how the company is rated, this would provide useful intelligence on probable market pricing.

Irrespective of how vendor performance evaluation is done by customers, whether with paper and pencil, with or without the aid of a calculator, it is very quickly done in a spreadsheet program on a PC. Though not of primary interest to sellers, if the information about customers' basic criteria and perhaps individual ratings can be obtained, to reproduce it as in exhibit 7.3 will enable many 'what if' situations to be appraised. The exhibit is a general layout with specimen weights; ratings would be entered for each supplier. The completed form is illustrated in exhibit 7.4.

Ratings of the criteria for the supplier are entered in column [C]. The formulae for the other relevant cells are:

```
[D5]  +B5*C5/B15
[D6]  +B6*C6/B15
[D7]  +B7*C7/B15
[D8]  +B8*C8/B15
```

```
            [A]                    [B]            [C]           [D]
[1]  <Vendor>
[2]  Supplier:                 Product:              Date:
[3]
[4]     CRITERIA               WEIGHT          RATING    PERFORMANCE
[5]  Price                      19.00
[6]  Delivery                   17.00
[7]  Quality                    16.00
[8]  Reliability of delivery    13.00
[9]  Service                    12.00
[10] Emergency supplies          8.00
[11] Accessibility               6.00
[12] Uniqueness of product       5.00
[13] Subsidiary criteria         4.00
[14]                           ------                        ------
[15]                           100.00
```

Exhibit 7.3 Evaluation form with weights

```
            [A]                    [B]            [C]           [D]
[1]  <Vendor>
[2]  Supplier: RST Ltd        Product:  Red Balls    Date: Oct 89
[3]
[4]     CRITERIA               WEIGHT          RATING    PERFORMANCE
[5]  Price                      19.00          64.00        12.16
[6]  Delivery                   17.00          63.00        10.71
[7]  Quality                    16.00          77.00        12.32
[8]  Reliability of delivery    13.00          90.00        11.70
[9]  Service                    12.00          72.00         8.64
[10] Emergency supplies          8.00          45.00         3.60
[11] Accessibility               6.00          54.00         3.24
[12] Uniqueness of product       5.00          72.00         3.60
[13] Subsidiary criteria         4.00          68.00         2.72
[14]                           ------                       ------
[15]                           100.00                        68.69
```

Exhibit 7.4 Completed evaluation form

```
[D9]   +B9*C9/B15
(formulae from p.169 cont)
[D10]  +B10*C10/B15
[D11]  +B11*C11/B15
[D12]  +B12*C12/B15
[D13]  +B13*C13/B15
[B15]  @SUM(B5..B13)
[D15]  @SUM(D5..D13)
```

The weights allocated by the company to the criteria will doubtless need to be amended from time to time. They should add to a round figure of, say, 100.

If the total of the weights is varied, the individual criteria weights will not be *relevant* weights, so the total must be kept constant. With a spreadsheet this is a simple matter. Alterations of any of the criteria will automatically alter the total in [B15]. By maintaining an agreed total, weights for individual criteria have to be allocated so that the total stays at this figure. In this example, suppose that the company decided that price was becoming a more important factor in their purchasing decisions and increased its weight in [B5] to 21, the total in [B15] would be 102. Adjustments would have to made to other criteria so that the total in [B15] became 100.

A LONDON EXPERIENCE

Exhibits 7.5 and 7.6 are completed vendor performance evaluation forms for a London manufacturer's two main suppliers. They have been slightly modified to conceal the identities of manufacturer and suppliers, but the weights and ratings are as used by the company.

Because of the higher overall performance rating, 72.32, manufacturer XYZ, was the favoured supplier and received the bulk of the business. The ABC company, with 69.49, was used for second sourcing.

The London company wrote to all their suppliers telling them that, because of increasing costs, they were looking for keener prices. At the next meeting of the purchasing committee in September 1988 they increased weighting for price in the evaluation form from 18 to 20, and lowered the weight for emergency supplies from 10 to 8.

The XYZ company knew from other sources that, although they received a large bulk of the business from the London company, they were at a slight price disadvantage to the ABC company. They thought that they were obtaining business because of better service

171

	[A]	[B]	[C]	[D]
[1]	<Vendor>			
[2]	Supplier: ABC Ltd	Product:		Date: 20 Jun 88
[3]				
[4]	CRITERIA	WEIGHT	RATING	PERFORMANCE
[5]	Price	18.00	95.00	17.10
[6]	Delivery	18.00	36.00	6.48
[7]	Quality	14.00	81.00	11.34
[8]	Reliability of delivery	12.00	90.00	10.80
[9]	Service	11.00	72.00	7.92
[10]	Emergency supplies	10.00	45.00	4.50
[11]	Uniqueness of product	6.00	72.00	4.32
[12]	Accessibility of personnel	5.00	65.00	3.25
[13]	Subsidiary criteria	6.00	63.00	3.78

				69.49

Exhibit 7.5 Evaluation of supplier ABC

	[A]	[B]	[C]	[D]
[1]	<Vendor>			
[2]	Supplier: XYZ Ltd	Product:		Date: 15 Aug 88
[3]				
[4]	CRITERIA	WEIGHT	RATING	PERFORMANCE
[5]	Price	18.00	90.00	16.20
[6]	Delivery	18.00	60.00	10.80
[7]	Quality	14.00	75.00	10.50
[8]	Reliability of delivery	12.00	88.00	10.56
[9]	Service	11.00	70.00	7.70
[10]	Emergency supplies	10.00	55.00	5.50
[11]	Uniqueness of product	6.00	68.00	4.08
[12]	Accessibility of personnel	5.00	70.00	3.50
[13]	Subsidiary criteria	6.00	58.00	3.48

				72.32

Exhibit 7.6 Evaluation of supplier XYZ

and backup. On receiving the letter from their customer, though they appreciated its importance, they were unsure of the relative importance of price in the future. They decided to lower their price by a substantial margin that would also take into consideration the likely reduction that would be made by the XYZ company.

Exhibit 7.7 Comparative evaluation of two suppliers

	Overall rating		
	ABC	XYZ	Advantage of XYZ over ABC
Price 18, Emergency 10	69.49	72.32	2.83
Price 20, Emergency 8	70.49	73.02	2.53
Price 20, Emergency 8 and both rated 95 for price	70.49	74.02	3.53

Subsequently both suppliers' prices were rated at 95 per cent by the London company, and, with the amended weights, the evaluation situation was as in exhibit 7.7.

XYZ company were obviously not in possession of all the facts and over-reacted to the situation by lowering their price too quickly and by too much. Because of the volume of business, this had a significant adverse effect on their profits. The circumstance, of which they were unaware, was that the current protracted delivery period for the product of the ABC company earned ABC a low rating of 36 per cent for delivery.

When, some months later, ABC's delivery situation improved and matched that of XYZ company, they were rated equally at 60 per cent for delivery, but ABC's overall performance rating increased to 74.81. Their share of the customer's business rose steadily, as did their profits. Their improving delivery position and larger volume of business enabled them to shade price even more, to the point where the original roles were reversed: ABC became the major supplier, and XYZ the second source.

This example illustrates the central importance of price in all purchasing decisions. Although price is pivotal, other factors often have an impact by turning the situation about the pivot. In the long run, purchasing decisions are made on the price and profit resulting from the acquisition of materials. The supplier should seldom, if ever, change the price without assessing the other criteria in the situation.

PRICING CONSUMABLES

Pricing of industrial consumables is a similar process to pricing consumer products, except that a greater buying skill is encountered: the emotional content in the professional buying situation is low. Industrial buyers are not impressed with product attribute claims that cannot be proved or backed up with evidence.

As with consumer marketing, it is the total package which determines who gets the order, but, whereas price is not the main factor in consumer product purchasing, it tends to be so in industry. Quality, delivery, reliability of delivery, and servicing are assessed by buyers in relation to the price.

PRICING CAPITAL GOODS

Pricing capital goods is in a different category. Usually there is only one chance to get the price 'right', that is, somewhere near the figure the professional buyer is expecting to pay. To secure an acceptable profit through prudent pricing of industrial capital goods a company must have an effective pricing procedure and an efficient staff to implement the procedure and monitor results. Those responsible for setting prices, or advising on them, must have a thorough knowledge of costs of production at various levels of operation, an appreciation of competitive pricing methods, and an understanding of customers' behaviour.

Where appropriate, in addition to the price submitted for capital equipment, a lifetime cost analysis such as a discounted cash flow calculation at a modest discount rate should be appended to the quotation. While it may be assumed that a potential buyer's financial managers or accountants would examine the cost of any capital acquisition, the fact that the intending supplier sets out the financial implications adds a great deal of professionalism to the quotation.

Most large capital goods markets are oligopolistic; that is, they have relatively few sellers. None controls the market, but each is able to influence it to one degree or another. Thus, there are not a great many aircraft constructors, container shipbuilders, mainframe computer manufacturers, jet engine manufacturers.

Exhibit 7.8 MEL's five-year summary

	19x1 (£000)	19x2 (£000)	19x3 (£000)	19x4 (£000)	19x5 (£000)
Sales	2,916	3,427	3,625	4,168	5,550
Costs					
Direct materials	496	548	566	713	855
Direct labour	729	754	848	896	1,332
Variable o/h	175	171	199	188	344
Fixed overhead	927	1,028	1,164	1,209	1,665
Total cost	2,327	2,501	2,777	3,006	4,196
Profit	589	926	848	1,162	1,354
% Profit	20.2%	27.0%	23.4%	27.9%	24.4%

To consider a typical industrial pricing problem, the following situation confronted the divisional manager of a company in the UK. The figures and names have been altered to preserve anonymity of the company.

MAJOR ENGINEERING'S PRICING PROBLEM

Major Engineering Limited (MEL) specializes in the production of industrial equipment, components, measuring and testing equipment used in the motor car, truck, engineering and allied industries.

Summary results of the company's operations for the past five years are shown in exhibit 7.8. For the current year, the company has forecast its sales turnover at £6,530,000 and a 23 per cent profit as summarized in exhibit 7.9.

The company has four divisions, each run by a director who reports to the chief executive. Divisional directors agree annual sales and profit objectives and report progress to the main board every quarter. The profit objective set for each division is related to their usual profitability, normally between 20 and 25 per cent of sales before tax.

The agreed turnover and profit objectives for the year are shown in exhibit 7.10.

Industrial products pricing

	£	£
Estimated total company sales		6,530,000
Costs		
Materials	1,077,000	
Labour	1,633,000	
Variable overheads	359,000	
Fixed overhead including admin	1,959,000	
Total cost of goods sold		5,028,000
Forecast profit		1,502,000
Percentage profit forecast		23%

Exhibit 7.9   MEL forecast for the year

Exhibit 7.10   Divisional targets

Division	Estimated sales (£)	Forecast profit (£)
Electronic	1,800,000	442,000
Mechanical	1,700,000	390,000
Instruments	1,650,000	394,000
Tools	1,380,000	276,000

The first three divisions are each running at approximately 125 per cent of their target by the middle of the financial year, but the Tools Division is currently at about 80 per cent of target. Orders already booked and pending for the Tools division are expected to reach about 70 per cent of normal capacity over the next six months. The division's forecast for the year breaks down as in exhibit 7.11.

Divisional directors are responsible for obtaining their own enquiries, tendering for contracts, submitting quotations and organizing production to ensure that delivery dates are met. Production of all divisions is carried out within the large complex at Birmingham.

	£	£
Forecast divisional sales		1,380,000
Costs		
Materials	255,000	
Components from other divisions	103,000	
Labour	262,000	
Variable overheads	70,000	
Fixed overhead and administration	414,000	
Total cost of goods sold		1,104,000
Forecast profit		276,000
Percentage profit forecast		20%

Exhibit 7.11 Tools Division forecast for the year

The company has an interrelated components system enabling it to offer a range of equipment to suit most customers' needs. They offer standard units and variations that suit the particular requirements of operations, size, weight and output for most installations.

All components have a standard price which is based on standard cost of materials, labour, machine time and production overheads.

Standard price is standard cost plus 30 per cent for general administration and selling expenses, plus 25 per cent for profit. A product with standard cost of, say, £100,000 would have a standard price of £162,500.

Company policy is to base all quotations on standard price, but directors normally quote higher to retain a degree of bargaining power during subsequent negotiations. No discounts are given on any interdivisional purchases, although divisions commonly add a percentage to the price paid for components from other divisions when invoicing their own customers.

THE TANDY ENQUIRY

During the middle of the financial year, Tom Fox, the Tools Division director, received an enquiry for a control unit from a large car subsidiary company in Coventry, Tandy Engineering. The control unit was required for machining operations on a new car component, which Tandy had to start supplying in six months. MEL's normal delivery for the unit is three months.

Fox phoned Ken Johnson, the works director of Tandy, and told him that the quotation would be sent in a day or so and would be around £170,000 to £180,000. Johnson had said that the price seemed to be on the high side, but that he would wait for the official quotation before commenting further.

Tandy Engineering is one of MEL's main customers and places orders for about £750,000 a year spread fairly evenly over the four divisions of the company. Considerable goodwill has been built up over the years between the two companies because MEL maintains a very high level of quality control, their delivery schedules are most reliable, and the service engineers and fitters have been with the company for many years, and are well known to MEL's customers.

Naturally, there are competitors in this industry, but MEL is one of the high-quality, high-price suppliers. It is widely accepted in the industry that most of the companies operate on about 20 per cent profit, while selling expenses and servicing range from around 18 to 25 per cent. The main competitor most likely to quote against MEL is Warwick Engineering of Leamington Spa.

Warwick's operations are not as complex as MEL's and they tend not to concentrate on the motor car components market. Their price is normally about 10 per cent below MEL's. With their knowledge of previous business, they would be able to estimate that MEL's quotation for this enquiry would be somewhere between £157,500 and £175,000.

Fox's problem was that he could not see any real prospect of further orders being received during the remaining six months of the financial year and he had either to price to get the order, or price in line with his division's objectives.

The standard price of £170,930 contains an allowance of approximately £7,000 for 'free' servicing during the first year of the equipment's operation, although the servicing allowance was seldom all used. Also, this figure is not shown, or even implied, in the quotation, and there is no understanding that such service is free.

He looked at the quotation, exhibit 7.12, particularly at the £45,500 worth of components bought from other divisions, thought about ringing his divisional co-directors to ask for a price reduction, then thought better of it. He decided to ask one of his senior executives to review the whole situation and recommend the price to quote Tandy.

Exhibit 7.12 Tandy Engineering quotation

Quotation for Tandy Engineering Ltd		
Standard T38 Control Unit	£100,260*	
Standard extras:		
Rubber wheels	530	
AC/DC adaptor and governor	970	
Transfer unit	1,040	
Optical and focusing unit	3,220	
Metric/imperial converter	920	
		£106,940
Accessories:		
Collector unit	550	
Electronic counter	2,070	
Pneumatic alignment adjuster	14,490	
		17,110
Customer variations:		
Square configuration	10,350	
Satin chroming	8,120	
Design changes (Drwg. TE/034)	7,480	
		25,950
Assembly on site and commissioning		20,930
		£170,930

* Includes components from other divisions at cost of £45,500

HOW THE PRICE WAS RECOMMENDED FOR TANDY

Divisional records indicated that sales were normally fairly regular throughout the year. This meant that after six months Tools Division turnover should be about half, that is, around £690,000. The executive who had been asked to recommend a price had the latest returns and knew that the six months' turnover was £552,000, or 80 per cent of what it should have been. The break-even chart for the division is illustrated in exhibit 7.13, and shows that break-even does not usually occur until July or August each year.

From the recent sales engineers' reports and forecasts, and because of the long lead time to secure orders, there was little prospect

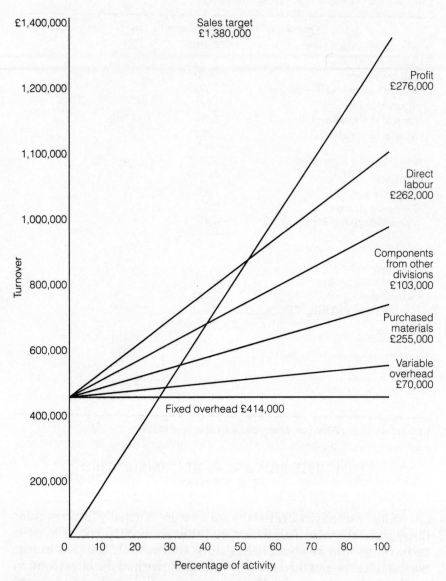

Exhibit 7.13 Break-even chart for Tools Division

of the division achieving sales of more than about £480,000 to £500,000 for the remaining six months. The executive used this

Sales for 6 months should be: £690,000

	£
First 6 months' sales	552,000
Likely sales for a second 6 months	490,000
Likely turnover for the year	1,042,000
less Fixed costs	414,000
	628,000

Average Variable Percentages

Materials	18.5%	
Components from other divisions	7.5%	
Labour	19.0%	
Variable overheads	5.0%	
Total average variable percentages	50.0%	
less 50% of likely turnover £1,042,000		521,000
Likely profit for the year		107,000
Agreed profit objective		276,000
Likely profit shortfall		£(169,000)

Exhibit 7.14 Calculation of profit shortfall

probable turnover for the year, as it appeared to be developing, as a basis for setting a price for the Tandy Engineering enquiry.

Sales to date were listed and added to the figure likely to be achieved for the second six months of the year. From this sales figure he deducted the division's fixed cost for the year.

The average variable percentages for materials, components normally purchased from other divisions, direct labour and overheads were computed, totalled and applied to the total sales figure that was estimated would be achieved. His workings are set out in exhibit 7.14.

The profit of £107,000 is just over 10 per cent of the likely turnover, £1,042,000, estimated by the executive; half what should normally be achieved. This is because the fixed costs of £414,000, already a high 30 per cent of turnover objective, would take almost 40 per cent of the likely turnover.

	£
Standard price for Tandy control unit	170,930
Profit content for Tools Division	
20% of £125,430 is £25,086	
Deduct cost of other divisions' components	45,500
Standard price of Tools Division content	125,430
Reduce division's standard price	
to standard cost (£125,430 × 61.54%)	77,190
Add back cost of other divisions'	
components to Tools Division's standard cost	45,500
Lowest possible price to cover variable costs	122,690

Normally, standard price of £170,930 would give a profit of £25,086. This is deducted from the likely profit shortfall of £169,000, estimated in Exhibit 7.14 and added to the standard price of £170,930.

Likely profit shortfall (exhibit 7.14)	169,000
Profit already in Tandy quotation	25,086
Amended profit shortfall	143,915
Standard price for Tandy quotation (exhibit 7.12)	170,930
Price to achieve profit objective	314,844

Exhibit 7.15 Minimum and maximum price for Tandy

He used a 'minimum–maximum' approach to establish the price range in which the final recommendation had to be made.

First, from the draft quotation of £170,930, the cost of components from other divisions was deducted to get at the Tools Division's net figure. This he reduced to standard cost.

Standard price is obtained by adding 30 per cent, then 25 per cent, to standard cost. Thus 1 multiplied by 1.3 and 1.25 gives 1.625.

Reversing the process, standard cost is found by multiplying standard price by the reciprocal of 1.625, which is 0.6154, and means that standard cost is 61.54 per cent of standard price.

Exhibit 7.16 Range of possible prices for Tandy

Possible prices for Tandy's quotation	
The price that would probably achieve the division's profit objective for the year	£314,844
Standard price, as per draft quotation	£170,930
Price that the main competitor Warwick would be expected to quote (90% of MEL's price)	£153,837
Lowest price possible and most likely to secure the order but makes no profit	£122,690

By adding back the total of other divisions' components to standard cost, he obtained a 'minimum' price to cover variable costs that could be quoted, but which would make no profit for the division.

He then added the likely shortfall in profit, from exhibit 7.14, to the standard price for Tandy in exhibit 7.12. This gave a 'maximum' price that would go some way to achieving the division's profit objective. His further workings are shown in exhibit 7.15.

The executive argued that the price that could be quoted Tandy ranged from £122,690 to £314,844. These, with other relevant prices are shown in exhibit 7.16.

SUBJECTIVE PROBABILITY ESTIMATES

At a subsequent meeting, Mr Fox and four of his staff reviewed the possible range of prices that the executive suggested could be quoted to Tandy. They agreed that setting a high price to try to reach the year's profit objective would ensure that they would not get the order. Also, they considered that there was always a chance that an unexpected order would be received during the second six months of the year as a result of their continuing efforts in the market.

Their suggestions for the price ranged between £165,000 and £175,000. The lower figure was suggested because it was about 3 per cent below standard price; the higher figure was justified because

Exhibit 7.17 Subjective probability profit

Price (£)	Probability of getting order	Profit (£)	'Subjective profit' (£)
178,500	0.639	32,656	20,867
177,000	0.675	31,156	21,030
175,500	0.747	29,656	22,153
174,000	0.775	28,156	21,821
172,500	0.784	26,656	20,898
171,000	0.811	25,156	20,402
169,500	0.850	23,656	20,108
168,000	0.896	22,156	19,852
166,500	0.941	20,656	19,437
165,000	0.982	19,156	18,811

Tandy had already been told on the phone that the price would be 'between £170,000 and £180,000'.

They agreed that price would be sensitive to customer reaction in amounts of about £1,500. The maximum and minimum range they had suggested indicated four possible prices below the standard price and five above. They then committed on paper, individually, without any of the others knowing, their estimates of getting the order at the various prices. Their percentage estimates were averaged, set against the respective price and profit, and multiplied to give a 'subjective profit' figure. These figures are shown in exhibit 7.17.

The price that gave the best 'pay-off' was £175,500. The executives devoted considerable time and thought to their estimates. In their subsequent discussion, all agreed that they had been cautious in their estimates of percentage probability. In particular, the estimate of approximately 75 per cent probability of getting the order at the best pay-off price was lower than they thought. The following points were noted in this meeting when the price was finally agreed.

- MEL is the price leader; their quality products carry a price premium of between 10 and 15 per cent higher than competition.
- Tandy's works director had been told on the phone that the price would between £170,000 and £180,000. He is likely to

have been conditioned to expect a price nearer to £180,000 than £170,000.

- His reaction that the price was on the high side was deemed to be a normal response; no buyer complains that the price is too low.
- MEL's engineers and fitters are known to the customer.
- MEL has a first-class servicing record.

Mr Fox decided to quote £174,850, an odd amount just below the 'best price' that had emerged from the discussion with his staff.

PRESENTING THE TANDY QUOTE

MEL's marketing staff were competent in their analysis and planning; they were also meticulous in their implementation. With the Tandy quotation prepared, the secretary of the senior sales engineer handling the account phoned Ken Johnson's secretary and asked for an appointment with Johnson for the engineer. She had been instructed not to speak with Johnson, but to restrict her call to making the appointment.

The reason was to avoid any of MEL's staff having to discuss the quotation and disclose the price over the phone. It was essential for a face-to-face situation for the presentation of the quotation.

Mr Fox briefed the engineer prior to his call on Tandy. They agreed that the main reactions likely as Johnson received the quotation would be:

- He would accept it without a great deal of argument.
- He would say nothing, but his face and body language would express dissatisfaction.
- He would say something similar to, 'I'm sorry, but it's too high.'
- He would display no reaction that could be interpreted.

In view of the previous relationship, it was thought that the fourth reaction could be discounted, as it would not occur. The first possible reaction presented no problems. The second required the engineer to remain absolutely silent and wait for Johnson to speak.

Exhibit 7.18 MEL's negotiation check list

Negotiations

Decision-makers, influencers and recommenders in the prospect's organization have been identified.	1 [ ]
The main aims, perhaps objectives, of the prospect's production, finance and sales functions are known.	2 [ ]
The prospect's priorities have been established.	3 [ ]
The prospect's negotiating points have been ranked in order of importance to the prospect.	4 [ ]
The concessions likely to be asked by the prospect have been quantified and listed.	5 [ ]
The concessions we are prepared to concede have been quantified and listed.	6 [ ]
The concessions most difficult to concede have been quantified and listed.	7 [ ]
Common ground has been established.	8 [ ]
We know how far apart we are likely to be.	9 [ ]
Sequence of presentation we favour has been listed.	10 [ ]
All who will attend the negotiations have been thoroughly briefed.	11 [ ]
Strength of competitive quotes.	12 [ ]
Advantages and disadvantages of our product compared with competitive offers have been noted.	13 [ ]
Documentary proof of all statements, advantages of our product for use in negotiations have been collated.	14 [ ]

The third would be normal for most buyers but, in view of Tandy's past knowledge of working with MEL, it might not arise.

Fox thought that the engineer should take the trouble to rehearse his responses to 'I'm sorry, but it's too high.' The question that the engineer would want answered was, 'How much is it too high?'

It is better to obtain the answer by an indirect question which throws some of the burden for the high price onto the potential buyer. So if this objection arose, the engineer was advised to respond by looking at his copy of the quotation, pause for a moment as though looking through it, and say, 'Satin chroming – is that absolutely necessary?' What the question is really asking is, 'If the price is reduced by £8,120, would it be acceptable?' The buyer might be willing to settle for a two or three per cent reduction, and £8,000 is nearly 5 per cent of the price.

Pricing a capital product is an important part of business; presenting the price to the potential buyer equally important. The price has to be justified, and sales people should be thoroughly trained in price negotiation skills. A negotiation checklist that the company uses for important sales negotiations is reproduced in exhibit 7.18.

In the event the sales engineer used the price of the metric converter as an exploratory question in the negotiation. Johnson agreed that it was not essential and the order was placed at £173,500.

COST OF OWNERSHIP

Today's professional buyers are well trained in purchasing procedures. Their job is to obtain for their companies, with specification or by search and comparison, the most satisfactory plant, equipment, components, materials and supplies, in the most convenient quantities, and delivered at the right time. Within these general limits, they have to buy at the lowest possible price. This does not mean the lowest initial price, but the lowest cost of obtaining *and using* the products and services; that is the full cost of ownership.

When comparing the merits of two machines which are priced close to each other, a professional buyer will be interested in their operating costs as well as the initial outlay. The 'lower' priced machine may be the more costly if it has to be serviced more often. By exploring the frequency and cost of maintenance, the buyer is able to calculate the true cost of ownership – that is, the cost of the machine in first-class operation.

The responsibility of preparing documentation for the price, cost of operating, and cost of maintenance and servicing is the task of the pricing executive. By a skilfully prepared presentation of 'cost of ownership', a company can often win orders against competitors whose products are apparently lower in price. This might best be accomplished with a sales proposal rather than a simple quotation.

PROPOSALS AND QUOTATIONS

A quotation is a traditional document used to specify the product, price, delivery and terms of payment. Often printed on the reverse of the document are the 'terms and conditions' which state practically every reason why the customer should *not* buy from you.

A proposal is a selling tool, and contains the same information as a quotation but also the reasons why the prospective customer *should* buy from you. Five main sections of a proposal are:

- the customer's objectives;
- your recommendations;
- additional benefits;
- financial justification;
- stated guarantee and service.

Customer's objectives   Find out what the customer wants to achieve before accepting the invitation to quote. Objectives should be listed in order of importance. Short statements of what the customer wants to achieve should ensure that the proposal is read.

Recommendations   Say how each objective will be met by your recommendations. If the proposal is for complex equipment, a detailed specification should be appended, with each section keyed so it is clear which recommendation relates to which objective.

Additional benefits   Recommendations will relate to the main objectives and indicate the main benefits. There may be additional benefits that the customer will enjoy.

Financial justification   State this simply so that the justification is clear in the first few sentences. If the financial justification is complicated, use a separate appendix and 'key' to the appropriate sections. If the purchase of your product 'pays for itself' in a period, explain in the appendix with a modest example that does not rely on maximum usage of your product to pay for itself. While the customer will investigate and justify the expenditure, don't assume this. Illustrate the justification to show that you have given it adequate thought from the prospective customer's viewpoint. If there is more than one way to illustrate financial justification, use them.

188

Guarantee and service   Don't rely on the pale print on the back of your official quotations for your guarantee, warranty and after-sales service. State what you are prepared to do. Often the fact that this is stated as a major part of the proposal, clinches the business. To underwrite what you offer for your guarantee and service, use third-party references where appropriate. If necessary, the company's official quotation should be included as an appendix.

A specimen proposal is given in exhibit 7.19.

Exhibit 7.19   Specimen proposal

Moulding Machines Limited

4 September 1989

Dear Mr Smith

Further to my letter of 4 April, following Mr Brown's call, I am now able to quote you for a moulding machine.
You require a machine that will:

* Replace your existing system.
* Operate automatically and increase current production by a minimum of 25 per cent within three months.
* Produce mouldings up to 250 mm diameter.

We recommend model SJR25. For the moderate capital outlay and operating costs, this automatic model will achieve these objectives and the following benefits:

* Constant temperature control for consistent moulding texture.
* Automatic cycling operation providing maximum output.
* Self-replenishing system requiring only one operator.
* Mouldings ejected into front-loading container for convenience of production and quality control.
* Unique, easy-clean filter system which reduces ingress of foreign material into valves and mechanism.
* All working parts readily accessible for speedy maintenance.

The SJR25 model has the following accessories:

Complete tool kit
Gloves and goggles
Digital thermometer
Air-gun
Silicone spray
Extension leads and adaptors for air and gas hoses.

Our own engineers will install and commission the machine and
train your operators in its running and maintenance. The machine will stand on any of your concrete floors.
Price delivered, installed, commissioned, and your operators
trained:

> US$xx,xxx (£xx,xxx) *[Price given first in customer's
> currency, then in sterling, and both in words.]* There
> are no extras.

In terms of cost per moulding produced:

* Your present plant produces 400 units a day.
* The new plant, SJR25, will produce up to 650 units
  daily, single-shift working; an approximate additional
  55,000 mouldings annually.
* If only, say, 60 per cent of this extra capacity (=
  33,000 units) is used, the annual charge over five
  years is US$xxx (£xxx).
* The capital cost per moulding produced at this level
  of operation will be US$x.xx (£x.xx).

Appended is a discounted cash flow calculation at various discount rates for you to compare with other quotations. *[not
shown]*
Similar machines have been installed in the companies listed
in the appendix. I know that none of them will mind your making enquiries.
Attached is our official quotation and technical literature
setting out the specification of the SJR25 model.

Yours sincerely

8

Discounts and price cutting

THE SOURCE OF DISCOUNTS

An important feature in pricing is the granting of discounts. Basically, a discount is a reduction from list price or normal price; it serves a legitimate marketing purpose. As illustrated in exhibit 8.1, discounts are either planned and come from the oncost component of price or are used as a tactical weapon, and are taken from the profit component.

TACTICAL DISCOUNTS

A frequently employed manoeuvre is to use discount to repel intending entrants to a market or market segment. Provided that the profit component in the price is adequate, a guerrilla attack can be mounted against new entrants. An attractive discount is offered to customers for increased orders, and to potential customers to place an initial order. This attack extends over the period of time it is estimated that the new market entrant would need to gain a foothold in the market. The perceived value of a product would appear to have been increased as result of a tactical discount.

Five main requirements need to be considered for tactical discounting to succeed. First, market intelligence should be able to identify potential and early entrants, and to forecast the type and price of a new product. Secondly, the discount must be sufficiently attractive to customers. Thirdly, the profit component must be large

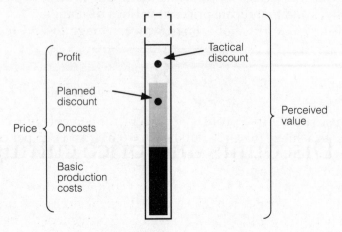

Exhibit 8.1 Where discounts come from

enough to absorb the discount without seriously affecting reasonable percentage profit. Fourthly, the period over which the discount is continued must be long enough to burn off the newcomer. Fifthly, the company must have a competent sales and marketing organization to implement the 'hit and run' tactics.

HIDDEN DISCOUNTS

Hidden discounts, as the name implies, are not generally seen, but will normally have been allowed for in the oncost component of price. They are granted to distributors, large buying organizations and major customers in the form of advertising allowances. Sometimes hidden discounts are given in the form of incentive allowances. This will be seen in the worked example for the hair product in chapter 11, exhibit 11.46.

PROGRAMMED DISCOUNTS

Consider the costing sheet shown as exhibit 3.2 of chapter 3 for a product transferred to the sales and marketing department at £18.50. The Midlands plastics company that originated the form subsequently set it up on a PC spreadsheet program: the computerized version of exhibit 3.2 is shown in exhibit 5.29 of chapter 5 for a product with a factory transfer price of £55. The form was extended to include the oncosts for sales and marketing to achieve their profit objectives and to indicate prices at various discounts.

The formula for establishing the percentage to add to cost to achieve a desired profit on return is:

$$\text{profit on cost} = \frac{\text{desired profit}}{(100 - \text{desired profit})}$$

Thus, if the desired profit is 20 per cent, the percentage to be added to cost to achieve this is $20/(100 - 20) = 0.25$ (that is, 25 per cent). To achieve a profit of, say, 25 per cent on return, $25/(100 - 25) = 33\frac{1}{3}$ per cent must be added.

If a product has a basic cost of, say, £80, and the desired profit is 20 per cent, 25 per cent of £80 is added for the necessary profit: the customer price is £100. The £20 profit is 25 per cent of the basic cost, 20 per cent of the customer price.

If this product, which has a normal price of £100, is offered at a discount of 5 per cent (that is, £95), profit is reduced by £5 to £15. The percentage profit is reduced from 20 per cent to $£15/95 = 15.8$ per cent.

The plastics company factory oncost of 20 per cent provides the factory operating profit. The sales department operates on a 30 per cent profit margin and adds 43 per cent ($30/70 = 0.43$) to the transfer price to provide 30 per cent. Any discount given has to come from this.

The company's full standard form with their range of discounts programmed in the file is shown in exhibit 8.2.

The main formulae for this form have already been given in chapter 5; those for the marketing oncost, discounted prices, and profit are as follows:

```
[D39]  @IF(D36,D36*43/100,@NA)
[D40]  @IF($D$39,$D$36+D39,@NA)
[E40]  +D40-$D$36
[F40]  @IF(D40,E40/D40,@NA) copy [F41]..[F50]
```

[C41] to [C50] are formatted for percentage to three decimal places.

```
[C41]  0.025
[C42]  0.05
[C43]  0.075
[C44]  0.1
[C45]  0.125
[C46]  0.15
```

```
             [A]         [B]        [C]        [D]       [E]        [F]
[1]
[2]                      COSTING SHEET FOR PRICING
[3]
[4]  Product _____            Date:    _____
[5]
[6]  Prepared by _____             Last updated: _____
[7]
[8]                       £          £          £
[9]  Raw materials                 24.00
[10] Bought-in                      8.50
[11]                                          32.50
[12] Inward transport    0.49
[13] Warehousing         0.91
[14] Internal handling   0.59
[15] Finsh. Goods Store  0.57
[16]                                2.55
[17] Direct labour       2.50
[18] Servicing labour    0.54
[19] Machine shop 1      1.50
[20] Machine shop 2
[21] Finishing           0.75
[22]                                5.29
[23]                                           7.84
[24] G & A               1.46
[25] Management          0.98
[26] HQ                  2.44
[27] Contingencies       0.65
[28]                                5.53
[29]                                          -----
[30]                                          45.86
[31]                                          -----
[32] Oncost                                    9.17
[33]                                          -----
[34] Min. Transfer price                      55.04
[35]                                          -----
[36]                    Transferred at:       55.00
[37]                                          =====
[38]                                                   Profit
[39] Standard marketing oncost                23.65     £         %
[40]              Standard price:             78.65   23.65    30.07%
[41]              Discount:    2.5%           76.68   21.68    28.28%
[42]              Discount:    5.0%           74.72   19.72    26.39%
[43]              Discount:    7.5%           72.75   17.75    24.40%
[44]              Discount:   10.0%           70.79   15.79    22.30%
[45]              Discount:   12.5%           68.82   13.82    20.08%
[46]              Discount:   15.0%           66.85   11.85    17.73%
[47]              Discount:   17.5%           64.89    9.89    15.24%
[48]              Discount:   20.0%           62.92    7.92    12.59%
[49]              Discount:   22.5%           60.95    5.95     9.77%
[50]              Discount:   25.0%           58.99    3.99     6.76%
```

Exhibit 8.2 Plastics company prices and discounts form

```
[C47]  0.175
[C48]  0.2
[C49]  0.225
[C50]  0.25
[D41]  @IF($D$39,$D$40-$D$40*C41.@NA)
                              copy [D42]..[D50]
[E41]  @IF(D41,D41-$D$36,@NA) copy [E42]..[E50]
```

QUANTITY DISCOUNTS

To induce buyers to purchase larger quantities, a discount is often granted. This is a reduction in the unit price, and varies depending on the size of the order placed. In many industries, unit cost of products falls considerably as volume is increased: all or part of this reduction is passed on to the buyer in the form of discount.

We read in chapter 1 of a company's price schedule that enabled buyers to buy ten machines for less than nine. Discount structures conceal similar traps. Discounts should be calculated at all levels to ensure that no such anomalies persist.

Where unit cost remains the same, or is reduced only very slightly even with large increase in volume, quantity discounts are seldom possible. Two types of quantity discount may be considered – cumulative and non-cumulative.

CUMULATIVE DISCOUNT

The discount granted to a buyer depends on the total purchases made during a period – usually a year. The purpose of a cumulative discount structure is to encourage the buyer to concentrate purchases of a product with the one supplier. While not necessarily a good example, the price schedule might look like exhibit 8.3.

If the market is highly competitive and customers buy keenly, a cumulative discount schedule can be constructed to appear to give them an advantage over the supplier as they increase their orders through the year.

The scheme does not have to follow the company's financial year, nor run from January to December. If the supplier's sales records indicate that there is a month when sales are normally depressed, the year over which the cumulative discount operates can be arranged to end in this previously depressed month.

Exhibit 8.3 Cumulative discounts

Volume ordered during 12 months	Unit price
up to 10	Net list
11–24	List less 1.0% on all sales to date
25–49	List less 1.5% on all sales to date
50–74	List less 2.0% on all sales to date
75–99	List less 2.5% on all sales to date

Exhibit 8.4 Quantity discounts

Quantity	Price (£)	Discount
up to 10	8.50	10.0%
11–49	8.50	12.5%
50–99	8.50	15.0%
100 upwards	on application	

NON-CUMULATIVE DISCOUNT

A non-cumulative discount applies only to any one order and is determined by the size of the order, hence the name 'quantity discount'. The amount of sales previously placed by the customer has no bearing on the price of a current order. The purpose of a non-cumulative discount is to encourage buyers to place larger orders and so enjoy a lower unit price. Where buyers place several orders during the season or year, if they increase the average order size they gain the advantage of a higher discount per order.

The price schedule is similar to the cumulative discount scheme. Exhibit 8.4 illustrates a typical scheme.

Whenever a discount scheme has been drafted, it should be analysed from the viewpoint of the potential buyer. Particular attention should be given to the discounts being offered at the various quantity changes.

Exhibit 8.5 Exhibit 8.4 extended

10 @ £8.50 less 10%	(£85 – £8.5)	= £76.50 (£7.65 each)
11 @ £8.50 less 12.5%	(£96.50 – £11.69)	= £81.81 (£7.44 each)
.	.	.
.	.	.
.	.	.
49 @ £8.50 less 12.5%	(£416.50 – £52)	= £364.44 (£7.44 each)
50 @ £8.50 less 15%	(£425 – £63.75)	= £361.25 (£7.23 each)

Exhibit 8.6 A distributor's discount schedule

Quantity	Price per dozen (£)	Discount
1 dozen	2	-
1 gross	2	10%
10 gross	2	19%
100 gross	2	27%

The schedule shown in exhibit 8.4 hides inconsistencies: the unit cost to the buyer of orders for quantities of 10, 11, 49 and 50 is set out in exhibit 8.5. This reveals that there is no inducement in the unit price at 49 over 11. A buyer at the higher level, investing in well over four times the amount of stock as at the lower level, would gain nothing. This type of schedule will encourage buyers to restrict orders to the lower level.

Discount structure discrepancies such as these are not as rare as one would think. Exhibit 8.6 is the schedule that was issued in 1987 by a Bristol-based distributor of a fast moving consumer product.

At first sight the odd percentages are confusing, but on investigation, it is apparent that the distributor had arrived at them by reducing the original price of £2 a dozen by successive amounts of ten per cent. This is shown in exhibit 8.7.

Exhibit 8.7   Exhibit 8.6 analysed

Quantity	Price per dozen (£)	Equivalent to a discount of
1 dozen	2 net	-
1 gross	1.80 (10% less)	10%
10 gross	1.62 (10% less)	19%
100 gross	1.46 (10% less)	27%

Exhibit 8.8   Exhibit 8.6 extended

Quantity	Price per dozen (£)	Total (£)
1 dozen	2 net	2.00
11 dozen	2 net	22.00
1 gross	2 less 10%	21.60
9 gross	2 less 10%	194.40
10 gross	2 less 19%	194.40
99 gross	2 less 19%	1,924.56
100 gross	2 less 27%	1,752.00

If this schedule is extended from the viewpoint of the potential customer, focusing on the total cost at the order size changes, exhibit 8.8 shows some interesting anomalies.

Clearly, the schedule is faulty because it costs less to buy a gross than 11 dozen; 9 gross and 10 gross lots cost the same; and 100 gross costs less than 99 gross. Obviously, the distributor had never extended the discount schedule to show the total amounts that customers would pay.

Customers' average order size had not been considered in the original construction of the discount schedule. The vast majority of customers ordered in quantities of 1 to 3 gross lots and the pricing structure should have been prepared to reflect this purchasing pattern and encourage buyers to order a slightly larger amount to obtain a higher discount.

The anomalies were pointed out to the distributor, who amended it. The 10 per cent discount was retained for the gross lot size, but

Exhibit 8.9 Distributor's amended discount schedule

Quantity	Price per dozen (£)	Total (£)
1 dozen	2 net	2.00
11 dozen	2 net	22.00
1 gross	2 less 10%	21.60
9 gross	2 less 10%	194.40
10 gross	2 less 20%	192.00
99 gross	2 less 20%	1,900.80
100 gross	2 less 25%	1,800.00

Exhibit 8.10 Distributor's discount workings

Quantity	Unit price (£)	Total (£)	@ £2 dozen (£)	Difference (£)	Discount (%)
1 gross (144)	0.15	21.60	24.00	2.40	10%
4 gross (576)	0.145	83.52	96.00	12.48	13%
6 gross (864)	0.14	120.96	144.00	23.04	16%
8 gross (1,152)	0.135	155.52	192.00	36.48	19%
10 gross (1,440)	0.13	187.20	240.00	52.80	22%

for 10 gross lots it was increased to 20 per cent; for the 100 gross lots it was reduced to 25 per cent. The extension from the point of view of the customer is set out in exhibit 8.9.

The pricing discrepancies remained, so the distributor took a different approach. He related the discount pattern to typical order sizes, and based price on the unit cost of the product. Net price was 15p and, at the 10 gross lot, 13p. He used an ordinary calculator, paper and ball-point. His workings are shown in exhibit 8.10, and the new price list in exhibit 8.11.

Exhibit 8.11   Distributor's new discount schedule

Quantity	Price per dozen (£)	Discount
1 dozen	2	-
1–3 gross	2	10%
4–5 gross	2	13%
6–7 gross	2	16%
8–9 gross	2	19%
10 gross	2	22%

TRADE DISCOUNT

A trade discount is given to middlemen who use the products to carry out marketing or technical services to others, and is often a substantial percentage of the oncost component of price. Wholesalers receive a trade discount because they carry out the functions that would otherwise have to be done by the manufacturer. They buy in bulk, store, supply in smaller quantities, finance their customers, promote products and generally extend the distribution network for manufacturers. Trade discount is to cover all these services and supply middlemen with their profit.

Service middlemen such as electricians, plumbers, hairdressers and builders use the products in their services to clients. The practice used to be that such servicing organizations received a trade discount on products, the full price of which was passed on to clients. With the growth of cash-and-carry wholesalers and do-it-yourself stores the practice has been largely eroded.

The type of distribution used by a manufacturer will obviously indicate the discount structure. In hi-tech fields such as computer software, prices reflect the amount of customer support necessary, such as training, development and upgrading. Typically, the hi-tech distribution network consists of main distributors, distributors, value-added remarketers and users. Trade discounts accorded to each type of middleman are related to the amount of service to be provided to others lower in the distribution network.

This importance of pricing to software manufacturers may be appreciated by the fact that a program, even of great value and flexibility, may consist of ten floppy disks and a manual – perhaps a cost of £20 – yet is priced at anything from £300 to £3,000 or more. It is not the actual raw materials of the product that matters so much as the support that has to be supplied for the customer to gain maximum benefits from using it.

Whether or not a company grants trade discounts, the type and size of those discounts must be influenced by the practice currently operating in the industry.

Packaged products sold through wholesalers and retailers may be priced at 25 per cent discount for retailers and an additional 15 per cent for wholesalers. An item with a list price of £100 would be invoiced at 'list less 25%' (= £75) to the retailer, and 'list, less 25% and 15%', to the wholesaler (= £63.75).

When trade discounts are given, these are usually deducted from the list price net of any tax, and then any quantity discount applied to the reduced base. Tax is added to the final computed figure.

CASH DISCOUNT

The vast majority of sales in industry and commerce is conducted on a credit basis; even consumer purchasing is now normal with credit or charge card operations. Payment of cash on delivery or cash in advance is rare except for certain mail order operations and poor credit risks.

A company's *terms* are the percentage reductions they are prepared to grant to debtors who pay the invoice within a stated time period.

All price schedules should include a percentage oncost to cover the normal credit provided. This is usually 30 days after receipt of statement and can, effectively, provide nearly two months' credit to customers. If the cost of money is, say, 12 per cent a year, then the cost of funding debtors is 1 per cent a month. If interest rate rises above 12 per cent a year, the cost of funding debtors also rises.

For these reasons, a cash discount is sometimes offered for early payment. A typical offer is 2 per cent within ten days, net 30 days; sometimes shortened on invoices to '2/10 net 30'. This means that if the invoice is paid within ten days of date of invoice, the buyer may deduct 2 per cent from the net-of-tax total, alternatively, pay the full amount 30 days from receipt. When interest rates are high and money costly, suppliers sometimes apply an interest charge to their accounts if not paid on or before the due date.

For the buyer, the 2 per cent cash discount for paying in ten days rather than 30 days is paying 20 days early. If 2 per cent is earned in 20 days, this represents a saving at the rate of about 36 per cent a year.

For the seller, early payments mean that less working capital has to be invested in debtors and less time and resources are needed to collect accounts.

Cash discount is the final deduction made from the net-of-tax figure. Suppliers should make it easy for buyers to pay invoices and include a statement on the invoice as to how much may be deducted for cash if paid within the allotted period. Where industry practice is 5 per cent for cash by return, 3.75 per cent seven days, 2½ per cent monthly, a statement of the amounts that may be deducted for *receipt of payment* at the various dates will avoid subsequent arguments.

Suppliers must also appreciate that offering 5 per cent for cash by return – say two working days – represents a rate of over 900 per cent a year! The formula for calculating the annual interest rate necessary to cover the granting of percentage discounts for quick payment is:

(365/number of days credit foregone) × discount rate

Thus, if terms are 2½ per cent seven days, net 30, by paying in seven days the customer deducts 2½ per cent of the net-of-tax total and forgoes 23 days of credit. This is the same as saying that for 23 days the customer earns 2½ per cent interest. Therefore, (365/23) × 2½ per cent = 39.6 per cent.

Company practice must influence cash discount procedures. Goods are supplied to buyers every day of the month, from day 1 to day 31. Some companies can enclose an invoice with the shipment; others send the invoice after advice of dispatch notes have been processed. Some cannot issue an invoice until collation of internal stores' notes and labour calculations have been made; such invoices are liable to arrive a week or more after the product or service has been supplied. If it is the custom to send customers' statements towards the end of each month, the credit being granted will vary from a few days to nearly two months. The oncost component of the price should contain a percentage for credit.

Immediately a sale is made and the product delivered or service supplied, what the customer owes is the suppliers' money. Assuming that the sale has been made on credit, the moment that payment changes from being due to being overdue, that money is a free loan to the customer. Some companies have a definite policy of delaying payment to their creditors so as to increase their working capital. Any customers who use your money in this way require you to increase your working capital to fund them. Money outstanding from debtors can often rise to an exorbitant figure as high as 40 per cent of current assets.

To determine how much a cash discount will cost your company, establish the cost of credit control etc. as a percentage of sales, and add this to the current annual interest rate for borrowing money. One-twelfth of this percentage is the monthly cost of carrying overdue debtors. Thus, if the current interest rate is 12 per cent, company credit control etc. is 2 per cent, this is 14/12 = 1.167 per cent monthly financing cost. If your company operates on a percentage of, say, 10 per cent, an overdue account of two months reduces this profit to 7.67 per cent.

ANALYSIS OF TURNOVER AND PROFITS

Before a quantity discount table is prepared, an analysis of the company's sales should be made as in the forms in exhibits 8.12 and 8.13. Use the first form to list the company's products in descending order of sales revenue, starting with the product with the largest turnover. Cumulative turnover percentages are inserted in the final column.

The second form is used for profits. The products are listed in descending order, starting with the product providing the greatest actual profit. As with the form for turnover figures, cumulative profit percentages are entered in the last column.

It is probably adequate in both forms to rely on the *pareto principle* and enter the number of products that provide approximately 80 per cent of turnover and profits. In both cases this is likely to be around 20 per cent of the products.

Exhibit 8.12   Turnover from products

	Product turnover			
	Product	*Sales value*	*% of T*	*Cumulative %*
1				
2				
3				
4				
5				
6				
7				
8				
9				
10				
11				
12				
13				
14				
15				
16				

The so-called pareto principle is frequently observed with 80 per cent of the effects coming from 20 per cent of the causes. While there is no statistical or logical reason for this 80:20 tendency, it is frequently found. It stems from the work of Vilfredo Pareto (1848–1923), an Italian sociologist and economist. He was a keen observer of social behaviour, investigated many statistical series, and wrote about Fascist principles of government in his *Mind and Society* (1916). 'Pareto' is now used as a modifying adjective, and denotes this 4:1 ratio tendency in natural phenomena and frequency distributions.

With the two forms completed, you have evidence of which products provide turnover and profit, and whether there is any correlation between them. You should aim to increase sales of those

Exhibit 8.13 Product profitability

	Profits from products			
	Product	*Profit*	*Profit %*	*Cumulative %*
1				
2				
3				
4				
5				
6				
7				
8				
9				
10				
11				
12				
13				
14				
15				
16				

products that provide your company with profit rather than those which provide mainly sales volume. At the same time you must consider the market and not overlook potential high growth products.

Discount policy may be designed to stimulate greater interest and demand for your most popular products, or to encourage buyers to buy the products you wish to push. Discount schemes should be used mainly as a promotional tool and certainly not constructed on 'compartmentalized thinking', that is, creating a table of discounts that relate to assumed groups, or compartments, of numbers – 1 to 9, 10 to 24, 25 to 49, and so on. The scheme should take into consideration the size of order you would prefer to handle; the most popular size of order from the customers' viewpoint, that is, the average size of orders placed by the bulk of customers; the cost to the customer of holding this average stock; the physical requirements of holding stock; the savings likely from larger sized orders.

Review all draft schemes to remove any inconsistencies similar to the examples in this chapter that enable buyers to purchase a higher quantity for less outlay.

PRICE CUTTING

As a promotional tool, price cutting is normally effective and has been used by countless organizations as a marketing strategy, when entering a new market, or attempting to extend their share of a market. Price cutting in supermarkets, in the form of 'loss-leading', was a strategy that held sway for several years. A number of highly popular lines were priced at cost, or near to it, to attract customers into the store. Once there, they continued with their other purchases. The thinking was that, since customers had probably travelled several kilometres by public transport or private car to purchase their goods from the store, they were unlikely to compare prices of less popular products.

Manufacturers normally oppose any of their products being loss-led in this way, especially for heavily branded products. They are concerned that products that are regularly loss-led will become associated in customers' minds with the cut price and that customers will tend to buy the product only when it is on offer at that price. Their legitimate complaint caused subsequent legislation in the UK to forbid loss-leading of products without pre-arrangement with the manufacturer concerned, and effectively ended this as a widespread practice.

What is more usual now is the use of *price leaders*, which are items offered at a cut price, often by special purchases from the manufacturer. They are sold above actual cost but below the normal retail price. They are called *special offers*, and are usually advertised in the local weekly newspapers that circulate within the store's catchment area.

Of all the marketing tools available to a company, price cutting is the easiest and quickest to implement, and requires no injection of cash to put into practice, although the returns will be less. However, other things being equal, price cutting is the same as giving discounts: it erodes profits. The thinking is that sales will increase to a level which will offset the loss of profit.

The validity of this line of thought depends largely on the degree of elasticity of demand. It must be high enough for the percentage increase in demand to be considerably more than the percentage decrease in price.

Distributors at Slough, near London, had sold 50 air conditioning units at a net-of-tax figure of £1,000 – a sales turnover of £50,000. Faced with a competitor who was offering a similar product at a slightly lower price, they considered that a 15 per cent price reduction would not only combat competition but would also achieve greater sales. For their price cut to be effective, the increase in sales had to be greater than the 15 per cent cut.

It is easy to see that, to maintain the same sales turnover of £50,000, the proposed new price of £850 is divided into 50,000 = 59 units. This would achieve a sales turnover of £50,150.

In the event, over a similar period of time they sold 80 units – an increase of 60 per cent; their turnover increased to £68,000.

THE PRICE CUT TRAP

While in the short term the distributors successfully combated the competition, increased their share of the market, and increased their sales turnover, the object of pricing is to obtain satisfactory profit.

They purchased the air conditioning units at £650 from the manufacturer. This gave them a gross profit of £350 when selling at £1,000, but only £200 when selling at £850.

At the previous price of £1,000, they made 50 × £350 = £17,500 gross profit. At the cut price of £850, they made 80 × £200 = £16,000 gross profit. For the extra effort and lower price, they were £1,500 worse off.

Price cutting as a long-term strategy has only a limited possibility of success, as Freddy Laker discovered. His Laker Airways cut-price policy brought transatlantic crossing within reach of many thousands of people who would otherwise not have flown. Sadly, in the face of united competition from other airlines with much deeper pockets, his UK-based company was forced into liquidation.

Similarly, in the USA, Donald Burr founded People Express Airlines Inc. in 1980 and started the first scheduled flights from Newark in 1981. His strategy was simple – heavy price cutting of fares on popular flights, well below competitors. Five years later, after the major carriers had aggressively cut their air fares, Burr was forced out of the business and sold out to Texas Air.

COMPETITIVE REACTIONS

Whether you are constructing a pricing schedule on entering a new market, or already operating in a market, you must assume that if you price your product lower than that of your competitors, it will attract their attention. This attention can be unwelcome, depending on the size, importance and timing of your price cut, and the position of the product in the market. You could make a general assumption, and work on the basis that, for every price cut you make, competitors will copy; the net result would be that profits are lowered all round.

While it is not always possible to quantify business decisions, far less to quantify likely events in the future, nevertheless, by tapping the experience, skills and innate ability of executives, you can often arrive at a combined decision which is better than one made by an individual. This can be particularly useful when contemplating pricing decisions or changes and the likely response from competitors.

Just such a situation occurred in the chemical industry. A company who supplied certain agents and additives was about to enter a market which had been the sole province of a competitor with a legally protected product for many years. With the protection having lapsed, the market was open.

Despite the competitor's having had free rein in the market, their pricing was keen, as they had adopted a penetration pricing policy at the start and maintained a low-price policy for many years. The price of their product was £7.60 per litre and the current size of the total market was in the region of 6 million litres.

The new entrant decided on the basis of evidence from several market surveys carried out elsewhere that the market was unlikely to be influenced by a price difference of under 10 per cent. They based their investigations on a variation of approximate 15 per cent below and above the current price of £7.60, that is, £6.50 and £8.75. The situation is set out in exhibit 8.14.

Exhibit 8.14 Chemical manufacturer's demand estimate

Price (£)	Likely demand Quantity (litres)
6.50	?
7.60	6,000,000
8.75	?

They judged that demand for the product would be inelastic; how inelastic they didn't know, but they started with an elasticity coefficient of unity. (As you will recall from the discussion earlier in the book, the COE is the proportionate change in quantity divided by the proportionate change in price.) They assumed that, at a lower price of £6.50, x, the quantity likely to be sold, would be greater than 6 million; at a higher price of £8.75, x would be less. Thus, their first calculation with £6.50 was:

$$\frac{x-6}{x+6} \div \frac{1.1}{7.60+6.50} = 1$$

$$\frac{x-6}{x+6} \times \frac{7.60+6.50}{1.1} = 1$$

$$\frac{14.1\,(x-6)}{1.1x+6.6} = 1$$

$$14.1x - 86.4 = 1.1x + 6.6$$

$$13x = 91.2$$

$$x = 7.015$$

which is 7,015,000 litres.

At £8.75, with x less than 6,000,000:

$$\frac{6 - x}{x + 6} \times \frac{7.60 + 8.75}{1.15} = 1$$

$$\frac{16.35 \, (6 - x)}{1.15 \, (x + 6)} = 1$$

$$16.35 \, (6 - x) = 1.15 \, (x + 6)$$

$$98.1 - 16.35x = 1.15x + 6.9$$

$$x = 5.21$$

which is 5,210,000 litres.

The marketing executive argued that, if elasticity of demand was considerably less than unity, perhaps only 0.25, the effect on sales of price changes would be slight. This coefficient was substituted for unity in the equations for the lower and higher prices:

$$\frac{x - 6}{x + 6} \times \frac{7.60 + 6.50}{1.1} = 0.25$$

$$14.1x - 84.6 = 0.25 \, (1.1x + 6.6)$$

$$14.1x - 84.6 = 0.275x + 1.65$$

$$x = 6.239$$

Thus, at price £6.50 and elasticity 0.25, likely sales would be 6,240,000 litres. For a price increase to £8.75 and the same elasticity:

$$\frac{6 - x}{x + 6} \times \frac{7.60 + 8.75}{1.15} = 0.25$$

$$\frac{16.35 \, (6 - x)}{1.15 \, (x + 6)} = 0.25$$

$$\frac{98.1 - 16.35x}{1.15x + 6.9} = 0.25$$

$$98.1 - 16.35x = 0.25 \, (1.15x + 6.9)$$

$$98.1 - 16.35x = 0.29x + 1.73$$

$$x = 5.79$$

which is the equivalent of 5,790,000 litres at £8.75 and elasticity of about a quarter.

The variable cost of the product including delivery charge was £4.16 per litre and the expenses for the first year's operation, covering factory space costs, production overheads, depreciation of machinery, wages and salaries of factory and sales staff, administration, management and promotion, amounted to £1,962,670. Their break-even figures at the three possible prices are calculated in exhibit 8.15.

At a price of £7.60 the company needed to capture nearly 10 per cent of the estimated market of 6 million litres to break even in the first year. At £8.75 they needed about 7 per cent market share, and at £6.50, 14 per cent.

Before the analysis, executives had regarded their pricing strategy as having three possibilities: the same price as the competitor, a higher price, and a lower price. Subsequently, they appreciated that cutting price would not offer an incentive to customers to buy from them, nor greatly affect market potential, but would depress their profits and require greater effort to achieve a viable market share.

Exhibit 8.15 Break-even volumes at three prices

Price of £7.60:

$$\frac{1,962,670}{7.60 - 4.16} = 570,500 \text{ litres}$$

Price of £6.50:

$$\frac{1,962,670}{6.50 - 4.16} = 838,700 \text{ litres}$$

Price of £8.75:

$$\frac{1,962,670}{8.75 - 4.16} = 427,600 \text{ litres}$$

The likely reactions by the competitor to their entering the market were also discussed at some length.

THE EXECUTIVE CRYSTAL BALL

At this point they decided to tap the experience and judgement of the senior executives involved in the project, and asked each one to estimate how the competitor might react to their entering the market. Would the competitor maintain the present price of £7.60 irrespective of the company's launch price, match it, cut it, or increase it and increase their promotion? The executives were asked to include a probability percentage with their estimates.

To facilitate this exercise, the three prices of £8.75, £7.60 and £6.50 were used, but executives were free to apply any percentage probability figure they thought appropriate. Obviously, the total possible price responses from the competitor must add up to 100 per cent. When all the estimates were received, they were averaged to the nearest whole number; they are shown in exhibit 8.16.

		Company's price		
		£8.75	£7.60	£6.50
Competitor's likely price	£8.75	6%	5%	1%
	£7.60	94%	85%	75%
	£6.50	<1%	10%	24%
		100%	100%	100%

Exhibit 8.16 Subjective probability estimates

The points to note about these probabilities are: first, that they are subjective, and are not related to any objective data; second, they have forced the executives to think clearly about the pricing problem, and apply a quantitative estimate to a qualitative opinion.

Exhibit 8.17 Chemical company's price list

Quantity (litres)	Price per litre (£)	Discount (%)	Quantity price (£)
up to 100	8.50	-	8.50
101–249	8.50	2.5%	8.287
250–749	8.50	5.0%	8.075
750–999	8.50	7.5%	7.863
1,000 and up	8.50	10.0%	7.65

UNEVALUATED DISCOUNTS LEAD TO PRICE LIST TRAPS

Subsequent discussions were more fruitful because of the analysis. The executives were unanimous in deciding that, because of its inelastic demand, the product should not be launched at less than £7.60 per litre. In fact, because the product had an advantage over the competition with an improved formulation, their opinions favoured pricing the product at £8.50 and offering a range of discounts based on quantity ordered.

They had spent a lot of time investigating the discount structure and the various financial implications that would result, and were glad to agree a price schedule. This is shown in exhibit 8.17.

Unfortunately, the executives had fallen into the price list trap because they did not evaluate the total paid by the customer at the quantity changes. An analysis of exhibit 8.17 is given in exhibit 8.18.

In each of the four quantity/price changes, the customer pays less for a greater quantity. At the lowest quantity of 100 litres and highest price of £8.50, 101 and 102 litres can be purchased for less than 100. The deviation becomes more marked as the quantities increase.

At the second price change, 250 to 255 litres can be purchased for a lower sum than 249. At the third change, 750 to 769 litres cost less than 749. Finally, 1,000 to 1,033 litres cost less than 999.

On learning of this, the marketing executive set up the problem on a PC and noted that there are nine steps of 10p between £8.50 and £7.60, and the same number of steps could be applied to quantities between 100 and 1,000 litres. The workings are arrayed in exhibit 8.19.

Exhibit 8.18 Analysis of chemical company's price list

Price change	Quantity (litres)	Price per litre (£)	Total (£)
	100	8.50	850
(1)	101	8.287	837
	103	8.287	854
	249	8.287	2,063
(2)	250	8.075	2,019
	256	8.075	2,067
	749	8.075	6,048
(3)	750	7.863	5,897
	770	7.863	6,054
	999	7.863	7,855
(4)	1,000	7.60	7,600
	1,034	7.60	7,858

	[B]	[C]	[D]	[E]
	<File name>			
[2]	Quantity	Price (£)	Total (£)	%
[3]	100	8.50	850.00	
[4]	199	8.50	1,691.50	
[5]	200	8.40	1,680.00	1.18%
[6]	299	8.40	2,511.60	
[7]	300	8.30	2,490.00	2.35%
[8]	399	8.30	3,311.70	
[9]	400	8.20	3,280.00	3.53%
[10]	499	8.20	4,091.80	
[11]	500	8.10	4,050.00	4.71%
[12]	599	8.10	4,851.90	
[13]	600	8.00	4,800.00	5.88%
[14]	699	8.00	5,592.00	
[15]	700	7.90	5,530.00	7.06%
[16]	799	7.90	6,312.10	
[17]	800	7.80	6,240.00	8.24%
[18]	899	7.80	7,012.20	
[19]	900	7.70	6,930.00	9.41%
[20]	999	7.70	7,692.30	
[21]	1,000	7.60	7,600.00	10.59%

Exhibit 8.19 Chemical company's price sheet workings

Exhibit 8.20 Chemical company's amended price list

Quantity (litres)	Price per litre (£)	Discount equivalent to
100–199	8.50	net
200–299	8.40	1.18%
300–399	8.30	2.35%
400–499	8.20	3.53%
500–599	8.10	4.71%
600–699	8.00	5.88%
700–799	7.90	7.06%
800–899	7.80	8.24%
900–999	7.70	9.41%
1,000 and up	7.60	10.59%

The formulae used in exhibit 8.19 are:

```
[D3] +B3*C3 copy down [D4]..[D21]
```

Column [E] is formatted for percentage to two decimal places.

```
[E5] (+$C$3-C5)/$C$3
```

Copy [E5] to cells [E7], [E9], [E11], [E13], [E15], [E17], [E19] and [E21].

From these workings the price list was amended with discounts ranging from 1.18 per cent for quantities of 200 to 299 litres, up to 10.59 per cent for quantities of 1,000 litres and above. It is set out in exhibit 8.20.

COLLECTING ACCOUNTS

Being too generous with your settlement terms or lax in the way you collect monies due to your company has the same effect as cutting your prices. If you obtain a certain volume of business because you allow customers liberal credit and do not press for payment, you must calculate the true profit from such transactions and compare it with what you consider is desirable. Because of the amount of money that can be lost by offering unwise cash discounts, and by not collecting outstanding debts early enough, a company should periodically analyse its credit arrangements, overhaul its settlement terms and review the way that customers vary them.

Classify customers into a convenient scheme that represents their creditworthiness and punctuality in paying. For example, you could place them into three categories and code them: blue, green, red.

Blue companies are well organized and pay their invoices on time as required by the settlement terms stated on the invoice. They include organizations such as central government departments, local authorities, public sector companies, banks, insurance companies, 'blue chip' companies, multinational groups and large well-capitalized companies.

Green companies take as much credit as they can get and often more than the invoice states. They are prepared to use your money as long as you will allow them, but are not bad debt risks. Even well-known and financially sound companies will be found in this category.

Red companies are strictly on 'cash by return' basis. They are given very limited credit because they represent an unknown risk.

Determine the total amount of credit outstanding at a specified day for each category of customer, and establish how much of this is overdue.

Inspect every invoice and statement issued by the company and make a note of the terms printed on them.

Using the information already gained of products that supply the most turnover and profit, similar to the suggestions in exhibits 8.12 and 8.13, obtain copies of recent invoices which have been paid by a cross-section of customers who have purchased those products. If terms are printed on invoices, see if they have been varied in any way by other data having been inserted on the invoices by anyone in your company.

Note the length of time taken to pay by blue, green and red category customers and calculate the average period of credit taken by each category. In this way you can determine the true profitability of each category of customer, and for the very large customers.

Find out the average time taken to pay in the industry in which you are operating.

You will then have a thorough analysis of what your settlement terms are; what kinds of cash discounts you are offering to various categories of account; how your stated terms are being interpreted in practice; what your terms and practice ought to be.

Even the exercise of finding out how much money is owed to your organization on a specified day might surprise you.

Armed with the results of your investigation, you can now decide how your settlement terms should be operated in the future. It would be futile to think that you can reduce the sum owed by debtors quickly. One financial director of a multinational organization told me that it took him ten years to reduce the debtors position to a satisfactory level.

You can clear your creditors overnight. By arranging for the necessary funds, you can send cheques in settlement to every one. Clearing debtors is much more difficult. It takes months, and possibly years, of patient pressure to reduce the size of debtors. However, from the moment you have analysed your terms and understand the true position, you can inform all customers of how you intend to conduct business in the future.

AVOID UNWANTED PRICE CUTS

Avoid hidden price reductions and lower profit by adopting the following procedure:

- Ensure that the format of all invoices is easy to understand, with subtotals, discounts and value added tax clearly marked, leading to the total sum to be paid. If customers order products using their own or a traditional description, use this on the invoice with the correct name in brackets below. Thus, 'Battery acid' ordered by a customer would be so described, but with the correct description 'Sulphuric acid' bracketed immediately underneath.
- Invoice the same day that advices of dispatch are issued by warehouse or factory.
- Give priority to all internal documents relating to materials used and labour involved in the fulfilment of customers' orders; none should be left over for the following day. Invoices not issued and kept pending receipt of costs from your suppliers should only be allowed for emergency orders.

217

- Make up statements regularly, twice a month if appropriate, listing payments received, invoices submitted but not due for payment, invoices and their total due for payment, invoices overdue.
- Arrange to have a computer printout of payments due each day, or at least each week, depending on the volume of work and money involved. On this same printout, list all amounts overdue and how long overdue.
- Issue overdue statements. Have a rigid procedure that reminds slow-paying customers, say, five days or less, after payment is due, if the amount is still outstanding. Issue a statement listing the invoices not paid and endorse with words such as, 'This statement contains items which are now overdue. Please phone ... if there is any reason why payment is being withheld.'
- If no response or payment is received after an overdue statement has been issued, telephone the customer, establish contact with someone with appropriate authority, and make sure that there are no queries on the invoices. If there is a dispute over one item, immediately after the call send an amended statement listing the amounts not in dispute but overdue for payment, and show the disputed item separately.
- Put the substance of the telephone conversation in writing to the person concerned.

You can also improve your cash flow situation by negotiating an initial payment in advance for unusually large orders; offer a budget account and regular standing order payments; offer a discount for prompt payment; deposit cheques at least once a day and have large cheques specially cleared. If cash flow does become difficult, you can consider the effect on your profit of factoring your invoices – that is, selling them to a specialized broker.

UNPLANNED DISCOUNTS COME FROM PROFITS

Exhibit 8.21 illustrates the increase in sales volume required at different contribution rates, to equal the cost of any unplanned discount granted. Calculate the percentage unit contribution for any

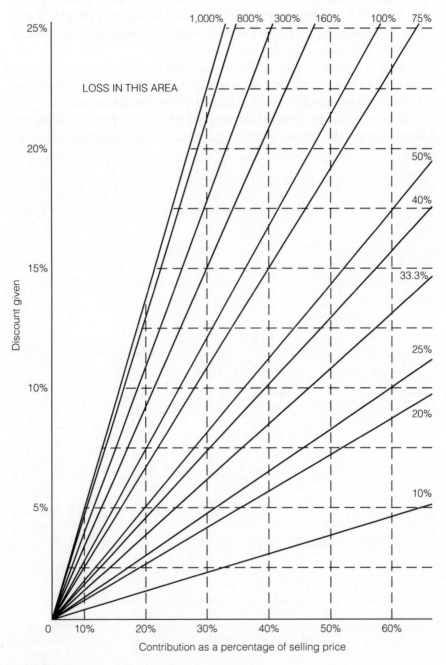

Exhibit 8.21 Offsetting the discount granted

219

product, read up from the base line at that point to the corresponding discount figure concerned. Look for the nearest diagonal and
note its percentage. This is the percentage increase in sales volume
required to balance the discount being given.

Thus, at a contribution of 20 per cent, giving a 10 per cent discount
requires a 100 per cent increase in sales to balance this discount; that
is, sales would need to be doubled to offset the discount.

At a contribution level of 10 per cent, giving 2½ per cent discount
would need to be balanced by an increase in sales volume of 33.3 per
cent.

9

Service industry pricing

SERVICE INDUSTRIES

The 'products' of non-manufacturing organizations are the services they supply: financial, commercial, insurance, transportation, technical, consultancy, advertising etc. Such services are an amalgam of the experience, skills and innate abilities of the people supplying them.

They range from the worldwide networks of banking, insurance and transport companies to the small hairdressing salon operated by its owner. As with manufacturing industries, price is geared to the cost of production – that is, the cost of supplying the service, what the market will pay and the profit that can be made.

IMPACT OF DECISIONS ON PROFITS

The technical director of a French service company of modest size that specialized in computer-aided design decided to relocate the demonstration and training room in order to make space for new electrostatic printers. The change, although quite substantial, was made at a cost of only FFr 20,000. The director had taken what he thought was a FFr 20,000 decision.

However, the relocation of the training room meant that the computer workstations were not as convenient as they had been previously. In the weeks that followed, the resulting disruption affected the efficiency of the instruction. The effectiveness of demonstrations declined markedly, and there was a noticeable lack of customer satisfaction. There was a dramatic fall in the number of conversions of demonstrations to orders. The director had actually made a FFr 500,000 decision without realizing it, and had to make amends to correct the situation.

Profit is not easily generated in today's fiercely competitive business environment. Directors, managers and executives have a continuing battle to keep prices high enough above costs to earn a reasonable profit. The relocating of the service company's training room is typical of a speedy decision being made in what is an extensive service industry without sufficient consideration of the likely impact on profit.

Decisions in manufacturing industry are usually based on more tangible items – the cost of raw materials, bought-in components, machine rates, labour costs etc. In the service industry, which is largely non-asset based, decisions frequently have to be made on intangibles.

There are distinct differences between the pricing procedures of different types of service industry, depending on the type of activity in which they are engaged.

TRANSPORTATION

The pricing of transportation is carried out according to the type of materials or products to be carried, ease of loading and handling, access at pickup and destination, weight, possibility of return load, any particular characteristic such as refrigeration or high security, availability of transport route and facilities – road, rail, river, canal, airport – distance, cross-border customs necessary, time and distance involved.

It is basically a cost-plus exercise, because the cost component cannot readily be reduced, nor is it subject to economies of scale. If something has to be transported by road from, say, London to Stuttgart, the distance is 970 km; it cannot be made shorter.

Even the swiftest method, air transportation, requires consideration of the distance of the airports from the city. From the centre of London to the centre of Stuttgart, by air is about 3 ¾ hours, an average of 260 kph (160 mph); London to Paris, about 345 km, takes 3½ hours, an average of 98 kph (61 mph). Such is the amount of road traffic congestion in large cities that moving goods in the centre of London or Paris is now about as quick as it was with horse transport a hundred years ago!

The types of goods dictate how they have to be transported, and directly affect the cost component of price. Highly perishable foods need refrigerated transport; diamonds and currency need high-security transportation; iron, steel and similar heavy materials require high space-to-value facilities. Widely differing goods will have vastly different prices for being transported over the same distance because of the importance of this element in the cost component.

Yet transportation is a typical example where introducing the marketing concept can change the fortunes of a company.

Transport contractors near the South Coast of England started with one vehicle and two main aims: to expand the business by ploughing back the profits; to give customers service, rather than just transporting their goods and chattels.

They maintained pressure on the basic cost component of their price by continually introducing the most modern, economic and cost-saving equipment and procedures. The bulk of the oncosts were devoted to providing a high-quality service; marketing costs were kept to a minimum, and publicity was targeted to minimize advertising wastage. The profit component was sufficient to fund the regular acquisition of cost-saving and labour-saving handling equipment

The company now has a large fleet of vehicles suitable for most types of transportation; they have a high repeat business and their reputation for satisfying the customer is widely known. This has been achieved by attention to detail: in addition to their attention to pricing, this is seen in the colour and cleanliness of the inside and outside of their transport, the care and attention to customers' goods and property, as well as the style of their letter headings and presentation of documents.

Though their prices are keen, these are not always lower than those of their rivals, but their competitors just transport goods; this company has expanded its reputation and trade by giving service.

CONSULTANCY

Consultancy, especially management consultancy, is of two basic types; resource consulting and process consulting. With resource consulting, the consultant brings knowledge, expertise and experience to an organization and recommends a programme of action based on the transference of that expertise. Process consulting is helping the organization to diagnose and construct remedies to solve its own problems.

Price cannot be based on the cost component as in the transportation industry; it is related to perceived value.

In a year of 52 weeks, assuming holidays of four weeks, there are 48 weeks of 5 days for a consultant's clients. This leaves Saturdays and Sundays for social activities, extra work, reading and the occasional panic job.

Thus, there are $48 \times 5 = 240$ days for client work, both face-to-face on the client's premises and away from clients, but working on their problems. The ratio is approximately 3 to 1; three days with the client requires one day's work away analysing findings, developing advice, preparing reports, 'recharging consultant batteries', or just recuperating and relaxing.

Therefore, of the 240 days available, 180 will be face-to-face with clients, and no consultant should be engaged on a face-to-face basis with clients for more than 180 days a year. Irrespective of whether this figure is accepted, it makes a reasonable basis for costing consultancy work and pricing proposals.

The perceived value that the client is buying consists of experience, resources, skills and know-how that are not possessed in the organization. If such skills were possessed, they would have to be paid for by employing full-time employees and paying salary, bonuses, social security payments, holiday pay, pensions etc.

A useful method of setting price in consultancy work is to establish the top rate that would normally have to be paid by the client for a full-time member of staff to do the work. This is multiplied by a factor of between 2 and 3 to reflect the degree of experience and expertise of the consultancy required.

The top rate is used because the company should employ the best talent available; doubling this rate reflects the payments that do not have to be made for employers' contribution to social security, holiday pay, severance pay etc. In addition, the consultant can be dispensed with at very short notice without further payment. This figure is divided by 180 to arrive at the daily rate exclusive of expenses.

Suppose a client requires marketing consultancy because there is no one in the company with sufficient expertise and know-how. Salaries range up to, say, £27,000 (the actual amount is immaterial to the method of calculating the daily rate). The experience of a good marketing person can be rated at a factor of, say, 2; £27,000 doubled equals £54,000. This divided by 180 gives the daily rate of £300 a day.

Similarly, a computer consultancy would probably consider the multiplying factor of its expertise as worth 3. A computer expert is worth, say, £40,000 a year. Multiplying £40,000 by 3, and dividing the result by 180, gives £667 as the daily rate. Therefore, the consultancy price is approximately £650 to £700 a day.

TRAINING

Training is a specialized form of consultancy. In the main, it is possible for a consultant to give the same lectures and inputs on a more or less constant basis, with only the need to update figures and references. The preparation of material for the initial inputs will take considerable time, but this will be spread over the number of times the consultant conducts the same course.

An additional problem has to be considered when pricing training: the number of persons who will attend the training course.

Starting with the formula already discussed for consultancy, a full-time training person could be employed for, say, £30,000. The multiplying factor is deemed to be 2, giving the rate of £60,000. This divided by 180 gives a daily rate of £333 – say, £350.

However, if there are ten delegates on the course, the company would be buying a course for the equivalent of £35 per day per delegate – a very low figure compared with 10 or 20 times this figure for open courses.

The consultant will normally supply all the necessary course material, loose-leaf ring binders, note pads, notes and exercises, but is being offered a group of delegates without having to advertise for them as with an open course.

The company is getting a course that is 'tailor-made' for their needs and would expect both to pay a little extra for this advantage, and at the same time would expect to pay a little less because it is supplying a complete number of delegates.

The consultant must consider the extent to which the course has to be adapted to the company's needs, the extra time required for this, any visits necessary to the company, and whether existing material can be used. By reviewing the current prices charged for similar courses by competing training organizations, the consultant can judge the going rate. The amount of extra work involved in adapting the course to the client's needs can be compared with the advantage of having a ready-made course of delegates, and priced accordingly.

If little adaptation of an existing course is necessary, the price can be set at a substantial percentage, say, 50 per cent, below the delegate-day cost of a public, open course. If the rate were, say, £400, then for a day's course for ten delegates the training organization could charge ten times £200, equals £2,000. The company gains by having a course for substantially less than the cost of sending delegates to an open course.

In contrast, if a course has to be specially devised for the client, this usually involves at least one visit to the client's company, and the training organization can consider charging at 100 per cent of the rate for an open course. Thus, for ten delegates it would quote a fee of £4,000. The client gains by having a specially tailored course for the price of a general, open course.

HOTEL PRICING

The pricing of hotel rooms is similar to the pricing of airline seats. It is a commodity that is perishable daily; if not sold today, the revenue is lost. However, if trade declines for the airline, it is able to transfer its planes to other, more profitable routes; a hotel has to remain where it is built. Crucial to its profitable operation is the occupancy rate of its rooms; this is the number of times the rooms are occupied during a year. If all the rooms were occupied every night of the year, this would be 100 per cent occupancy. However, even the most popular hotels seldom, if ever, reach maximum occupancy rate.

A heavily patronized 1,200-room hotel in the centre of a large UK conurbation has a current room occupancy rate of 87.5 per cent. This represents $1,200 \times 365 \times 0.875 = 383,250$ room nights. The average length of stay at this hotel is two nights, indicating that it has nearly

200,000 visitors, not all different of course because many of them visit more than once.

A hotel has high fixed costs, and a large cost component in the price of rooms and meals. For this reason, a hotel that is not situated in a high-demand area must produce strong seasonal revenue to counter the low- and off-season revenues. Pricing is the main tool for doing this.

The basic, normal room rate must first relate to the standard of the room: the amount of space, quality of furniture, carpeting, bed, covers, curtains, decoration, bath, toilet, shower, telephone (perhaps with direct dialling), colour television, in-house movies, radio, telephone, fridge, tea- and coffee-making equipment, hair-dryer, trouser press etc. Room rates should also include an element in the oncost for necessary periodic redecorating and refurbishing. When rooms are substantially upgraded, the new room rate must reflect this cost.

Secondly, the room rate is related to the market. A primary market would be located in a fashionable area with ample parking and garaging, frequented by high-class business people and groups.

Thirdly, the room rate should reflect the facilities available in the hotel for personal comforts: lounge, bar, restaurants, standard of cuisine, shops, hairdressing salon etc. If the hotel offers conference facilities, then lecture rooms, small group rooms and standard of equipment are particularly important.

Typically, a hotel's peak season occurs during spring and autumn when appeals are directed to its primary market. For the non-peak periods, hoteliers target their secondary market with reduced rates.

A large 1,000-room hotel would normally be sited in an area which would receive business and social visitors, and would experience a high occupancy rate upwards of 75 per cent. Not all 1,000 rooms would be offered at the same price, but targeted to well-defined market segments. A typical pricing policy for such a hotel is shown in exhibit 9.1.

The pricing policy is similar to product line pricing discussed in chapter 3, and, if there are six price categories, as in exhibit 9.1, the pricing pattern is as in exhibit 9.2. The basic cost and oncost components of the room price are similar, but different numbers of rooms are offered to different segments at different times of the year. The aim is to maximize to total revenue.

Exhibit 9.1 Peak and off-peak room rates

Period	Market segment	Room rate
Peak	'Chance'	100%
	Company rate with minimum numbers	70–80%
	National groups bulk booking	65–80%
Off-peak	Local groups	60–70%
	Training, education	40–55%
	Weekend breaks	50%

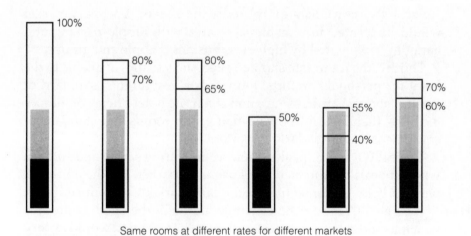

Same rooms at different rates for different markets

Exhibit 9.2 Hotel room prices

TARGETED HOTEL ROOM PRICING

In such a business, where demand is seasonal and coupled with a product that has to be sold the same day or lost forever, demand has to be managed by a daily allocation of rooms. This is a daily inventory of rooms that are offered at different prices to different market segments. This will improve customer service, stimulate customer use and strengthen revenue and profitability. While the practice

Exhibit 9.3 Rooms allocated to market segments

Period	Market segment	Room allocation
Peak	Company bookings and company 'chance'	50%
	National groups	20%
	'Chance'	30%
Off-peak	Company bookings company specials	60%
	National groups	24%
	Weekend breaks and special promotions	16%

might reduce revenue and profit during peak periods, the increased revenue achieved during off-peak periods increases the total long-term profitability of the hotel.

Preparing a differential room rate is part of the pricing task. The next is to promote these rate offers to the various market segments. This is controlled by *availability discounting*. The aim is to capture as much of the price-elastic demand as possible without affecting the price-inelastic demand. While the total supply of rooms is fixed, the number offered to the different market segments varies according to the changing demand from those segments. It is an important, continuing marketing research task for a hotelier to estimate the number of rooms in the market available to comparable market segments.

One large hotel has identified six market segments and, at the beginning of 1990 had the room allocation as in exhibit 9.3. Promotional efforts are directed to the market segments, with the highest price for the particular segment quoted, and discounts offered according to numbers, or other conditions.

For example, the promotion to selected companies for peak periods is at 80 per cent of 'normal' room rate, and further discounts of up to 12½ per cent, depending on the number of bookings. Thus, if the room rate is, say, £80 a night, this is offered to companies at a 'standard' £64 (80 per cent of full rate) but less discounts to a

229

maximum of 12½ per cent that can bring the price of rooms down to £56 when a minimum number are booked.

GENERAL HOTEL PRICING STRATEGY

In general, the lucrative trade for hotels is with companies who hold meetings, conferences and training sessions. In the popular centres, demand almost always exceeds supply and hoteliers have greater control over rates. As the year moves towards the off-peak periods, large hotels no longer have their company conferences, medium-sized hotels have few prime groups; supply exceeds demand and room inventories are changed and re-changed in a truly dynamic marketing situation.

Secondary markets are cultivated to maintain adequate revenue and a contribution to fixed overheads and profit; price becomes a major marketing tool with these more price-sensitive customers. Though more sensitive to price, these customers are able to negotiate with power, often playing off one hotel against another. This presents the hotelier with a problem of how low the rates can be reduced to prevent the business from going to a competitor.

As with all businesses, the costs of running the hotel can be divided broadly into two categories: fixed costs that have to paid irrespective of the amount of business, and variable costs that vary directly with the number of clients. In hotel operation, variable costs are relatively low, and, depending on the services provided by the hotel, are typically between 10 and 25 per cent of the price of the room.

Obviously, the fixed costs will reflect the location of the hotel and its appointments. A large, well-built hotel in the centre of London will have shatteringly high local taxes; a small hotel situated in rural Somerset or the sparsely inhabited area of south-western France will have correspondingly low local taxes. In all cases, the fixed costs have to be paid, and once the variable costs of room cleaning, laundry and amenities have been covered, the excess is a contribution towards fixed cost and profit.

There are two schools of thought on contribution towards the payment of fixed overheads. One is that any revenue that exceeds the variable cost contributes something towards overheads, which is more worth having than nothing at all. The other view is that every product should contribute towards the fixed costs.

Clearly, the second view is relevant to a non-service business. In a manufacturing industry, products that do not contribute their due proportion to the total fixed costs can be dropped from the range. This is explored further in a later chapter.

In hotel operation, the variable cost of a room is relevant to the pricing decision. Any revenue in excess of this cost is welcome. It cannot be sold tomorrow.

For these reasons, hoteliers should not be over-concerned with profit margins; market-related, manipulated, revenue is more important. The pricing strategy must be pricing for revenue, with long-term profit used to measure the success of the strategy.

SMALL HOTEL PRICING

Small hotels are often run as family businesses with part of the hotel also accommodating the family. To some extent, a more flexible operation is possible than with a large hotel, but pricing is nevertheless important. To ignore it and the likely revenue it can, or cannot, generate is to court disaster.

First, the average occupancy of other hotels in the area should be determined. This can be done by tactful conversations with known hoteliers, wine and brewery representatives, and other sales people who call on hotels, as well as making use of information available through various local associations and hotel and catering publications. A vast amount of market intelligence can be obtained by talking with people in the same trade; because hotels are open to all visitors, regular visits should be made to other establishments at different times during the year to observe their trade.

While all hoteliers try to obtain the maximum business from visitors, their restaurants are unlikely to be frequented by the same people all the time. Even the finest restaurant has a changing market, and will see its 'regulars' periodically and not necessarily every week. The fortunate thing about the trade is that, no matter how well we have eaten today, we will be hungry tomorrow!

Occupancy is unlikely to be evenly spread throughout the year; the various peak periods must be identified. The kind of area, its usual weather pattern and attractions will indicate which seasons

231

are popular with visitors. Local newspapers possess a mass of data, and often so do local authority staff. If the hotel is in a 'holiday region', summer is likely to be the big peak season, with Easter, Christmas and other festive holidays forming secondary peaks.

In many 'backwaters', hotel occupancy can be abysmally low, barely reaching double figures. Such hotels are often run by people in or nearing retirement and with little interest in stimulating business. Thus, a small family-run hotel with 15 bedrooms has $365 \times 15 = 5,475$ possible room nights. If the occupancy of the hotel is only 15 per cent, this means that there were only $365 \times 15 \times 0.15 = 821$ lettings during the year. If the average stay was, say, 2 nights, this means that 410 people stayed at the hotel. Decreasing the rate of the room is unlikely to stimulate trade, and increasing it would probably dramatically lower total revenue.

If the room rate is, say, £25, the total revenue for rooms is £20,525. More revenue would need to be generated from meals and bar takings if this hotel is to be a viable proposition. While increasing the price to £30 would generate an additional sum of just over £4,000, unless the hotel has some other attraction, such as excellent food, this is unlikely to work. At £25 the existing clientele might be prepared to continue patronizing it; at £30 they might not.

Reducing the price might stimulate more trade, but a simple arithmetical proportion sum indicates the position. Current revenue is £20,525 with 821 lettings. Reducing the price to £20 would require £20,525/20 = 1,026 lettings to maintain the same revenue. While this number of lettings means an increase in occupancy from 15 per cent to nearly 19 per cent, more importantly, in terms of effort, it requires an increase in trade of 25 per cent. With the additional cleaning and laundry caused by the increased lettings, it is likely that profit will fall.

POSITIONING THE HOTEL

'Positioning' here refers not to the physical location of a hotel but to determining its image and comparing its facilities with others in the area.

A hotel exists to satisfy expected demand from a range of market segments. Its 'catchment' area may be comparatively small, such as a small seaside town in Wales or a French country village; it may be large, such as the English Lake District, the Scottish Highlands, Tenerife, or the Grand Duchy of Luxembourg. Every other hotel in the area must be regarded as a potential competitor, but this should be with respect to competition in the various market segments and not generally. An obvious example is a discotheque, which will only appeal to a narrow segment of the market. Other examples are afternoon tea dances, bridge and whist parties, bingo, in-house films, snooker room, sauna and health club. The facilities offered by the hotels are noted and weighted according to their attraction to potential visitors. At this stage, a degree of product differentiation will be discerned, and the facilities are seen to be relevant to specific market segments and not to all visitors to the area.

Thus, while initially all other hotels are regarded as potential competitors, on analysis, they will be categorized as competitive in particular market segments. If there are, say, a dozen hotels or more, they can be considered in their various categories, and lists made of those which are truly competing with each other in market segments. If the number of hotels is relatively small, they may need to be considered altogether.

Hotels are ranked according to their weighting, but with their normal room rates indicated alongside. The hotel with the highest weighting will be top of the list and may be regarded as the 'best' hotel. It will probably have the highest room rate in the area.

By this means it is possible to 'position' a hotel and, if improvements are being considered to an existing hotel, a repositioning can be made, with appropriate adjustment to the room rates.

SMALL SERVICE COMPANIES

In recent years there has been a growth of small businesses in the service industry: hairdressers, jobbing gardeners, audio-video contractors, trainers, computer-aided designers, consultants etc. They have unique pricing problems in view of their selling a service rather than products, their small size, and the fact that their work is labour-intensive. Service companies usually have limited assets and do not carry substantial stocks, therefore trying to use pricing methods such as target ROI (return on investment) are inappropriate. The assets employed in supplying the service are insignificant compared with the human asset which is normally the accumulated experience and acquired skills of the persons carrying out the service.

Thus, setting price basically on variable costs has no point in the service company; full-cost pricing is essential, with an eye kept on competitive offers.

In many service industries, the experience and skill of the supplier of the service will largely dictate the price or fee charged. A contract gardener with extensive experience of 20 seasons or more will be able to charge a higher price than a person with only limited experience. Similarly, hairdressers' prices reflect not only the situation of the shop, but also the professional skills and artistry of the operator. A consultant with over 30 years' practical experience in on-the-job management and marketing will attract a much higher fee than a newly qualified consultant with a year's experience in a large consultancy firm.

In general, the full absorption cost of all fixed overheads and variable costs should serve as the lower limit in pricing. While total costs might be the same for both tiro and master and each have similar floor prices, the ceiling prices of the two will be completely different. The height of the ceiling above the floor is determined by the abilities, skills and experience that can be applied to the job.

The price quoted for any particular job will be the full absorption cost plus the mark-up. Despite this general approach to service industry pricing, different mark-ups should be applied for various market segments, and in the light of competition. Thus, it is common for men's hairdressers to have a lower price on one day of the week to accommodate old age pensioners. Consultants who are particularly interested in a new field of study might charge a relatively lower fee for work in that direction in order to enlarge their experience. Cartoonists will charge different rates for work depending on the medium in which their work is to be reproduced.

CAMBERLEY CONSULTANCY

A training and consultancy company based in Camberley had an annual turnover in 1988 of £291,460, two-thirds of which was for training, one-third for consultancy. The summary breakdown of the company's results is shown in exhibit 9.4.

Exhibit 9.4 Camberley Consultants' results

	Consultancy (£)	Training (£)	Total (£)
Fees	97,760	193,700	291,460
less Direct costs	36,374	50,466	86,840
Margin	61,386	143,234	204,620
less Indirect costs	22,230	51,870	74,100
Net profit	39,156	91,364	130,520
Percentage of total profit	30%	70%	100%

Indirect costs in the Camberley Consultancy included general administrative support not directly allocated to a department. Indirect costs were allocated to each department based on the percentage of total profit it contributed. Thus, the consultancy department supplied 30 per cent of the profit and was allocated 30 per cent of the total indirect costs of £74,100.

Early in 1989 this method of allocating indirect costs was challenged because it was arbitrary, and did not relate to the amount of support services that each department received. An analysis of the year's consultancy and training activities showed that there were 18 different consultancy commissions undertaken during the year and 24 courses were run, attended by 320 delegates.

The method of allocating indirect costs had been in operation since the company had started in business. For the training department, it was based on the number of delegates attending. This resulted in indirect costs about 2.3 times that for the consultancy department. It was agreed that the cost of servicing a training course was generally higher than that for consultancy, but all costs that could be attributed to the training department were already allocated as direct costs: the indirect costs were the same, irrespective of the number of people attending a course.

A new basis for apportioning indirect costs was to be in the ratio of consultancy commissions to courses, 18:24 or 43 per cent and 57 per cent. The year's performance with the more accurate apportion of indirect costs is shown in exhibit 9.5.

Exhibit 9.5 Camberley Consultants' more accurate results

	Consultancy (£)	Training (£)	Total (£)
Fees	97,760	193,700	291,460
less Direct costs	36,374	50,466	86,840
Margin	61,386	143,234	204,620
less Indirect costs	31,863	42,237	74,100
Net profit	29,523	100,997	130,520
Percentage of total profit	22.6%	77.4%	100%

In a service industry, where the emphasis is on the service supplied and not on a product, the basis for pricing must be costs and added value. Wherever possible, the allocation of costs should not be an entirely arbitrary relationship to direct labour hours, direct labour cost, machine hours, administrative hours etc.

The basis for allocation should be the factors that cause the cost to arise and increase. It is the number of courses processed, not the number of delegates attending, the number of purchase orders processed, not the volume purchased, and so on.

MARKET SEGMENTATION

Throughout this discussion of service industry pricing, the need to price for particular market segments has been stressed. This requires that homogeneous parts of the market are identified and attacked.

Segmentation is important to consumer and industrial markets, and particularly to service industries. Chapter 4 listed some of the characteristics that can be used to segment a market, and stressed the five main qualities to be an acceptable market segment: it must be measurable, accessible, different enough to be distinguishable, substantial and durable.

Accessible means that it should be a reasonably straightforward matter to advertise to the people making up the segment, and to contact them with a view to selling the product or service. If they are scattered throughout the country and belong to no association or have no common communication channel, it is doubtful if they are accessible.

As an example, it would be possible to segment the total market by salary and wages received by people. Suppose you wished to appeal to a segment of the market whose remuneration fell within certain limits. Such a group exists, but they are not accessible.

A segment must be measurable. If its members cannot be counted, the segment may be fictitious or the numbers insignificant. A segment that cannot be measured is an enigma; you don't know what sales and marketing resources to devote to it because you don't know how big it is. As with all marketing, a certain amount of advertising and promotion is essential to get over the threshold of inertia. If you cannot measure the segment, you do not know what weight of advertising would be adequate. The measurement of a segment will indicate the likely potential sales you can achieve; if you cannot measure it, you may be wasting your time.

A market segment must be substantial. It is no use highly defining a market segment and then finding that it contains very few potential customers. How substantial is 'substantial' will depend on the type of service you are providing. If it is a hotel with restaurant and you wish to develop the restaurant trade, you know how many you can seat at each lunch and dinner. Your pricing policy will be largely determined by the quality and standard of your food and the size of the market segment you are aiming at. Simple calculations will determine viability.

Suppose that your initial pricing policy indicates that you expect to see customers about six times a year, and, assume that they arrive in couples. If your restaurant seats 50 people, and you are open six nights a week, in a year, $6 \times 52 \times 50 = 15,600$ people could dine with you. If the people in your market segment visit you, say, four times a year, you need a segment containing 3,900 people (15,600/4). If they visit you only twice a year, you need a market of 7,800.

Your pricing policy will obviously influence the size of the market segment. Reduce your prices by 50 per cent and you *may* increase the size of your potential market, but it may just as readily be reduced because people tend to relate price with quality. If your market segment is spread over a wide area, you would be wise to adopt a high-price policy for meals. People do not normally travel long distances to eat cheap. In fact, the distance people are prepared to travel to restaurants is generally relevant to the price of the meal. The longer the distance away, the better the meal is expected to be, and, naturally, the higher its price.

Furthermore, it takes time to build up business in this trade; two to three years is normal before a satisfactory level is reached. Reducing price will not create an early increase in business, merely an immediate drop in profits.

The same simple calculation to determine the size of the segment may be used for many service industries. A window cleaner would need to establish the average length of time it takes to clean the windows of the average type of building in the area. Then, the number of potential clients must be substantial enough for a viable business to be maintained. A sensible percentage of the total market should be estimated as the likely customer base; assuming an initial 5 per cent penetration would be wise.

The frequency of cleaning is about every six to eight weeks. It must neither be too frequent nor too infrequent otherwise customer dissatisfaction is created. Assuming the cleaner can cope with, say, 20 buildings a day on a five-day week, this is 100 buildings a week. If a 48-week year is worked, this would be 4,800 cleanings a year. If they are cleaned six times a year, this indicates an active market of $4,800/6 = 800$. However, if only 5 per cent of the market is achieved initially, the total potential market segment has to be a substantial 20 times this, or 16,000.

This analysis indicates that, if the window cleaner wishes to earn a gross £20,000 a year, this is an average of $£20,000/4,800 = £4.16$ a visit.

The weather must be considered in this industry. If rain, snow, frost and other things sufficient to rule out window cleaning occur for say, 50 per cent of the year, the cleaner has to base all calculations on a '6-month year'. Increasing the price to £8.32 would put the figure right but undoubtedly reduce the number of takers.

A market segment must be sufficiently different from other parts of the market for products and prices made to appeal only to that distinguishable segment. If you cannot restrict your marketing thrust to the segment, there is little point in having it. Prices offered to a market thought to be unique may be taken up by the market generally. If the market cannot be distinguished it is doubtful whether sufficiently differentiated appeals can be made to it.

A market segment should be durable, not volatile. If a business is to be built by concentrating on particular segments, they should be there next year and the year after. If not, a lot of goodwill and investment in marketing activities will be wasted.

SEGMENT CHARACTERISTICS

Some of the specific indicators that can be used to segment a market for a product are:

- usage of the service (or product);
- type of products to be serviced;
- periodicity of service;
- level of service;
- type and average cost of service;
- where service carried out;
- size of organization requiring service;
- specific servicing requirements.

10

New product pricing

NEW PRODUCTS AND SERVICES

The comments in this chapter on new product pricing also apply to new services, though for convenience the word 'product' will mainly be used.

The distinction must be drawn between products that are entirely new to the market, such as computers with chip technology based on quantum electronics, and products that are only new to the company.

With products that are new only to a company, pricing strategy would need to be guided by an assessment of how competitors price similar products already on the market.

A product that is new to the market is probably unique in some important aspects and will pass through distinctive stages in its life cycle. Its pricing strategy will need to be related to those different stages. Such a product, which is obviously also new to the company, often possesses some form of protection that lasts for as long as it takes competitors to copy it. If it is highly protected with patents or technical difficulties of manufacture, as is the Polaroid camera that was discussed in chapter 3, the period of protection will obviously be longer. With a product in this category, provided it possesses a strong market appeal, a manufacturer has considerable flexibility in pricing.

New product pricing

THE GILLETTE SENSOR

Such a situation confronted Gillette early in 1990 with the introduction of Sensor, their new razor which had started life in 1977. It is a high-technology product consisting of spring-mounted, twin ultra-thin blades laser-welded to steel carriers, housed in a new plastic cartridge, and used with an elegant steel handle. It required a capital investment of $125 million, and $75 million in research and development. This new venture was the single most expensive product that the company had ever taken on.

The shaving market is compounded by the general division into dry electric shavers and wet razors, and the razors further subdivided into disposables and permanents which take replacement blades. An insignificant part of the market, but one that could develop into big business, is the small, battery-powered wet razor, which gives a gentle, vibrating action to the blade for safer and more efficient shaving. This cheap electric wet-razor takes any refill blade.

Gillette make both permanent and disposable wet razors and have about two-thirds of the market in North America and Europe. They make 8¢ to 10¢ gross profit on each disposable razor, compared with 25¢ to 30¢ on a pack of refill blades for its Atra and Trac II system razors. Opinion was sharply divided on whether to make the Sensor a permanent, or a disposable, or both. Against the permanent type was the fact that competitors – Wilkinson, Schick and others – already made cheaper refills for Gillette's other two systems, and despite the Sensor's 22 patents, the possibility of cheaper clones being developed could not be ruled out.

However, the substantial investment necessary in new manufacturing facilities, complicated production and 30-odd assembly processes, and its higher profit, persuaded them to opt for the permanent version.

They were faced with a 'Polaroid' pricing problem: what price to set for the new razor, and what for its unique, well-protected refills.

Acknowledging that sales make profits, they priced the Sensor, with three blades, at $3.75, well below their Atra and Trac II razors. The aim was to attract men away from the older systems that used clone blades. The price for a Sensor five-blade refill pack was pitched at $3.79, which is about 25 per cent higher than a refill pack for their older systems. It is estimated that they make about 3 per cent gross on the old packs and about 4 per cent gross on the new Sensor packs.

241

They invested heavily in promotion, and in 1990 their advertising budget was $110 million. Just to recoup the large promotional cost required an increase of about 5 per cent in market share.

Any company introducing a new product to the market has to assess its distinctiveness and regard this as subject to progressive erosion from competing products. A pricing plan should be prepared in outline ready to be invoked as required. When new competitors enter the market, as the advantage gap narrows, the company's degree of discretion in pricing is reduced. At the same time, a product development plan should ensure that new ideas are being tested. Already, before the results of Sensor are known, Gillette have a curved blade and a ceramic blade in view.

PRICING IBM'S NEW PRODUCT

When IBM introduced its Personal System/2 computer to the market in late 1988, it too had a new product pricing problem. The PS/2 innovation was its Micro Channel, an IBM-only product that enables the computer to operate more than one processor at the same time. The resulting increase in speed of processing time is little short of phenomenal.

Pepsi-Cola set up a system of nearly 300 PCs connected to one Micro Channel PS/2 which co-ordinated the entire system. Such is the power of the new system that distribution orders to bottlers, fax transmissions, electronic mail and other internal data flow without interruption.

The PS/2 is not compatible with the older PCs, and little software for it exists. In effect, although the PS/2 introduced a large measure of obsolescence into the PC market, customers were reluctant to buy the new machine because of its incompatibility: all their existing programs would need to be changed.

A number of competitive computer manufacturers, led by Compaq Computer Corporation, joined together and proposed an alternative hardware design compatible with the older PCs, although not with Micro Channel.

While IBM retained its usual high-pricing policy reflecting the high quality of its product, it nevertheless pushed hard with the new PS/2, offering special discounts to large dealers, hosted many briefings for the press and interested parties, and backed it up with television commercials at peak viewing time.

242

PRODUCT LIFE CYCLE

Like human beings, all products have a pattern of life: they are born, develop, mature and eventually die. There are exceptions, things like salt which are essential to human life, and product groups which exhibit no market growth and decline, such as whisky, beer etc. Individual products in the groups have their own life patterns and often undergo marked changes during their lifetime. An example is Cadbury's Milk Tray chocolates, which have received many 'face lifts' during their lifetime to prevent the pack from becoming too familiar, taken for granted, and so losing market share.

Some products, as soon as they are introduced to the market, take off and reach very high sales; some of these plummet into early maturity and death just as quickly, others gradually decline with age. Some products are slow to catch on, but once they have secured a hold on the market just keep on going; their sales keep in line with population growth.

Speciality products, such as certain pharmaceuticals for the treatment of particular ailments, achieve level sales as soon as they are introduced, and this level remains fairly constant.

Apart from the notable and special exceptions, all products exhibit a pattern of introduction, growth, maturity, decline: the product life cycle (PLC). What differs between products is the time scale and rate of change from one stage to another. During the progress of a product through its PLC, changes will occur in the three components: basic costs; oncosts, especially for distribution, sales and promotion; profit. Provided that the company obtains an equitable market share, basic costs will fall, and the appropriate element in oncosts used to increase perceived value and take advantage of price elasticity. The profit component should increase, and may be shared with customers by adjusting price.

Exhibit 10.1 illustrates the four-stage life cycle, together with typical price compositions for each stage. Some products have a PLC that extends, as do people, for the full 'three score years and ten' and more; others are in and out of the market within two or three years.

With any product, we know when we are in the introductory and growth stages; we also know when we are in the decline stage. What is generally not known is where we are from the end of the growth until the beginning of decline stage. In other words, we can never really be sure of the time span of the maturity stage.

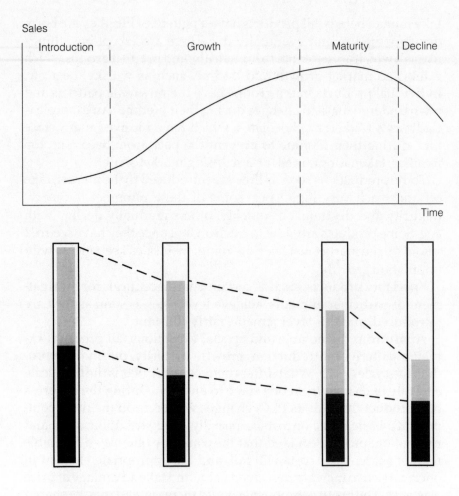

Pricing component tendencies associated with the four stages

Exhibit 10.1   Product life cycle

While pricing strategy changes over the life of the product, so must product policy in general, and new product policy in particular, relate to the various PLC stages of company products.

As a product advances towards its maturity stage, three different aspects of maturity are encountered although not necessarily coincidental: technical maturity; market maturity; competitive maturity.

TECHNICAL MATURITY

Technical maturity gradually becomes apparent when development and innovative changes in the product have slowed down, and little real difference exists between it and competing products. Furthermore, manufacturing processes will have become widely known and similar in competitors' plants, neutralizing any previously held competitive advantage in the basic cost component.

MARKET MATURITY

Market maturity is reached when customers are able to evaluate competitive offers with competence and can distinguish the various differences in the competing products. No longer do they require persuading or convincing as to the value or use of the product, and it is accepted for what it is. Perceived value tends to become equal to actual value.

An example is the domestic television set. Early in its life cycle, especially before the 1939–45 conflict, the tube was not entirely free from faults, and was guaranteed by the supplier for only three months. It was normal practice to insure it against failure during the first year or so. Today the tube is taken for granted; it is no longer necessary to insure it. It has a long life and is, with normal use, free from imperfections that would cause its early demise. Customers are able to pick and choose with considerable skill between television sets. Market maturity has been reached.

COMPETITIVE MATURITY

Competitive maturity is reached when the market shares of competitors do not change greatly, and have settled to a reasonably stable relationship. At this stage, prices reflect the respective quality and value of the products. To some extent it is possible to reduce the input for advertising in the oncost component.

PLC TACTICS

Some products have a short and merry life, especially those in the hi-tech industries. Their price should contain a high oncost component to recoup as much as possible of the R&D, and an element to intensify perceived value. If sufficient volume can be generated

New product pricing

Exhibit 10.2 Welsh company's product life cycle tactics

	Introduction	Growth	Maturity	Decline
Product	Basic	Expand range with more models and styles.	Modification and improvement especially of marketing and image.	Eliminate product or let it die.
Price	Low or high relative to its perceived value in the market.	Lower if competition strong; consider raising if not. Some of profit might be needed to strengthen marketing activities.	Discounts and pricing tactics.	Relate activities to profits.
Place	Concentrate on one segment if funds are limited.	Widen distribution and cultivate new markets and sub-markets.	Intensive distribution if appropriate.	Distribute on a selective basis with minimum order size to maximize profit.
Promotion	Heavy to make sufficient impact.	Increase investment in all forms of publicity.	Only sufficient promotion to maintain market share.	'Milk' product by maintaining as high a price as possible and siphoning the profits.
Service	Centralize if appropriate and possible.	Maintain control, but decentralize if possible.	Transfer control to service centres.	Use service to generate new sales leads.

before the product dies, the profit component should provide satisfactory overall profit. Such is the speed of development in some hi-tech industries that, by the time the developing company is in a position to take advantage of demand stimulated, a new product enters the market.

Demand exhibits different characteristics over the PLC, and prices behave differently. Sometimes the pace of growth, sales, and competitive reactions require strong, positive responses from the seller. On occasions, new products are introduced, falter and create a market for a similar product from another producer.

Pricing strategy cannot be developed in a vacuum; it must be related to the other elements in the marketing mix. New products

246

are particularly vulnerable to a lack of strategy or poor pricing tactics. Over the life of a product, tactical changes and adjustments are essential if momentum is to be maintained. There are no rules governing how price should be adjusted at each stage of the PLC, but other companies' experience is often helpful. Exhibit 10.2 has been edited from the business plans of a Welsh company that markets industrial consumables, a sizeable percentage of which have been developed during the past five years. Since the decline of coal mining in the region, many companies have started up in light industry and numerous new products have been developed and marketed.

THE IMPORTANCE OF THE MARKET

Over a period of time there is a tendency for many competitive products to become similar to each other in their quest to satisfy the collective demands of the market. It is sometimes contended that this process of degeneration depends on the extent to which the environment has to be modified to adapt the innovation effectively.

This view is possibly encouraged by the lengthy gestation periods for some products; a number of major innovations have taken long periods from conception to realization. Exhibit 10.3 lists 16 of the more notable of these.

In 1989 Professor Steven Schnaars, in his book *Megamistakes*, reported that in his investigations of the previous 30 years of product forecasts, 80 per cent had failed to materialize. He listed, among many other proposed new products, a robotic lawn-mower, a bed-making machine, the electric motor car, home dry-cleaning, a domestic sonic-shower and tooth decay vaccine, all of which failed to emerge.

The two main reasons given are technological obsession and *price*. Companies become so involved with technical innovation that they are blinkered to what the customer wants. Also, the products that are developed, are marketed at the wrong price.

In the Evoluon, the permanent exhibition in Eindhoven, Holland, are displayed some of the electrical products that were technically imaginative but developed too early and were too costly for the market. They include a dynamo lighting set for pedal-cycles, and a hand-generated electric torch.

Exhibit 10.3 Gestation period for some products

	Date conceived (approx.)	Date realized (approx.)	Gestation period (years)
photography	1785	1838	53
television	1884	1936	52
zip fastener	1875	1914	39
radar	1904	1938	34
antibiotics	1910	1940	30
nuclear energy	1919	1945	26
instant coffee	1934	1956	22
dry soup mixes	1943	1962	19
self-winding wrist-watch	1923	1939	16
photocopying	1935	1950	15
frozen foods	1908	1923	15
nylon	1927	1939	12
automatic transmission	1930	1940	10
liquid shampoo	1950	1958	8
videotape recorder	1950	1956	6
ball-point pen	1937	1943	6

Products mentioned by Professor Schnaars that didn't miss include microwave ovens, video-recorders, video games, electronic calculators, digital watches, ball-point pens and paperback books. All offered primarily what the customer wanted or needed.

All the new product misses occurred because they offered no additional benefits to customers over existing products or they were *too costly*.

THE INCREASING IMPORTANCE OF PRICE

The importance of pricing in marketing, especially with regard to the pursuit of profits, has been increasing since the 1960s, when marketing started to develop as a serious business activity.

In the mid-sixties pricing was ranked about sixth in order of importance in marketing; research and development, sales planning, sales management, advertising, and product servicing were all ranked by industrial and consumer products manufacturers as more important. By the mid-seventies just over half of the leading companies who were asked reported that they were conducting pricing studies, and that price had become a major factor in their marketing.

Only ten years later, a similar investigation into the importance of pricing in companies revealed that well over 80 per cent of the same leading companies actively studied pricing. Now, in the early 1990s, pricing ranks as the number one marketing pressure point, and, for new products and services, getting the price right is critical for its successful marketing.

NEW PRODUCT STAGES

Up to ten stages need to be considered when planning the price and launch of a new product or service onto the market:

- product/market evaluation;
- initial customer research;
- detailed market appraisal;
- development and testing of ideas;
- preliminary assessment;
- developing the marketing plan;
- test marketing;
- regional launches;
- national launch;
- continuous improvement.

PRODUCT/MARKET EVALUATION

Once management has established the criteria for short-term and long-term planning of new products, the first marketing stage is to seek target product/markets presenting the best opportunities for profit-making at prices envisaged by the company. The search for new products should not be considered in isolation but in relation to the target markets they can satisfy.

Before a market can be adequately assessed it must be screened and its make-up analysed. It is not good marketing practice to conduct an analysis before executives have a strong understanding of the product and target market. The estimate of potential demand in the market is only valid if this is linked with a firm idea of the price of the product.

POSSIBLE AND PROBABLE PROFIT

The likely profit that could be generated over the PLC, relative to the price envisaged for each stage, will qualify the attractiveness of the new product. Some companies require an assured minimum profit level before proceeding with a new product; others are more interested in growth and future potential rather than large profits.

The degree of stability in likely profits will have an impact on the company's cash flow situation and indicate the pattern of profits acceptable from a new venture.

Of equal importance with profit, especially if the product is marketed through middlemen, is resaleability. A product with a very high profit component is of little use if it does not readily resell. The level of price has a high influence on the degree of resaleability.

The wider the geographic spread of customers, the more costly it is to penetrate the market. In this respect, perhaps the most attractive product is the one that will sell immediately outside the factory gates. A new product that can be sold to existing markets is very attractive, but if a new market has to be developed for a product, or it requires a new marketing mix – new promotion, perhaps even different distribution channels and another sales organization – it is far less attractive.

The company that is highly regarded in the market in which the new product is to be launched will automatically transfer its reputation to the new product, giving it what is called the halo effect. This can usually be reflected in a slightly higher price.

If appropriate, the company should be able to supply a full technical backup service and support middlemen and users with existing resources.

If the new product rounds out a line, pricing should be relative to the total line and not just for itself.

Sometimes competition is created within the company by the introduction of a product. Although it may not compete directly with any of the company's existing products, it might adversely affect their sales. It will need to be priced in tandem with the potentially competing product.

A new product does not always enter the market evenly, but has a skewed distribution and appeals to a small number of customers. It may be necessary to circumvent this with segmental pricing, to forestall the effects of some of the customers withdrawing their support from the new product.

A product that can be packaged and given point-of-sale appeal must contain sufficient oncost in the price to exploit this promotional advantage. In contrast, one that needs special packing for protective transportation must also have sufficient allowance in the oncost, but here there is no promotional advantage – it is purely functional.

If only a single model of the product is possible, pricing is a much simpler task. If a number of models have to be made, or special versions that require additional production costs, line-pricing is advisable and this could make it a less acceptable proposition.

Ordinary seasonality should not unduly affect price, but it may be possible to take advantage of seasonality and harden prices, perhaps by differential discounts, to increase the profit component.

PRODUCTION CAPABILITIES

The longer the manufacturing cycle, in general, the higher the price. This needs careful assessment because some products cannot be produced without a long cycle. Wine, whisky and fruit, especially avocados, are examples. If the product can be made very quickly it may need to be priced low to dissuade competitors from entering the market before the company has gained a foothold.

A proposed new product that makes use of existing facilities (better still, currently idle equipment) and techniques familiar to the company is attractive because a low-price strategy is possible. This must not blind executives to the need to relate the product to the market; production capabilities must not over-influence new product selection. Alternatively, if the new product requires the acquisition of new plant and equipment, this will increase the size of the basic cost component and the subsequent price.

Some assessment of labour costs is needed because they are often the largest element in basic costs. If the new product can make more extensive use of personnel currently employed or it can be automated, it could be keenly priced.

FUTURE EXPANSION

The existence of reasonably assured future sales influences the level of initial price. Sometimes a product, such as the Gillette Sensor, is more or less unique either in its manufacture or operation and is covered by patents. Reliable technical and market data on competitive products and processes should be obtained. How far the proposed new product will fulfil an unsatisfied need or replace a higher-priced product, the greater the flexibility in pricing.

Two aspects of technology, the speed of technological change and the impact on the company, were discussed in some detail in chapter 6. If change or high impact is likely in the near future, the product may carry a low price, but if you are reasonably sure that the product is in a stable market it could carry a higher price tag.

If the product could be exported and there are no serious obstacles or barriers to prevent this, fundamental decisions have to be taken on recovery of overheads and the extent to which this is done in the home market.

POTENTIAL MARKET SIZE

The size of the potential market is vitally important to some companies, who will not venture into a market unless a minimum turnover and profit return are feasible. Large multinationals like Philips, Shell, Unilever and IBM will not market a product that cannot generate sufficient volume for their needs.

At the other end of the scale, some small organizations require small markets and are unable to cope with large volume. An initial assessment of market size will indicate to a company whether or not the new product is a viable proposition. If the potential market is very small, few large competitors are likely to be encountered, and high prices could be set.

One company in the UK specializing in small transformers is able to charge very high prices for its products because most of their orders are one-off. They have practically no competition because the large transformer manufacturers look for volume sales.

TARGET MARKET TYPE

Normally, a market in recession is not one in which a new product should be launched. Occasionally, while total business may be in recession, the target market may be stable. Some products and services have this characteristic of remaining buoyant even though others are faltering: these include liquidators who specialize in the disposal of plant, equipment and furniture of companies who go out of business.

A product's elasticity of demand will be affected by the degree of stability of the market. A new product with a highly elastic demand should be directed to a compatible, stable market. If the market is not entirely suitable it is a very dubious proposition.

The potential width of the market both for the new product and the company's total range should be assessed; if the product appeals to only a narrow range of customers it should not be offered at a low price.

A product which has a captive market, such as a potential market within the organization, should be highly priced, but if an equivalent product can be readily purchased in the market a low price is indicated.

A product which is a basic ingredient or component for which there will always be a demand is likely to have many competitors. Normally the price must be low, as should components for products in an advanced life cycle stage.

LOCATION OF INDUSTRY

A small, scattered market is costly to service, and may have limited potential sales; but if it is concentrated in one area it can be more readily reached, and selling and servicing costs are less. Relating the product to the size of the market and the degree to which it is geographically dispersed will determine level of price to be set.

CONSUMER GROUP

Consumer products often appeal to one or two age groups, and may be more attractive to those with a greater amount of disposable

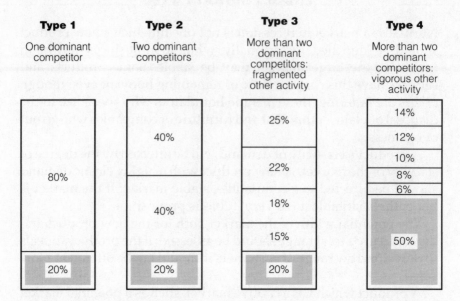

Exhibit 10.4 Four main types of markets

income. The target market for a new consumer item should be defined in terms of age, social grading and geographic location to provide a sound basis on which to judge the price level.

NATURE OF THE MARKET

The nature of the market can be crucial to the success of launching a new product or service. In general, markets may be categorized into four main types:

- one dominant competitor;
- two dominant competitors;
- more than two dominant competitors, fragmented other activity;
- more than two dominant competitors, dynamic other activity.

Exhibit 10.4 illustrates the four types with approximate, but typical, market shares. The clear areas represent the dominant products; the shaded parts, 'all other products'.

Experience of marketing products over the past ten years indicates that, providing the pricing has been competently carried out, two types of market offer good opportunities for new products.

The highest proportion of successful new entries into a market was in Type 2 – a market with two dominant competitors. The second best for new products was Type 4, where few, if any, of the leading companies had much more than about 10 per cent each of the market, and up to about half of the total market was fragmented with many vigorously competing products.

The type of market in which new products failed most was in Type 3, where three or four products enjoyed a strong major share of the market.

INITIAL CUSTOMER RESEARCH

Some of the points that should be established before a new product or service is priced and launched are:

- Who buys and who uses the product?
- How frequently is the product purchased?
- What prices are paid?
- How often is the product used?
- What attributes about existing products do users like?
- What improvements would users like to have?
- Are there any criticisms of existing products?
- What needs are not being satisfied?

The user and buyer of a product may be the same person. If so, the user will undoubtedly know the price, and may be very interested in it. If the user and buyer are not the same person, such as is the case with consumer gifts or the vast majority of industrial products, pricing is directed primarily to the buyer and those who influence the buying decision. Claims for the product, detailing its benefits, are directed to the user.

Products that are purchased frequently would allow different pricing tactics to be used to stimulate sales during the year. A product that is purchased very seldom, or only once, has to be 'target priced'. That is, the price has to be pitched at a level which it is thought will achieve the sale, as was done with the Major Engineering Ltd quotation discussed in chapter 7.

To compare prices, all competitive products of similar quality and performance should be analysed and positioned, as described generally in chapter 6 and illustrated particularly in exhibits 6.11–6.16. Special attention should be given to products of near-equal performance and price. These are the products that are truly competitive, and whose prices are compared after an analysis of their respective sales and marketing activities as suggested in exhibit 6.18.

Frequency of use influences frequency of purchase, and will thus have an impact on quality and price. Products that are used only once – that is, those that are used up or destroyed in use, such as bread, soap, matches, petrol, lubricating oil – will normally be price sensitive; customers tend to look at price first, quality second.

Products that are used repetitively, as with consumer products – clothes, shoes, electric shaver, screwdriver, washing machine etc. – and industrial products – capstan mill, crane, lathe, lorry etc. – are considered carefully for quality, if not first, certainly early in their appraisal stage before the purchase is made. Such products are expected to have a long life. In particular, industrial buyers of products that have a high repetitive use will include in their deliberations the cost of ownership and amortization of the product over an appropriate number of years.

Qualitative aspects can only be superficially explored in the initial customer research, and it may be useful to organize informal discussions with some of the better known customers. While responses are likely to be biased, it is valuable to have customers' viewpoints on what they like about a product, and, even more importantly, what improvements they would like to see.

DETAILED MARKET APPRAISAL

After agreement has been reached on the chosen target market, it is investigated in depth and related to the known price structures of companies. This investigation will include:

- sales trends of comparable products;
- sales patterns – seasonal, regional, by industry or outlet;
- distribution channels and methods;

- advertising, and degree of 'pull' through channel;
- if 'pushed' through channel, support by middlemen;
- competitors' production potential;
- competitors' marketing potential;
- special warehousing, packaging etc.

Competitors' prices will reflect the way their products are distributed, advertised, promoted, sold and serviced.

Authoritative published statistics will form a major part of the desk research, but to obtain information on the latest marketing practice it is necessary to go into the market and find out.

For consumer markets there are a number of continuous *ad hoc* retail audits available. These report on the number of competitors, their market shares, strengths and weaknesses, sales trends and seasonal fluctuations, the relative importance of different types of retail outlets, and much other detailed information. Occasionally, surveys of industrial markets that have been conducted can be purchased, but considerable care must be taken in the interpretation of their findings. Before using them, they should be subjected to an examination by an independent analyst.

Market research reports are as good as the people who conduct them, the relevance of the data obtained, the collation and analysis of both quantitative and qualitative material, and the interpretations made from the investigation. The two examples that follow are from my own experience of pricing consultancies, and should serve to emphasize the need to evaluate all sources of information.

A MARKET SURVEY ON CLOCKS

A large multinational company sold, among a multitude of other products, quartz clocks. They decided to penetrate the domestic clock market and purchased a comprehensive market research on the European electric clock market. To stimulate interest in the product it was decided to introduce the project to successive groups of executives on international seminars in the form of an exercise that I constructed. They decided to concentrate on four countries: West Germany, France, the UK and Denmark.

The survey contained data on every conceivable aspect of marketing clocks: ownership, type and brand of clock, location in the home, power source, size of household, income class, professional activities or occupation, number of children, whether newly wed, and so on.

On closer inspection, the report was found to contain data on practically every country, but at various stages of completion. The data for West Germany were complete; France, incomplete; the UK, just a few insignificant figures; for Denmark, non-existent. Yet these were the four countries for which plans and prices were to be constructed.

Analyses were made of appropriate tables for every country to determine whether any useful relationships existed between the criteria and whether these were supported by an acceptable degree of statistical correlation. A surprising relationship was discovered. For practically every country, a coefficient of correlation of 0.995 was found between the estimated sizes of the electric clock markets and the total working population in the manufacturing industries of that country!

While perhaps even a high degree of correlation between these two sets of data might be presumed, nevertheless the coefficients would be expected to vary over a wide range. With the figure of 0.995 appearing so consistently, considerable doubt was cast on the validity of the rest of the research. To base plans and prices on such suspect data was thought inadvisable.

COMPUTER SOFTWARE PRICES

I discovered a similar occurrence with a leading computer software company in 1987. A research survey that had been conducted on the world software market had been purchased by the company, and was being used as a base for their expansion plans. The survey also contained five-year projections for the leading competitors, based on published prices.

On analysis, small discrepancies were discovered in some of the percentages but, though small, when extended with competitors' prices they created a deviation of estimated total sales from a minimum of $11,840,000 to a maximum of $23,350,000 over the five years.

Comparisons between the estimated sales for the four leading companies and exponential projections from their base sales figures revealed statistical correlations between the estimates and the exponential figures of 0.999, 0.997 and 0.992 (twice).

The forecasts were highly questionable, and were ignored in the company's plans. The originators of the research had used a simple exponential projection to generate a table of figures.

The moral from these tales is that no research should be taken at face value. Any pricing strategy based on marketing intelligence will be as sound as the information on which it is based.

DEVELOPING AND TESTING IDEAS

Developing new products and services within acceptable price brackets for a company's future markets, and allocating resources to achieve that future mix, require critical decisions by management.

A decision is:

- a choice of one or more *goals*;
- an *irrevocable* allocation of *resources* to reach that goal.

The three words in italics in this definition – 'goal', 'resources' and 'irrevocable' – are crucial in a decision.

The goal is, generally, the finish where you wish to be, and may consist of several objectives. An objective should be stated in terms of results to be achieved in a certain time period, otherwise it is not possible to judge whether it has been accomplished.

Resources are what the company has available now, and what they could have use of during progress towards the goal. They consist of the four 'Ms': men, money, materials, machines.

Irrevocability is the characteristic that, once committed to a course of action, it is impracticable, sometimes impossible, to reverse the situation. Even trying to change direction may be difficult and costly.

New products should be related to customer and market appraisals. Each new product idea should be screened, especially for its likely price bracket, and if accepted, priced in line with the company's present and future R&D, production and marketing capability.

When the long lead times necessary from product conception to commercialization are considered, the fact of irrevocability puts greater stress on management to take the 'right' product and price

259

Exhibit 10.5 Typical lead times for new products

Product development	2–6 years
Production facilities	1–4 years
Marketing operations	2–10 years

decisions. Typical lead times are given in exhibit 10.5. As will be seen, the time period from innovation to commercialization varies from about five to twenty years, depending on the product.

Two main questions should be continuously applied to new product ideas: Will customers buy it at the proposed price? At that price, will it make sufficient profit for the company?

Consumer products can be quickly tested; whether it is assessing the idea, its proposed price, variations in quality, formulation, packaging, or value, all can be undertaken by existing organizations. The cost of such research may be thought high until it is appreciated how much it can save a company from making expensive mistakes.

Industrial product testing is more difficult and time-consuming because of the multidimensional structure of industrial markets. Often a lengthy testing period with the product in actual operation is required before a decision can be made by the potential customer.

PRELIMINARY ASSESSMENT

One or more ideas will have passed through the screening process at this stage. Now is the time for more urgent co-ordination between R&D, production and marketing personnel to develop potential production plans that are in tune with marketing plans. It is undesirable to proceed with marginal products by adjusting the screening process to admit them. Regular reassessment of the screening parameters should be undertaken, especially those relating to price structure, but the standard of the evaluation procedures should remain demanding, and not allowed to become less rigorous or, worse still, lax.

Sourcing of raw materials and components and factory capacity must be appraised for the launch period of the product, and for a predetermined growth pattern. Any likely or foreseeable increases in costs must be taken into consideration in the pricing policy.

The additional investment of resources, manpower and finance for the new product should be assessed in the light of the requirements of existing products and services; this is more particularly so if sales of current products are increasing.

Risks will obviously need to be taken – some minor, some more fundamental. Quantifying such risks, where possible, in terms of probability of success or failure has a remarkable effect of clearing the mind of irrelevancies. Full use should be made of software programs that allow 'what if' scenarios with varying price levels. The effect of costs on prices and profits will be explored later in the book.

DEVELOPING THE MARKETING PLAN

When a 'go' decision has been taken for a product, the marketing plan, which has been progressed in step with product development plans, can be taken to an advanced stage, prices and discounts agreed. This plan should detail the actions to be taken to stimulate demand for the product at an optimum level of volume and profit, with an acceptable level of risk.

Battles of the market-place are first won in the boardroom. To give the marketing plan the best chance of being successful it should be the result of a co-operative effort: everyone involved, either directly or indirectly, should contribute to its construction. All should be convinced that the manner in which the product is to be presented to customers is as good as the company employees can make it. Collective responsibility for the marketing plan is the order of the day. In this way, the chances of success are multiplied.

TEST MARKETING

Irrespective of the testing and pre-testing carried out, there is no substitute for a product on offer at a specific price in the market-place in company with its competitors. It has to win sales in the cold light of reality in competition with other products, many of which might possess a higher perceived value.

Not only the product is tested, but also its brand name (if used), price, price structure to the middlemen, distribution method, selling

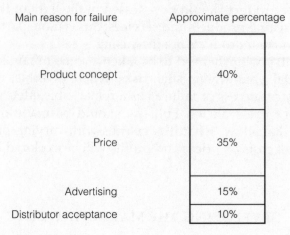

Main reason for failure	Approximate percentage
Product concept	40%
Price	35%
Advertising	15%
Distributor acceptance	10%

Exhibit 10.6 Why they failed

effort, packaging, advertising copy themes, media, promotion and service. There are many examples of products which are rated very highly through all the previous stages and then fail during test marketing.

Over many years of experience with consumer and industrial products I have found four main causes of product failure: the product concept was wrong; the price was wrong; there was insufficient or ineffective advertising; the product was not accepted by middlemen. The two most important reasons for failure were wrong product and wrong price. Exhibit 10.6 illustrates the spread of the reasons.

Products that meet their test marketing objectives tend to repeat the results when marketed nationally, or on a large scale. Exhibit 10.7 illustrates the experience with products observed in exhibit 10.6.

SUCCESSFUL TEST MARKETING

The test should form part of the general marketing plan. It should be designed to find the solution, or solutions, to a major problem and not a range of minor issues. The objectives of the test should reflect what is possible, or usual, nationally. Thus, if 1 per cent of potential sales would normally be appropriated to national advertising, the same percentage should be set for the market being tested.

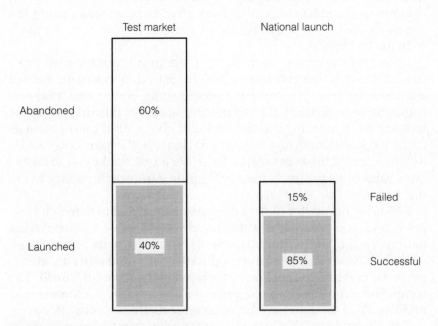

Exhibit 10.7 Test marketing justified

Increasing this 'to give the test a good chance of succeeding' will distort the conclusions that can be drawn from the results.

If the price for the national launch is to be, say, £100, attempting to boost the test by offering the product for, say, £80 will damage the value of the test. If a lower price is offered during the test, it must be repeated as a general policy when launched nationally. IBM adopted this strategy with the introduction of their PS/2 personal computers in 1988.

The choice of test market area is often critical in the evaluation of a new product or service. It should be restrictive enough to contain the advertising and promotional campaign, and not be subject to regular, massive influxes of people. The City of London, for example, would be a difficult general test market area for products, and probably only suitable for products and services appealing specifically to the financial, banking and insurance services conducted there. Some areas have been subject to so many new product tests that the population has developed a high degree of sophistication towards product testing, and provide unreliable results.

Serious underestimates are often made of the time necessary to mount a market test. Allow adequate time to plan and initiate the test, and establish a base against which to measure any subsequent changes in the marketing mix. If price has to be altered during the course of the test, take careful measurements of results to compare with the test base.

If, during the course of the test, competitors counter with price cuts, discounts, special offers and increased promotion, do not abandon the test, but compare your results before and after the competitive retaliation. If your product survives the onslaught, the test will have been invaluable, and will give a strong indication as to the likely outcome of a full national launch. Pay particular attention to a competitive price attack during a test marketing exercise. How sales of all products react will guide your pricing policy in the full-scale launch.

Should a competitor make a deep price cut, perhaps to match your price, and you weather the storm, when you extend your market nationally, the competitor is unable to raise price to its former level.

If you have costed your new product properly, and enjoy an adequate profit margin, you will be well placed in the national launch. The competitor who has lowered price will be seen by customers and middlemen, if used, to have been forced to do this by your efforts.

This occurred in 1988 in the UK in the computer software market. One company tested its comparatively low-priced product through a well-known chain of High Street stores, with the intention of expanding through other distribution channels if the test was successful. Competitors retaliated by reducing their prices, increasing their sales and promotional efforts, and stressing the service and backup they provided. Despite their well-intentioned efforts it created a strong suspicion in the market that their prices had previously been far too high.

From these comments it should be clear that methods should not be used in the test that cannot, or will not, be repeated in the national launch. If on average one sales person normally covers, say, every 10,000 accounts, it is pointless to re-allocate the sales force one to every 1,000 accounts during the test.

Price is of paramount importance in the test, and unless disaster is threatened, it should not be meddled with once the test has started.

REGIONAL AND NATIONAL LAUNCH

Lead times for establishing new products and services on the market can, as summarized in exhibit 10.5, take up to a couple of decades.

The longest requirement is for the development of marketing operations. The time that can elapse between the test and the regional or national launch can be as much as five years, especially with fast moving consumer goods.

Despite this proviso, if the test has been satisfactory, the product can be launched nationally as soon as possible, but in accordance with the marketing plan.

During every regional or national launch, price takes on a predominant and pivotal role. It is vitally important to the company introducing the new product; it is of major interest to every competitor waiting to pounce on the new intruder.

The new product will undoubtedly have been launched with venture capital. Profits will not flow immediately, and the investment already made in research, development, production, advertising, sales and marketing, has to be recovered. The level of price will, as we have seen in earlier chapters, influence sales according to the elasticity of demand for the product. The margin in the price will influence the rate of cost and expense recovery as well as eventually delivering profits.

This is the moment of maximum danger, because it is at this stage that the product is highly vulnerable to competitive attack. There are many examples of products that were successfully test-marketed but then viciously attacked, and even killed, by a shrewd competitor at the moment of national launch.

The main weapon used for the assault is price, with concentrated selling efforts, advertising and promotion in support.

Monitoring the progress of the product and competitive activity in the market, preferably using independent observers, will provide management with the intelligence necessary to secure a bridgehead in the market, and enable them to decide when to commit reserves of sales and advertising firepower. Price should not be altered; it is for this reason that an extensive analysis should be made of all aspects of price, including possible competitive reactions, before the national launch.

THE SERVICE ELEMENT

With the steady, and sometimes incredibly rapid, advance of technology, new products are becoming more esoteric and complicated.

The servicing element in the makeup of price assumes greater importance. While the pricing executive will doubtless include in the price of a new product a proportion of the total estimated cost of providing warranty, guarantee and the usual period of free servicing, this area can be a minefield.

A new product, especially one that uses a new or different system of operation, will often have a high incidence of free servicing calls during its guarantee period, simply because it is new, and users are not thoroughly familiar with it. This higher-than-normal servicing could be regarded as an advertising investment in the product, and an adequate allowance made in the price.

When introducing their early range of video-recorders to the market, the company mentioned in chapter 1 included in the price 5 per cent for the provision of warranty etc. during the first year of the guarantee. The product had performed faultlessly during its extensive 'soak' tests and passed all other performance tests without problems. The allowance of 5 per cent was thought to be a generous margin, within which the company would make a little extra profit. It proved to be woefully inadequate.

Companies marketing products that make use of the latest technology are particularly at risk. In 1988 General Electric of the USA ran into problems with its new, energy-efficient rotary compressor for a line of high-tech refrigerators. Each unit carried a five-year warranty. A design flaw caused many of them to fail. The company honoured its commitment to customers but no allowance for service in the price could possibly have covered this unforeseen problem. Each unit cost in the region of $200 to fix, and 700 service staff had to be recruited to help cope.

CONTINUOUS IMPROVEMENT

A constant improvement must be maintained in the product, its performance and its marketing. This makes all the difference between the 'end of the beginning' and 'the beginning of the end'.

CHAPTER

11

Pricing tools

PRICING TOOLS

In management information systems there are many tools available for setting prices to make profits: demand analysis, elasticity of demand, standard costing, cash budgeting, cash flow analysis etc. These financial tools are as useful and timely as the speed with which the market and accounting data can be collected, collated, analysed and circulated. Even today it is not uncommon for a company not to know how much profit it is making until a period revenue account has been prepared.

Profit must be planned and controlled; it cannot be left to chance. If profits are too small, insufficient funds are generated to develop adequate research, exploit market opportunities, cushion tomorrow's depressions, take action to neutralize threats, or keep shareholders happy.

If profits are too high, competition is encouraged, increasing demands by employees are stimulated, and complacency sets in, causing unwise or inappropriate allocation of excess funds. Occasionally, government investigations may be invited.

Of all the decisions made in business, those relating to price have the greatest effect on profit. A product that is improved and offered at the same price as its predecessor is, in effect, a price reduction.

Advertising may increase awareness of a product and its uses, and play an important role in persuading customers to buy, but advertising is an expense: it does not supply profit. Similarly, everything done inside the company costs money: only customers supply profits.

Although pricing is so important in establishing the level of profit, or even whether any profit is to be made, many pricing decisions are taken with inadequate financial and quantitative data.

Systems for the control of profits often take the form of regular reports which are issued monthly, weekly, or even daily, depending on their importance and relevance. Marketing managers receive reports on the sales mix, the product mix, disposition of customers and distributors, and responses to advertising and promotion. Sales managers receive regular, often daily, reports of regional sales by product. Production managers have regular summaries of labour hours, overtime, material costs and stock position, the frequency depending on the nature of the business.

These reports enable management to explore favourable trends, or to correct unfavourable situations, but they are historical, and often arrive too late to avoid losses or take advantage of any openings. More important, they are of little help in taking decisions related to profit.

COMPARING RESULTS

In all reports, actual results should be compared with planned results rather than with the previous period, or with the same period last year. Exhibit 11.1 shows the results for February compared with the same period last year.

Exhibit 11.1 Comparison of results with previous year

	This Feb (£)	Last Feb (£)	Variance (£)
Sales	72,270	65,700	+6,570
Selling expenses	19,710	18,340	+1,370
Production	38,000	36,000	+2,000
Profit	14,560	11,360	+3,200

Exhibit 11.2 Comparison of actual with planned results

	Planned (£)	Actual (£)	Variance (£)	Performance (%)
Sales	75,000	72,270	(2,730)	96.4%
Selling expenses	19,500	19,710	210	101.1%
Production	37,800	38,000	200	100.5%
Profit	17,700	14,560	(3,140)	82.3%

With exhibit 11.1 it is not possible to decide whether the results for February are good or poor and need attention. There is no base or yardstick with which to compare the results; no plan against which to measure the returns. Conditions are likely to have changed in the intervening year: there will be different customers, a modified, or different product range, and certainly costs will have changed. A crucial point is that the results of the previous February may not have been satisfactory. But the manager may think, 'Profit has improved by £3,200, so things can't be all that bad!'

Comparing results with a planned budget, as in exhibit 11.2, enables the position to be more readily evaluated.

With these comparisons, it is easy to see that, although sales this February are higher than a year ago, they are below target and profit is unsatisfactory. Comparing results with previous periods, or less satisfactory, a year ago, hides the profit performance.

PROFIT AND COSTS

Whereas price can be reasonably defined as the amount of money that is exchanged for goods or services, profit has many definitions. It can mean gross profit, net profit, net profit before tax, profit after tax, profit from manufacture, profit from trading, from operations, per customer, per unit of sale, for the year, and what tax inspectors regard as profit can frustrate many business people.

This book is concerned with the construction of prices to achieve desired profits. This means that price must cover all costs of making a product, stocking and distributing it, advertising, selling costs, discounts provided to middlemen, credit given to customers until they pay for it, and interest on the use of money to do all these things. Most of these costs can be accurately applied to products.

Some costs cannot be so easily apportioned, and are allocated to products according to relevant factors such as the hours required for manufacture, space occupied by the appropriate production machines in the factory, the direct production cost, sales volume, sales revenue etc. This allocation of general costs to specific outputs extends as far as they can be reasonably traced to individual products.

Many production, administration and selling facilities are common to all products, and their costs cannot always be allocated equitably to individual units of output. Examples are: salaries of people who supply various management, supervisory, and general services such as the company secretary, factory nurse and cleaners; the company canteen in which subsidized meals are available; provision and maintenance of fire-fighting equipment; upkeep of the grounds and gardens; the company social and sports club.

All general operating costs are paid from an overhead 'fund' which is the sum of all business costs that cannot be traced to specific units of output because it is inconvenient or too costly to do so. All products normally contribute to this general overhead.

TWO APPROACHES TO PRICING

Pricing for profit can be approached in two main ways. We can assign a price to a product or service and calculate profit after all costs have been absorbed, or we can set aside the general overhead and calculate the contribution the product makes to it.

Whichever method is adopted, the fixed costs have to be paid. If only one product or service is being marketed, it will have to bear the total fixed cost. With two or more products, the fixed costs can be paid by the products at different rates, and management is able to vary their prices accordingly.

The first method is an absorption costing procedure that emphasizes the need to allocate all costs, fixed and variable, because all costs have to be recovered before a profit can be determined. This is sometimes criticized because attempting to allocate what cannot be allocated merely misinforms decision-makers.

270

The second method is a marginal costing approach: only costs that vary with output, or that can be directly attributed, should be allocated to that output. Simple examples illustrate the two methods.

PRIME COSTS AND DIRECT COSTS

Prime costs are normally those that are incurred during the course of production. They are also called direct costs and are:

cost of materials + cost of production labour
+ production overheads

Materials are the raw materials, components and bought-ins to make and assemble a product; production labour includes the man-power costs used in the actual manufacture of a product; production overheads are those costs that are difficult to relate directly to a product and are an oncost to all products produced in the factory. Lighting, heating and cleaning the factory, for example, cannot readily be split up into smaller amounts, and their total cost is spread over the number of products. An output of 25,000 units and a production overhead of £20,000 would mean that each unit would carry about £1 production overhead, and allow for production falling to about 80 per cent of capacity.

To the prime cost has to be added any administration, selling and other costs. Fixed costs also have to be paid.

A company produces one product and has the costs and oncosts shown in exhibit 11.3. Their annual production is 2,500 units, and their forecast of sales for the year is shown as exhibit 11.4. In January

Exhibit 11.3 Company's costs and oncosts

Raw materials	£3 per unit
Production labour	£2 per unit
Production overheads	£1 per unit
Selling and administrative costs	50% of prime cost
Profit	25% of total cost
Fixed general overhead	£36,000 a year

Exhibit 11.4 Company's monthly sales forecast

Jan	Feb	Mar	Apl	May	Jun	Jul	Aug	Sep	Oct	Nov	Dec
50	100	150	200	300	400	500	450	150	100	50	50

their output was 50 units, in February it was 100 units, and in March 150 units.

FULL ABSORPTION COSTING

Using the first method, the absorption costing approach, a decision has to be taken on the allocation of the fixed cost of £36,000. This is easy: with only one product, all the fixed costs are charged to it. The allocation problem arises as soon as other products are added to the company's product range.

However, unless fixed costs are applied correctly in the price structure weird and wonderful prices can result. Each of the company's annual output of 2,500 products should pay its share towards fixed costs.

Assuming that the total production is sold, this is an average share of £36,000/2,500 = £14.40 for each product. To allow for less than 100 per cent activity, fixed overhead could be recovered at, say, 80 per cent, 2,000 units. £36,000/2,000 = £18 per unit. The two possible price structures are set out in exhibit 11.5.

There are a number of points to note about this structure. Because fixed cost recovery has been based on two different levels of activity, two prices have resulted. The lower price of £38.25 assumes that all 2,500 units will be sold; £45 assumes that only 2,000 will be sold. But in both cases the total fixed cost of £36,000 is recovered.

Prudence suggests a price of £45, but this is about 17.5 per cent higher than the lower price. If sales have been estimated at 2,500 on a price of under £40, because of unknown demand elasticity, pitching it at £45 might lower sales by a similar percentage to around 2,000.

Initially, the company favoured the lower price, and were confident that 2,500 units would be sold. The position, with recovery of

Pricing tools

Exhibit 11.5 Two suggested prices

| | Price with recovery at 100% capacity | | Price with recovery at 80% capacity | |
	Unit cost (£)	Total 2,500 (£)	Unit cost (£)	Total 2,000 (£)
Materials and labour	3.00	7,500	3.00	6,000
Production	2.00	5,000	2.00	4,000
Production overhead	1.00	2,500	1.00	2,000
	6.00	15,000	6.00	12,000
Fixed overhead	14.40	36,000	18.00	36,000
	20.40	51,000	24.00	48,000
Selling and admin (+50%)	10.20	25,500	12.00	24,000
	30.60	76,500	36.00	72,000
Profit (+25%)	7.65	19,125	9.00	18,000
Price and Revenue	38.25	95,625	45.00	90,000

fixed costs at 100 per cent level of operations, is summarized in exhibit 11.6.

Whichever price is chosen, if sales are less than the base on which the price was constructed, under-recovery of fixed costs will occur; if sales are more than the base, greater profit will be made. At a price of £38.25, sales of 2,500 recover the full £36,000. If sales are 80 per cent of this level, only 2,000 × £14.40 = £28,800 will be recovered, an under-recovery of £7,200. Fixed costs have to be paid, and therefore profit is reduced by the amount of the under-recovery.

Unfortunately, decisions on price, appropriations for administration, selling, advertising and distribution have to be made before operations are started.

Approximately £25,000 has been committed for administration and selling expenses at the start of operations, and although it is an oncost of £10.20 or £12 per unit, depending on the base, the total cannot be substantially reduced if less than forecast sales are being achieved. Raising price in an attempt to adjust such a position is liable to have the opposite effect. Irrespective of the number of units

Pricing tools

	£	£
Sales 2,500 units @ £38.25	95,625	
less Cost of goods @ £6.00	15,000	
Gross profit		80,625
less Fixed cost		36,000
		44,625
Selling and admin 2,500 @ £10.20		25,500
Profit 2,500 @ £7.65		19,125

Exhibit 11.6 Projected revenue account

	£	£
Sales 2,000 units @ £38.25	76,500	
less Cost of goods @ £6	12,000	
Gross profit		64,500
less Fixed cost		36,000
		28,500
Selling and administration		25,500
Profit		3,000

Exhibit 11.7 Sales of 2,000 with figures based on 2,500

sold, the commitment for such costs still has to be met: any shortfall has to come from profit.

When sales are falling short of what was planned, the profit is already being eroded. With sales of only 2,000, but operations based on 2,500, the situation would be as in exhibit 11.7. Profit is £16,125 less than was estimated. Exhibit 11.8 shows where it went.

If sales were more than the estimated 2,500, say, 2,800, then 2,800 × £14.40 = £40,320 would be recovered for fixed costs, an over-recovery of £4,320. This and other savings would boost profits

274

Exhibit 11.8 Where the profit went

	Estimated (£)	Achieved (£)	Difference (£)
Profit	19,125	15,300	3,825
Fixed costs	36,000	28,800	7,200
Selling & Admin	25,500	20,400	5,100
			16,125

	£	£
Sales 2,800 units @ £38.25	107,100	
less Cost of goods @ £6	16,800	
		90,300
less Fixed cost		36,000
		54,300
Selling and administration		25,500
Profit		28,800

Exhibit 11.9 Sales of 2,800 with figures based on 2,500

by £9,675 to £28,800, as in exhibit 11.9. How the increased profit would arise is shown in exhibit 11.10.

In the costings in exhibit 11.5, if the unit fixed cost element of £14.40 or £18 were inserted after the percentage oncosts, lower price calculations would result because 50 per cent and 25 per cent of the fixed cost, for other expenses, would not be included.

Using percentage oncosts in the pricing structure is normal practice, but the actual proposed amounts must be used when checking the figures. This is to ensure that the required totals will be achieved with the percentages inserted at the particular points in the price structure.

Provided that percentages in the costings are calculated one after the other, the combined percentage oncost total will be the same, but

Exhibit 11.10 How the increased profit would arise

	Estimated (£)	Achieved (£)	Difference (£)
Profit	19,125	21,420	2,295
Fixed costs	36,000	40,320	4,320
Selling & Admin	25,500	28,560	3,060
			9,675

the individual totals will differ. In this example, the company needed around £25,000 for selling and administration costs, and a profit of about £20,000 on sales of approximately £100,000. They had calculated that these figures would be achieved with oncosts of 50 per cent and 20 per cent applied to all other costs.

It may be assumed that the company would know in advance whether it was going to introduce a second product, and could organize its costing and price structure accordingly. But if another product is marketed without the advantage of previous knowledge, a costing problem has to be solved.

The first product has £14.40 included in its price so that sales of 2,500 will produce the necessary £36,000 fixed overhead. If the second product is about the same price, and will sell at least as many than the first, obviously it could carry half the cost of the fixed cost. If it is put on the market half way through the year, the first product is likely to have sold around 1,250 units and recovered £18,000 of the fixed costs.

The questions are: Should the first product continue to carry all the fixed cost burden? How could the remaining £18,000 fixed cost be recovered from the two products? The first product could be reduced by some £7 or more. How could this be explained away to customers? Or would it be better to pocket the difference as extra profit? Such problems become more intelligible with a marginal costing approach where products are taken to a 'contribution' stage.

As fixed costs relate to a time period rather than to production, one-twelfth could be added to each month's output. This is shown for the three months in exhibit 11.11.

Exhibit 11.11 Marginal costing for three months

| | Jan (50) | | Feb (100) | | Mar (150) | |
	Unit (£)	Total (£)	Unit (£)	Total (£)	Unit (£)	Total (£)
Materials, labour	5	250	5	500	5	750
Production o/h	1	50	1	100	1	150
Total direct cost	6	300	6	600	6	900
Fixed cost	60	3,000	60	3,000	60	3,000
	66	3,300	66	3,600	66	3,900
Monthly unit cost	66		36		26	

Total costs increase each month in line with production, but unit cost decreases. This is because the fixed cost element is spread over an increasing number of units. The unit prime cost does not vary: it is always £6 and is called the marginal cost.

Marginal cost is important in pricing, but unfortunately it has several different definitions depending on whether you view it as an accountant, an economist, or a business manager. For pricing purposes we define it thus:

Marginal costs are those costs that vary with volume.

The total of marginal costs is:

materials + production labour + production variable overheads

Consider exhibit 11.11 again. In January 50 units were produced. In February an extra 50 were produced, making a total of 100 units. The cost of those extra 50 units in February was the *addition to total cost* of producing January's total of 50. That is, £300. Similarly in March, another 50 units more than February were produced for an *addition to total cost* of £300. In both months, the additional 50 units cost £300, or £6 each, which is the marginal cost or direct cost.

Once the marginal cost has been found, any price can be established with additions for sales, commissions, marketing, administration, contribution to fixed overheads, profit.

From our previous workings, £25,500 has been estimated for selling and administration costs. This could be regarded as fixed, or rigid for the year, and lumped together with the other fixed costs of £36,000 to make a total of £61,500.

With one product, obviously, all the fixed overheads have to be carried by that product, and, whatever type of costing display is considered, sufficient must be added to recover the total at an estimated level of operations.

When more products are marketed, decisions have to be made on allocation of costs. It is not a waste of time to have a marginal costing statement for one product, because the product's contribution to fixed overhead and profit are clearly seen. When other products are added, apportionment of costs and pricing are made easier.

BREAK-EVEN POINT

From exhibit 11.12, using the unit cost figures, the break-even point is determined by dividing total fixed costs by the unit contribution, which is price less unit variable cost. The formula is similar to that in chapter 5.

$$\frac{\text{total fixed costs}}{\text{price - unit variable cost}}$$

$$\frac{£61,500}{£38.25 - £6}$$

which equals 1,907 units. Checking:

Sales 1,907 @ £38.25	£72,942.75
less Production @ £6	11,442.00
	£61,500.75

The wisdom or folly of setting price at £38.25 should be considered, because 1,907 is a little over 76 per cent of total capacity to break even. If sales were regular throughout the year it would mean that the company would not break even until early September.

Pricing tools

	£	£	£
Sales 2,500 @ £38.25		95,625	
Materials	7,500		
Production labour	5,000		
Production overhead	2,500		
Marginal production cost		15,000	
Contribution			80,625
Fixed costs			
Selling and administration		25,500	
Overhead		36,000	
			61,500
Profit			19,125

Exhibit 11.12 Marginal cost statement

CASH FLOW

The high percentage of maximum sales required to break even directs attention to the likely cash flow situation. Exhibit 11.13 expands the marginal cost statement of exhibit 11.12 into a cash flow statement and profit and loss summary in a PC spreadsheet. Since the spreadsheet is a wide one, it is divided into three parts in the exhibit, but it should be remembered that it is read horizontally across columns [A] to [Q]. Sales are on credit, cash being received after two months, and interest at one per cent per month charged on any borrowing. Exhibits 11.14–11.17 illustrate the position at prices £38.25 and £45, with sales 2,500, 2,125 and 1,875. The monthly sales have been adjusted in line with the original sales pattern.

The necessary formulae for the spreadsheet in exhibit 11.13 are as follows:

```
[E1]  38.25
[O4]  @SUM(B4..M4)
[B5]  +B4*$E$1 copy across [C5]..[M5]
[Q5]  @SUM(B5..M5)
```

	[A]	[B]	[C]	[D]	[E]	[F]	[G]
[1]	*<File name>*			Price:	£38.25		
[2]				Estimated Cash Flow (£s)			
[3]		Jan	Feb	Mar	Apl	May	Jun
[4]	Estimated sales	50	100	150	200	300	400
[5]	Revenue	1,913	3,825	5,738	7,650	11,475	15,300
[6]	Cash received			1,913	3,825	5,738	7,650
[7]	Manufacturing	300	600	900	1,200	1,800	2,400
[8]	Admin & Sales	2,125	2,125	2,125	2,125	2,125	2,125
[9]	Fixed cost			9,000			9,000
[10]	Cash out	2,425	2,725	12,025	3,325	3,925	13,525
[11]	Balance +/(-)	(2,425)	(2,725)	(10,113)	500	1,813	(5,875)
[12]	Balance b/fwd		(2,425)	(5,174)	(15,338)	(14,992)	(13,329)
[13]	Interest		(24)	(52)	(153)	(150)	(133)
[14]	Balance c/fwd	(2,425)	(5,174)	(15,338)	(14,992)	(13,329)	(19,338)

	[H]	[I]	[J]	[K]	[L]	[M]
[3]	Jul	Aug	Sep	Oct	Nov	Dec
[4]	500	450	150	100	50	50
[5]	19,125	17,213	5,738	3,825	1,913	1,913
[6]	11,475	15,300	19,125	17,213	5,738	3,825
[7]	3,000	2,700	900	600	300	300
[8]	2,125	2,125	2,125	2,125	2,125	2,125
[9]			9,000			9,000
[10]	5,125	4,825	12,025	2,725	2,425	11,425
[11]	6,350	10,475	7,100	14,488	3,313	(7,600)
[12]	(19,338)	(13,181)	(2,838)	4,234	18,721	22,034
[13]	(193)	(132)	(28)	0	0	0
[14]	(13,181)	(2,838)	4,234	18,721	22,034	14,434

	[N]	[O]	[P]	[Q]
[3]	Price	£38.25		
[4]	Sales Vol.	2,500		
[5]	Revenue			£95,625
[6]	Total cash	£91,800		
[7]	Production		£15,000	
[8]	Admin etc		£25,500	
[9]	Fixed costs		£36,000	
[10]	Interest		£866	
[11]				£77,366
[12]				
[13]	(£866)		Profit	£18,259

Exhibit 11.13 Profit and cash flow with 100 per cent sales at £38.25

```
[D6]  +B5 copy across [E6]..[M6]
[O6]  @SUM(B6..M6)
[B7]  +B4*6 copy across [C7]..[M7]
[P7]  @SUM(B7..M7)
[B8]  2125 copy across [C8]..[M8]
[P8]  @SUM(B8..M8)
[D9]  9000 copy in [G9], [J9] and [M9]
[P9]  @SUM(B9..M9)
[B10] @SUM(B7..B9) copy across [C10]..[M10]
[P10] -N13
[B11] +B6-B10 copy across [C11]..[M11]
[Q11] @SUM(P7..P11)
[C12] +B14 copy across [D12]..[M12]
[C13] @IF(B14<0,B14*0.01,0) copy across [D13]..[M13]
[N13] @SUM(B13..M13)
[Q13] +Q5-Q11
[B14] @SUM(B11..B13) copy across [C14]..[M14]
```

	Estimated sales	Balance c/fwd
Jan	50	(2,425)
Feb	100	(5,174)
Mar	150	(15,001)
Apl	200	(13,976)
May	300	(11,291)
Jun	400	(15,929)
Jul	500	(7,713)
Aug	450	5,385
Sep	150	15,860
Oct	100	33,385
Nov	50	37,710
Dec	50	30,785

	£	£
Sales 2,500 @ £45		112,500
Production	15,000	
Admin etc.	25,500	
Fixed costs	36,000	
Interest	715	
		77,215
Profit		£35,285

Exhibit 11.14 100 per cent sales at £45

281

	Estimated sales	Balance c/fwd
Jan	43	(2,383)
Feb	85	(5,042)
Mar	128	(15,340)
Apl	170	(15,388)
May	255	(14,301)
Jun	340	(21,106)
Jul	425	(16,238)
Aug	383	(7,819)
Sep	128	(3,534)
Oct	85	8,446
Nov	43	10,959
Dec	40	2,845

	£	£
Sales 2,125 @ £38.25		81,281
Production	12,750	
Admin etc.	25,500	
Fixed costs	36,000	
Interest	1,012	
		75,262
Profit		6,020

Exhibit 11.15 85 per cent sales at £38.25

	Estimated sales	Balance c/fwd
Jan	38	(2,353)
Feb	75	(4,952)
Mar	113	(15,351)
Apl	150	(15,660)
May	225	(14,970)
Jun	300	(22,307)
Jul	375	(18,299)
Aug	338	(11,160)
Sep	113	(8,731)
Oct	75	1,536
Nov	38	3,505
Dec	35	(4,961)

	£	£
Sales 1,875 @ £38.25		71,719
Production	11,250	
Admin etc.	25,500	
Fixed costs	36,000	
Interest	1,138	
		73,888
Profit		(2,169)

Exhibit 11.16   75 per cent sales at £38.25

	Estimated sales	Balance c/fwd
Jan	38	(2,353)
Feb	75	(4,952)
Mar	113	(15,094)
Apl	150	(14,895)
May	225	(13,434)
Jun	300	(19,743)
Jul	375	(14,191)
Aug	338	(4,986)
Sep	113	37
Oct	75	12,672
Nov	38	15,404
Dec	35	7,444

	£	£
Sales 1,875 @ £45		84,375
Production	11,250	
Admin etc.	25,500	
Fixed costs	36,000	
Interest	896	
		73,646
Profit		10,729

Exhibit 11.17 75 per cent sales at £45

284

CONTRIBUTION ANALYSIS

In contribution analysis, two kinds of costs are considered:

- fixed, or rigid, costs;
- variable costs.

Fixed costs are those costs that are regarded as fixed, rigid, or constant over a period of time, irrespective of the level of operations or volume of sales. Examples of true fixed costs are rent and insurance; costs that may be regarded as rigid are salaries, advertising and anything that management considers is fixed for the period, usually a year. Fixed costs are necessary to be in business, and will be incurred even if the company fails to make or sell one item.

Variable costs are incurred in proportion to the amount of products made and sold, or the quantity of service supplied. Materials used in manufacture will vary with the number of products; labour required for production will vary directly with the number of products made.

The difference between fixed and variable costs is that fixed costs are related to time, variable costs to level of operations.

A distinction should be made between costs and costings. Supposing a product includes raw material costing £20, and the company makes ten products a day. The total material costing for the ten products is £200. But the company buyer doesn't buy raw material in units, or even in tens, but negotiates prices with different suppliers. Sometimes special prices or discounts are available, and the actual unit cost of the raw material will vary. Over the year the material may be purchased at an average of £18 per unit. The cost would be £18, but £20 is the costing for raw material in the product.

The labour required to make the product may take 15 minutes. If the worker is paid at a rate of, say, £8 per hour, the actual cost of labour to make the product is £2, but the costing for the labour content may be at, say, £1 a minute. The labour cost would be £8, but £15 would be the costing for the labour content.

Pricing decisions can be taken with much greater confidence if costs are broken down into their fixed and variable elements, and the product's contribution calculated.

Exhibit 11.18 shows a statement from a factory in Kent for three of its products, before contribution analysis was applied. There is

Exhibit 11.18 Kent company full absorption statement

	A (£000)	B (£000)	C (£000)	Total (£000)
Sales	600	1,400	2,400	4,400
Materials	100	160	180	440
Direct labour	20	80	180	280
Direct overhead	10	40	30	80
Total direct cost	130	280	390	800
Production overhead	136	318	546	1,000
Selling expenses	158	370	632	1,160
Administration	46	108	186	340
Cost of sales	470	1,076	1,754	3,300
Net profit	130	324	646	1,100

Exhibit 11.19 Imbalance of sales turnover and profit

Product	Sales as percentage of total turnover	Profit as percentage of total profit
A	14%	12%
B	32%	29%
C	54%	59%

considerable imbalance of sales turnover and profit. Product C has 54 per cent of the turnover and supplies 59 per cent of the profit. The full situation is shown in exhibit 11.19.

The costs are broken down into their respective fixed and variable elements. After analysis of the company's records, it was agreed that £1,740,000 costs could be regarded as fixed, and were extracted from the costings of the three products. Exhibit 11.20 is a marginal cost statement of the same information, showing each product's contribution.

The marginal cost statement takes the analysis of costs as far as they can reasonably be apportioned to products. All costs that are truly general overheads, that cannot be readily apportioned to a product, or that management decides are rigid are lumped together

Exhibit 11.20   A marginal cost statement of exhibit 11.18

	A (£000)	B (£000)	C (£000)	Total (£000)
Sales	600	1,400	2,400	4,400
Materials	100	160	180	440
Direct labour	20	80	180	280
Direct overhead	10	40	30	80
Direct cost	130	280	390	800
Variable production o/h	20	105	135	260
Production cost	150	385	525	1,060
Variable selling expenses	38	122	300	460
Variable administration	0	0	40	40
Total marginal cost	188	507	865	1,560
Contribution	412	893	1,535	2,840
Fixed overheads not allocated to products				
Production				740
Selling				700
Administration				300
Total fixed overhead				1,740
Net profit				1,100

as fixed overhead. The important figure for comparison is contribution. Contribution means contribution to fixed costs and profit.

In the absorption costing statement, exhibit 11.18 production overhead of £1,000,000, selling expenses of £1,160,000, and administration of £340,000 have been allocated to the three products according to their turnover – 14, 32 and 54 per cent respectively for *A*, *B* and *C*. This takes no account of volume, administration needed to process orders, time required to achieve sales, incidence of product in advertising and publicity, and all the other activities particular to each product.

In the marginal cost statement in exhibit 11.20, £260,000 production overhead has been apportioned to the products, product *A*

Exhibit 11.21 A fairer distribution of costs

Product	Sales as percentage of total turnover	Contribution as percentage of total contribution	Contribution as percentage of product sales
A	14%	14%	69%
B	32%	31%	64%
C	54%	54%	64%

Exhibit 11.22 Effect of increasing product *A*'s sales by 50%

	A (£000)	*B* (£000)	*C* (£000)	Total (£000)
Sales	900	1,400	2,400	4,700
Materials	150	160	180	490
Direct labour	30	80	180	290
Direct overhead	15	40	30	85
Direct cost	195	280	390	865
Variable production o/h	30	105	135	270
Production cost	225	385	525	1,135
Variable selling expenses	57	122	300	479
Variable administration	0	0	40	40
Total marginal cost	282	507	865	1,654
Contribution	618	893	1,535	3,046
Fixed overheads not allocated to products				
Production				740
Selling				700
Administration				300
Total fixed overheads				1,740
Net profit				1,306

taking 8 per cent, product *B* 40 per cent and product *C* 52 per cent. Of the allocated amount of £460,000 for selling expenses, product *A* takes a low 8.2 per cent, *B* takes 27 per cent and *C* a high 65 per cent. Of the total of £340,000 for administration, product *C* has been apportioned £40,000; the remainder of £300,000 is regarded as a general overhead.

There has thus been a considerable change in the product costings and no product is carrying costs unjustly, see exhibit 11.21.

The profit figure of £1,100,000 is the same in both statements. All three products have a high contribution. Product *A* is the highest unit earner but lowest total contributor.

Action to increase sales of product *A* would be beneficial to the company. Increasing sales by 50 per cent would increase *A*'s contribution by 50 per cent to £618,000, an additional £206,000. This would increase profit from £1,100,000 to £1,306,000. Exhibit 11.22 illustrates this.

A division of another company has four main products. One product shows a loss on an absorption costing statement. The statement is in exhibit 11.23 and the marginal costing statement in exhibit 11.24.

Exhibit 11.23 Division with a loss-making product

	A (£000)	B (£000)	C (£000)	D (£000)	Total (£000)
Sales	800	400	1,300	1,000	3,500
Materials	210	140	350	280	980
Direct labour	90	60	150	120	420
Production o/h	186	124	310	250	870
Total direct cost	486	324	810	650	2,270
Selling expenses	93	62	153	122	430
Administration	60	40	100	80	280
Cost of sales	639	426	1,063	852	2,980
Net profit	161	(26)	237	148	520

Exhibit 11.24 Marginal cost statement of exhibit 11.23

	A (£000)	B (£000)	C (£000)	D (£000)	Total (£000)
Sales	800	400	1,300	1,000	3,500
Materials	210	140	350	280	980
Direct labour	90	60	150	120	420
Var. prod. o/h	60	50	90	70	270
Marg. prod. cost	360	250	590	470	1,670
Var. sell. exes.	30	10	40	50	130
Var. admin. cost	0	0	0	0	0
Marginal cost	390	260	630	520	1,800
Contribution	410	140	670	480	1,700
Fixed overheads					
Production					600
Selling					300
Administration					280
					1,180
Net profit					520

The profit is the same, but the marginal costs of making the products have been taken to their respective contributions. The 'losing' product, product *B*, is making a contribution of £140,000. If it is not possible to increase the price of product *B*, and it is dropped from the range, an amended marginal cost statement, exhibit 11.25, shows a loss of profit equal to the contribution by product *B*.

SUMMARY OF CONTRIBUTION ANALYSIS

- Costs are divided into two main categories: fixed and variable.
- Fixed costs accrue with time and, within broad limits, are normally independent of the level of sales.

Exhibit 11.25 Position with 'loss-making' product dropped

	A (£000)	B (£000)	C (£000)	D (£000)	Total (£000)
Sales	800		1,300	1,000	3,100
Materials	210		350	280	840
Direct labour	90		150	120	360
Var. prod. o/h	60		90	70	220
Marg. prod. cost	360		590	470	1,420
Var. sell. exes.	30		40	50	120
Var. admin. cost	0		0	0	0
Marginal cost	390		630	520	1,540
Contribution	410		670	480	1,560
Fixed overheads					
Production					600
Selling					300
Administration					280
					1,180
Net profit					380

- Variable costs are those needed to produce and handle the products or service and are directly proportionate to changes in volume.
- Unit price less unit variable cost is unit contribution.
- Unit contribution multiplied by the sales volume equals the total contribution.
- Break-even point is when total contribution equals total fixed costs.
- The amount that total contribution exceeds break-even point is profit.
- The amount of total contribution that is less than break-even point equals loss.
- Fixed, or rigid costs are not normally allocated to products but absorbed by the products' contributions.

- Contribution analysis can be applied to any time period, yearly, monthly, weekly and even daily.
- Contribution analysis is used to supply quick decisions while maintaining control of costs and profits.

BENEFITS OF CONTRIBUTION ANALYSIS

- Price setting and product-mix decisions are made easier because of a greater understanding of the cost-price relationship.
- There is more accurate and extensive knowledge of product profitability.
- Profit control is improved because more detailed and relevant financial information is available.
- There is more effective cost control.
- There is better understanding of how expenditures and capital investments affect profit.
- Losers can be more quickly and easily identified.
- Plans for expansion are made easier.
- Make-or-buy decisions are easier to assess.
- There is more confidence in bids and tenders.
- Financial projections can be quickly updated.

SETTING A PRICE

Irrespective of the method used to analyse costs when setting prices, the fixed costs of running an organization have to be paid for. While the contribution analysis approach has a number of benefits, there are occasions when it is necessary to consider the allocation of overheads in some detail in the construction of prices.

Various methods of apportioning overheads appropriate to the products and pricing problem should be explored; the one that is adopted should be equitable to all products. Periodic review may be necessary to remove minor inconsistencies, particularly if new products with widely disparate material and labour costs are added to the company's range.

	£	£
Estimated sales		120,000
less Production costs		
Materials	24,000	
Direct labour	12,000	
		36,000
		84,000
less General expenses		60,000
Projected profit (+25%)		24,000 = 20%

Exhibit 11.26 Projected profit and loss account

Exhibit 11.27 Year's projected sales and costs

	X	Y	Z	Totals
Sales (units)	360	1,200	200	1,760
	(£)	(£)	(£)	(£)
Cost materials	7,560	13,200	3,240	24,000
Direct labour	1,260	2,400	8,340	12,000
Total direct cost	8,820	15,600	11,580	36,000

A company is planning sales of £120,000. Production costs are £36,000 and all other costs and expenses come to £60,000. The company normally makes a profit of 20 per cent, and 25 per cent is added to costs to achieve this. This is illustrated in exhibit 11.26. There are three products X, Y and Z, and the individual product sales, costs of materials and labour are set out in exhibit 11.27.

The company wishes to set prices. When calculating the total cost of producing each product, the general overheads of £60,000 need to be apportioned in a way that is fair and reasonable to each one.

The simplest way of doing this, which we shall call Method 1, is to allocate a third of the total overhead to each. This is illustrated in exhibit 11.28.

Exhibit 11.28 Method 1: overheads allocated equally to products

	X	Y	Z	Totals
Sales (units)	360	1,200	200	1,760
	(£)	(£)	(£)	(£)
Total direct costs	8,820	15,600	11,580	36,000
Allocated overheads	20,000	20,000	20,000	60,000
Total cost	28,820	35,600	31,580	96,000
Unit cost	80.06	29.67	157.90	
Profit (+25%)	20.01	7.42	39.48	
Price	100.07	37.08	197.38	
Total profit	7,204	8,904	7,896	24,004

Exhibit 11.29 Method 1: a fourth product enters the scene

	X	Y	Z	N	Totals
Sales (units)	360	1,200	200	10	1,770
	(£)	(£)	(£)	(£)	(£)
Total direct costs	8,820	15,600	11,580	50	36,050
Allocated overheads	15,000	15,000	15,000	15,000	60,000
Total cost	23,820	30,600	26,580	15,050	96,000
Unit cost	66.17	25.50	132.90	1,505.00	
Profit (+25%)	16.54	6.38	33.23	376.25	
Price	82.71	31.88	166.13	1,881.25	

However, Method 1 fails to take into consideration sales volume. Product Y has six times the volume of product Z. Generally, the higher the sales volume, the greater the use of general overheads by a product. In addition, with this method of allocation, if a new product were introduced, it would have to carry an equal share of overhead from the start. Exhibit 11.29 shows what happens to exhibit 11.28 when we add a fourth product, N, with low sales. The price of N is seen to be completely unacceptable. There is no need to calculate total revenue!

The inclusion of N produces a dramatic decrease in the prices of X, Y and Z because each of them takes £5,000 less of the £60,000 overheads. While this is not a realistic exercise, it highlights the importance of the allocation of overheads.

Exhibit 11.30 Method 2: overheads according to volume

	X	Y	Z	*Totals*
Sales (units)	360	1,200	200	1,760
	(£)	(£)	(£)	(£)
Total direct costs	8,820	15,600	11,580	36,000
Allocated overheads	12,273	40,909	6,818	60,000
Total cost	21,093	56,509	18,398	96,000
Unit cost	58.59	47.09	92.00	
Profit (+25%)	14.65	11.77	23.00	
Price	73.24	58.86	115.00	
Total profit	5,274	14,124	4,600	23,998

Exhibit 11.31 Unit materials and labour costs

	X	Y	Z	Totals
Sales (units)	360	1,200	200	1,760
	(£)	(£)	(£)	(£)
Direct materials	7,560	13,200	3,240	24,000
Direct labour	1,260	2,400	8,340	12,000
Total direct cost	8,820	15,600	11,580	36,000
Unit materials cost	21.00	11.00	16.20	
Unit labour cost	3.50	2.00	41.70	

Method 2 is to apportion the general overhead according to volume. Thus:

$$X \text{ is } (60,000/1,760) \times 360 = 12,273$$
$$Y \text{ is } (60,000/1,760) \times 1,200 = 40,909$$
$$Z \text{ is } (60,000/1,760) \times 200 = 6,818$$

The result of applying Method 2 to X, Y and Z is shown in exhibit 11.30.

Method 3 makes use of unit material and labour costs of products, which are calculated in exhibit 11.31. Product X has the highest unit cost of materials; product Z requires much greater unit labour costs.

Exhibit 11.32 Method 3: 200 per cent materials and 100 per cent labour

	X	Y	Z	Totals
Sales (units)	360	1,200	200	1,760
	(£)	(£)	(£)	(£)
Direct materials	7,560	13,200	3,240	24,000
Direct labour	1,260	2,400	8,340	12,000
Unit materials cost	21.00	11.00	16.20	
Overhead (+200%)	42.00	22.00	32.40	48,000
Unit labour cost	3.50	2.00	41.70	
Overhead (+100%)	3.50	2.00	41.70	12,000
Total unit direct cost	70.00	37.00	132.00	
Profit (+25%)	17.50	9.25	33.00	
Price	87.50	46.25	165.00	
Total profit	6,300	11,100	6,600	24,000

Exhibit 11.33 Method 4: overheads based on direct costs

	X	Y	Z	Totals
Sales (units)	360	1,200	200	1,760
	(£)	(£)	(£)	(£)
Total direct costs	8,820	15,600	11,580	36,000
Allocated overheads	14,700	26,000	19,300	60,000
Total cost	23,520	41,600	30,880	96,000
Unit cost	65.33	34.67	154.40	
Profit (+25%)	16.33	8.67	38.60	
Price	81.66	43.34	193.00	
Total profit	5,879	10,404	7,720	24,003

Therefore, to allocate costs based on materials would penalize product X; to allocate them based on the labour content would penalize product Z with over 20 times as much labour content as product Y.

When there is a wide disparity between unit costs of materials and labour it is difficult to establish an equitable method of allocating costs based on them. To illustrate, in exhibit 11.32 the £60,000 has

Exhibit 11.34 Summary of the results of the four methods

	X (£)	Y (£)	Z (£)
Method 1	100.07	37.08	197.38
Method 2	73.24	58.86	114.99
Method 3	87.50	46.25	165.00
Method 4	81.67	43.34	193.00

Note: Unit and decimal discrepancies are the result of rounding up on computer.

Exhibit 11.35 Checking that the total profits are correct

	Product	Sales	Price (£)	Revenue (£)	Total profit (£)
Method 1	X	360	100.07	36,025	7,204
(⅓ to each)	Y	1,200	37.08	44,500	8,904
	Z	200	197.38	39,475	7,896
				120,000	24,004
Method 2	X	360	73.24	26,366	5,274
(by volume)	Y	1,200	58.86	70,632	14,124
	Z	200	115.00	23,000	4,600
				119,998	23,998
Method 3	X	360	87.50	31,500	6,300
(200% materials	Y	1,200	46.25	55,500	11,100
100% of labour)	Z	200	165.00	33,000	6,600
				120,000	24,000
Method 4	X	360	81.67	29,400	5,879
(on direct costs)	Y	1,200	43.34	52,008	10,404
	Z	200	193.00	38,600	7,720
				120,008	24,003

Note: Unit and decimal discrepancies are the result of rounding up on computer.

been apportioned by 200 per cent of the unit materials, 100 per cent of unit labour.

It appears to be more equitable to apportion general overheads to products according to their total direct costs. Thus:

$$X \quad 8,820/36,000 \times 60,000 = 14,700$$
$$Y \quad 15,600/36,000 \times 60,000 = 26,000$$
$$Z \quad 11,580/36,000 \times 60,000 = 19,300$$

This is the basis of Method 4, set out in exhibit 11.33.

Thus, with four different methods of allocating the £60,000 over-heads, four different suggested prices have been obtained. These are shown in exhibit 11.34; exhibit 11.35 checks that these figures produce the correct total profit.

THE SALES VERSUS ACCOUNTING PROBLEM

The pricing problem is made clearer when we compare the relative prices, total profits and percentage of total profits of the three products for each of the four methods of allocating overheads. Exhibit 11.36 summarizes the results.

If it is desired that product Z should be sold at the lowest price, then Method 2 should be adopted. But this puts a high burden on product Y, which is required to supply 59 per cent of the total profit.

Prices suggested using such costing methods should be used as a base on which to build the selected price after estimating likely demand responses from the target market.

WHEN WE DON'T MAKE QUOTA

From the discussions in previous chapters, you will appreciate that planning to recover fixed overheads on 100 per cent level of operations leaves no room for manoeuvre. Also, if prices are computed on the same basis, failing to achieve the sales estimate erodes profit.

The problem is two-edged. If you compute to recover fixed over-heads at less than 100 per cent of activity, prices will obviously be higher; if prices are higher, sales could be depressed.

Exhibit 11.36 Prices and profits using the four methods

	X	Y	Z	Totals
Sales estimate (units)	360	1,200	200	1,760
Method 1				
Price	£100.07	£37.08	£197.38	
Revenue	£6,025	£44,500	£39,475	£120,000
Total profit	£7,205	£8,900	£7,895	£24,000
Percentage of total profit	30%	37%	33%	
Method 2				
Price	£73.24	£58.86	£114.99	
Revenue	£26,366	£70,636	£22,998	£120,000
Total profit	£5,273	£14,127	£4,600	£24,000
Percentage of total profit	22%	59%	19%	
Method 3				
Price	£87.50	£46.25	£165.00	
Revenue	£31,500	£55,500	£33,000	£120,000
Total profit	£6,300	£11,100	£6,600	£24,000
Percentage of total profit	26%	46%	28%	
Method 4				
Price	£81.67	£43.33	£193.00	
Revenue	£29,400	£52,000	£38,600	£120,000
Total profit	£5,880	£10,400	£7,720	£24,000
Percentage of total profit	25%	43%	32%	

It is highly unlikely that all products will achieve the same percentage performance, and to be realistic the situation should be set up in a spreadsheet. Countless 'what if' situations can be reviewed with varying percentages of individual product sales being assessed. The situation could be further explored by varying the profit content of the products, using different prices and calculating potential results at various levels of product sales.

The various situations are shown in exhibit 11.37, using Method 4 to compute prices because it spreads the burden of overheads and also for the achievement of profit. Prices are first computed on 100 per cent of operations, where the forecast 1,760 units are sold; then the position is illustrated where instead only 80 per cent, 75 per cent or 70 per cent of each were sold.

Exhibit 11.37 Position at 100 per cent, 80 per cent, 75 per cent and 70 per cent of sales

	X	Y	Z	Totals
Forecast sales (units)	360	1,200	200	1,760
	(£)	(£)	(£)	(£)
Materials and labour	8,820	15,600	11,580	36,000
Method 4 overheads	14,700	26,000	19,300	60,000
Total cost	23,520	41,600	30,880	96,000
Forecast revenue	29,400	52,000	38,600	120,000
Method 4 prices	81.66	43.34	193.00	
80% sales achieved	288	960	160	1,408
	(£)	(£)	(£)	(£)
Reduced revenue	23,518	52,008	38,600	114,126
Profit at 80%	(2)	10,408	7,720	18,126
75% sales achieved	270	900	150	1,320
	(£)	(£)	(£)	(£)
Reduced revenue	22,048	39,006	28,950	90,004
Profit at 75%	(1,472)	(2,594)	(1,930)	(5,996)
70% sales achieved	252	840	140	1,232
	(£)	(£)	(£)	(£)
Reduced revenue	20,578	36,397	27,020	83,995
Profit at 70%	(2,942)	(5,203)	(3,860)	(12,005)

As with most pricing procedures, the calculations very quickly become complicated and tedious when too many 'what if' situations are considered. It is much easier and quicker to set up a file in a PC spreadsheet. Exhibit 11.38 is exhibit 11.37 set up to receive different total sales performances. The formulae are as follows:

Rows [3] [5] [6] [7] [8] and [9] take the data already known.

Row [11] is for data to be entered. In this first example, '90%' has been entered into [A11] and a formula for 90 per cent in [B11] copied across [C11] to [E11].

```
[B11]   +B3*0.9            copy across [C11]..[E11]
[B13]   +B11*B9            copy across [C13]..[D13]
[E13]   +B13+C13+D13
```

Pricing tools

	[A]	[B]	[C]	[D]	[E]
[1]	*<File name>*				
[2]		X	Y	Z	Totals
[3]	Forecast sales	360	1,200	200	1,760
[4]		(£)	(£)	(£)	(£)
[5]	Materials and labour	8,820	15,600	11,580	36,000
[6]	Method 4 overheads	14,700	26,000	19,300	60,000
[7]	Total cost	23,520	41,600	30,880	96,000
[8]	Forecast revenue	29,401	52,000	38,600	120,001
[9]	Method 4 prices	81.67	43.33	193.00	
[10]					
[11]	90 % achieved	324	1080	180	1,584
[12]		(£)	(£)	(£)	(£)
[13]	Reduced revenue	26,461	46,800	34,740	108,001
[14]	Profit at 90%	2,941	5,200	3,860	12,001

Exhibit 11.38 Layout for use by entering various sales levels

[11]	80 % achieved	288	960	160	1408
[12]		(£)	(£)	(£)	(£)
[13]	Reduced revenue	23,521	41,600	30,880	96,001
[14]	Profit at 80%	1	(0)	0	1

Exhibit 11.39 Layout of exhibit 11.38 with 80 per cent sales estimate

[11]	75 % achieved	270	900	150	1320
[12]		(£)	(£)	(£)	(£)
[13]	Reduced revenue	22,051	39,000	28,950	90,001
[14]	Profit at 75%	(1,469)	(2,600)	(1,930)	(5,999)

Exhibit 11.40 Layout of exhibit 11.38 with 75 per cent sales estimate

[A14] is amended from '90%' to whatever percentage is inserted in [A11] and in the formula in [B11].

```
[B14]  +B13-B7 copy across [C14]..[D14]
[E14]  +B14+C14+D14
```

With this basic spreadsheet layout, only row [11] and [A14] need to be amended. Exhibits 11.39–11.41 have been taken from the same layout, with different percentage levels having been inserted.

[11]	70 % achieved	252	840	140	1232
[12]		(£)	(£)	(£)	(£)
[13]	Reduced revenue	20,581	36,400	27,020	84,001
[14]	Profit at 75%	(2,939)	(5,200)	(3,860)	(11,999)

Exhibit 11.41 Layout of exhibit 11.38 with 70 per cent sales estimate

[31]		X	Y	Z	Totals
[32]	Forecast sales	360	1,200	200	1,760
[33]	Percentage likely	90%	75%	60%	
[34]	Resulting sales	324	900	120	
[35]		(£)	(£)	(£)	(£)
[36]	Method 4 prices	81.67	43.33	193.00	
[37]	Turnover likely	26,461	39,000	23,160	88,621
[38]	Total cost	23,520	41,600	30,880	96,000
[39]	Likely profit	2,941	(2,600)	(7,720)	(7,379)

Exhibit 11.42 Layout for product sales variations

The layout in exhibit 11.42 is slightly more complex to allow for different percentage sales performances to be entered into the row 'Percentage likely'. The modifications to the spreadsheet are as follows:

Rows [32] [36] and [38] take the data already known.

Row [32] is the same as row [3] above.

Row [36] same as row [9].

Row [38] same as row [7].

Row [33] is for entering the percentage sales thought likely to be achieved for each product. All the remaining figures are automatically adjusted.

```
[B37]  +B34*B36              copy across [C37]..[D37]
[E37]  +B37+C37+D37                 copy down [E38]
[B39]  +B37-B38              copy across [C39]..[E39]
```

In exhibits 11.43 and 11.44 the layout in exhibit 11.42 has been used with different percentage sales figures inserted for the three products in the 'Percentage likely' row.

[31]	X	Y	Z	Totals
[32] Forecast sales	360	1,200	200	1,760
[33] Percentage likely	75%	75%	60%	
[34] Resulting sales	270	900	120	
[35]	(£)	(£)	(£)	(£)
[36] Method 4 prices	81.67	43.33	193.00	
[37] Turnover likely	22,051	39,000	23,160	84,211
[38] Total cost	23,520	41,600	30,880	96,000
[39] Likely profit	(1,469)	(2,600)	(7,720)	(11,789)

Exhibit 11.43 Layout of exhibit 11.42 with product sales below forecast

[31]	X	Y	Z	Totals
[32] Forecast sales	360	1,200	200	1,760
[33] Percentage likely	60%	70%	50%	
[34] Resulting sales	216	840	100	
[35]	(£)	(£)	(£)	(£)
[36] Method 4 prices	81.67	43.33	193.00	
[37] Turnover likely	17,641	36,400	19,300	73,340
[38] Total cost	23,520	41,600	30,880	96,000
[39] Likely profit	(5,879)	(5,200)	(11,580)	(22,660)

Exhibit 11.44 Layout of exhibit 11.42 with product sales well below forecast

AN EXAMPLE FROM FMCG

Using contribution a product makes to fixed overheads as a basis for pricing has been developed to a fine art in fast moving consumer goods (FMCG), especially, in the toiletries market. In particular, the hair shampoo market has grown out of all recognition since the 1960s.

As listed in exhibit 10.1 of chapter 10, liquid shampoo was originally conceived in 1950, but it was not until 1958 that it was commercialized. In the 1960s only a handful of products was available, and consumer brand loyalty was very high. Ten years later approximately 80 per cent of customers maintained that they tried to purchase the same brand but by 1980 this number had fallen to around 60 per cent.

Hair is not merely washed now; it is shampooed, conditioned, treated, tinted, coloured, styled and lacquered in position. The UK

Exhibit 11.45 UK hair care market in 1989

Product	£ million
Hair colorants	50
Hair conditioners	65
Hairsprays	123
Setting agents: mousses, lotions, and gels	70
Shampoos	167
	475

market for hair products is worth around £475 million, as shown in exhibit 11.45.

The customer is besieged with manufacturers' offers of new products containing additives, conditioners, natural colouring, ozone-friendly propellants and a variety of publicity, refunds, coupons, contests and a host of promotional gimmicks. Brand proliferation is the order of the day and brand-switching is rife.

Manufacturers support their brands with extensive and aggressive marketing techniques, especially with consumer and trade promotions. Allowances and discounts are offered to retailers for use of some of their limited counter and display space. With the increasing adoption of checkout scanners, more accurate data is available to retailer and manufacturer on actual brand sales patterns. With all this information becoming common knowledge, pricing is a major factor in determining the success in the market of products of similar performance. Premium products have their own segment, maintaining their image with price, packaging, perfume, psychological appeal, or various combinations of the four.

Analytically assessing competition and likely competitive reactions and responses is as important as analysing prices, turnover and profits. When assessing the comparability of products, prior to constructing a product's price structure, all products in the same product/value/market should be considered, and a selection made of those judged to be comparable.

Exhibit 11.46 Prices and discounts of competitive products

Product	Average retail price (£)	Trade discount (%)	Incentive discount (%)	Unit price (£)	Retailer Margin (£)	(%)
A	1.80	20.0%	8.0%	1.32	0.48	26%
B	1.45	18.0%	10.0%	1.07	0.38	26%
C	1.25	20.0%	10.0%	0.90	0.35	28%
D	1.15	17.5%	12.5%	0.83	0.32	28%
E	0.95	15.0%	10.0%	0.73	0.22	23%
F	0.85	12.5%	8.0%	0.68	0.17	19%

First, the prices of products in the focus group are established; it is assumed that it will not be practicable to find out the costs of production, and these are omitted from the comparative analysis.

Early in 1989 a company had developed a product to sell at around £1.50 against six competitive products with similar performance, ranging in price from 85p to £1.80. Competitive costs and discounts were obtained from company sales people, by inspection at various retail outlets, and from friendly retailers. These are listed in exhibit 11.46.

The maximum retail price for a comparable product, was £1.80; the operating margins varied from 19 per cent to 28 per cent. Applying these two margins to £1.80, they estimated a lower and upper price for their product of £1.30 and £1.46. Their initial idea to price around £1.50 fell just outside this range of what the market would expect to pay, but they still aimed to position their product towards the top of the group.

Many companies encourage retailers to display their products by giving a display allowance, subject to certain conditions being met, such as minimum shelf exposure and period of time. Unfortunately it is not always possible to monitor retailers' performance in this respect, and the allowance becomes just another discount that is available. Exhibit 11.47 shows the display allowances given by the six competitors.

The price structure that the company thought would be acceptable in the market was a price at least equal to product A and a

Exhibit 11.47 Display allowances

Product	Retailer unit price (£)	Display allowance per dozen (£)	Unit net cost to retailer (£)	Display allowance margin (%)
A	1.32	1.25	1.22	8%
B	1.07	1.75	0.92	14%
C	0.90	1.50	0.78	14%
D	0.83	1.00	0.75	10%
E	0.73	0.50	0.69	6%
F	0.68	0.75	0.62	9%

Exhibit 11.48 Alternative pricing options

	Option (A) (£)		Option (B) (£)
Retail price		1.75	1.75
	less 20%	0.35	less 20% 0.35
		1.40	1.40
	less 10%	0.14	less 5% 0.07
Price to retailer		1.26	1.33
Display allowance	1.00/dozen		2.00/dozen

display allowance comparable with product *B*. Therefore, they set retail price at £1.75 and considered two possible structures: list less 20, less 10 per cent with a display allowance of £1 per dozen; list less 20, less 5 per cent with a display allowance of £2 per dozen. The two price structures are set out in exhibit 11.48, and profit analysis in exhibit 11.49.

If the company's objective is to get the lowest price at retail, option (A) is preferred. However, this puts an emphasis on price at the expense of promotion. If price is not considered to be crucial at the customer level, then option (B) is to be preferred because it has double the amount of display advertising.

Exhibit 11.49 Contribution for new product, based on projected sales of 5,000,000

	Option (A) (£000)		Option (B) (£000)
Revenue @ £1.26/unit	6,300	@£1.33/unit	6,650
Production cost	2,835		2,835
	3,465		3,815
Display allowance @ £1/dozen	417	@ £2/dozen	833
	3,048		2,982
Advertising (8%)	504		504
	2,544		2,478
Marketing expenses (25%)	1,575		1,575
Contribution	969		903
	15.4%		13.6%

While (A) provides £66,000 more contribution to the company, option (B) provides £350,000 more revenue. As the company wished to increase its image in the market, it chose option (B).

12

Creative pricing

DIFFERENT BASES

Creative pricing may be oriented to three main bases: cost-oriented, demand-oriented and competitive-oriented.

Cost-oriented pricing offers the least scope for creative pricing and is mainly an internally controlled activity. It focuses on any competitive advantages in the basic cost and the marketing element in the oncost component. Pricing related to basic cost depends largely on the skills of the buying and production departments, and the extent to which their managers are marketing oriented. Most of the creative content in cost-pricing relates to differential production costing, which is discussed later in this chapter.

The oncosts include all the percentage mark-ups and profit-targeted prices. Percentage mark-ups are inserted in the pricing structure at points where they achieve predetermined amounts for various overheads, middlemen's profit, advertising and selling expenses. The percentages may be compounded, that is, calculated as a percentage of a percentage, or added together and one oncost applied.

Subtle differences may be achieved with percentage discounts. A list price which is 'less 30, less 20, less 10' is 50.4 per cent of the original price. List less the total of the percentages, 60 per cent, is 40 per cent of the original price.

There is limited creativity in pricing based on costs. This might best be appreciated by comparing the basic cost component for a piece of canvas covered with different coloured pigments – say, £20 – and its price. Even with generous allowances for wear and tear of equipment and hefty overheads, the price for a painting by a celebrated painter would bear no relationship to its cost-price.

Cost-oriented pricing is appropriate in inelastic situations such as with certain pharmaceuticals, although products that emanate from research-based operations should not use a cost-oriented approach. Patents can protect company market position, but basing price on costs misses the opportunity of creative pricing possibilities, forgoes profit, and curtails the company's future ability to maintain its research activities.

Demand-oriented pricing is perceived value pricing strategy that may be implemented with differential pricing tactics. The product is priced according to the benefits perceived by customers. These may be estimated within the company or, if time and resources permit, developed with market research such as group interviews where the members' willingness to pay the suggested price is evaluated. When estimating price with this method, the focus groups must reflect the general tendencies of customers in the target market.

Differential pricing is charging the various segments different prices that reflect their perceived value and do not relate directly to marginal costs. The segments may be geographical, with different prices charged to different sub-markets, or they may be temporal, where different prices are charged at different times: these may be daily, seasonal, or related to the period over which the product is marketed, such as with fashion goods. Perhaps the most widely known temporal market is the 'happy hour' at hotels and bars, where prices are lower for a period early in the evening.

Competitive-oriented pricing is basing price on competitive products with similar performance or perceived value. Before this can be done, a thorough analysis of the market is essential, because the real competition is not always the company making similar products; it is often alternative products or new technology. It does not mean copying competitors' prices; it is setting price *in relation* to competitors. Thus, a comparatively high or low price could be adopted depending on the relative market positions of the competing products. Careful estimation of product positioning, as discussed in chapter 6, is necessary for a competitive-oriented pricing strategy and any associated tactics, such as penetrating the market, skimming the market, or focusing on a part of the market.

DIFFERENTIAL PRICING

When all fixed costs have been recovered or it is clear from the rate of sales being achieved that fixed costs will be recovered, marginal cost can be used as a basis for creative pricing. Marginal price, which is based on marginal cost, can be quoted for additional sales volume or other products.

A company sells 50,000 products, with a unit variable cost of £20, at a price of £60, and recovers the fixed costs of £250,000 with a £5 element in the price. Sales turnover is £3 million. If an enquiry to supply a new market is received, the lowest price that can be quoted is a marginal price based on the marginal cost of £20.

The company has scope for creative pricing and can set the price between £20 and £60. Competition, likely competitive response, and the present customer base, must be considered; analysing the figures alone is insufficient.

If the enquiry is to supply an identifiable product, pricing it at less than £60 in the new market requires that there is little or no communication between the customers in the current and new markets.

If the two markets are not discrete and independent of each other, pricing below £60 takes on a different aspect. Four main market situations are possible as set out in exhibit 12.1.

A necessary condition for the assessment of this particular pricing problem is that the fixed costs charge will be recovered from existing sales.

	Markets not discrete	Separate markets
Product identifiable	Market Type A High price near to £60	Market Type B Price £20–£60
Product not identifiable	Market Type C Price £20–£60	Market Type D Low Price near to £20

Exhibit 12.1 Four market types

What militates against setting a price towards marginal cost is that the sales mix can seldom be controlled. If the company was experiencing tough competition, and had the opportunity to supply to a market type *D*, an unidentifiable product to a completely separate market, it might be tempted to base price on the marginal cost of £20.

Marginal price contributes little, if anything, to fixed overhead. If the new market starts to expand at the marginal price, the company is committed to selling a product at an uneconomic price, and loses the opportunity of making considerable profits. If, at the same time, current market sales decrease, serious under-recovery of overheads will result.

Creative opportunities exist for companies selling in type *A* markets and willing to adopt a mixed brand, or mixed product strategy. The company sells at one price in the *A* type market, repackages the product, renames it, or both, and sets a lower price in a *C* or *D* market.

The potentially dangerous market is type *B*. The conditions that exist that make the markets interdependent must be such that they cannot subsequently be eroded. Obvious examples are overseas markets where it is possible to sell at a lower price than in the home market. But adopting this as a pricing strategy lays the seller open to serious financial difficulties if the overseas market expands. Where differential pricing is used, the oncost component should contain a substantial contribution to overheads.

If a fixed cost element is included in the price structure the price could then be regarded as the lowest base price. In this example the fixed cost contribution could be anything up to £5 per unit, making the lowest base price £25.

The company should be more concerned with profits. It would be better practice to price the product at £60 and negotiate discounts up to a maximum of, say, 40 per cent. This would provide a low price of £36 that would cover variable cost, contribution to fixed overhead, and £11 to profit and other expenses.

DIFFERENTIAL PRODUCTION COSTS

Consider the situation frequently observed in companies where a certain number of products can be produced at an average cost, and a greater number at a lower average cost.

	£
Sales	
100 @ £3,000	300,000
100 @ £2,200	220,000
	520,000
Manufactured	
200 units @ £2,400	480,000
Profit	40,000
	= 7.7%

Exhibit 12.2 Sales at two price levels

A company is able to produce 100 units of its product at an average cost of £3,200. If it produces 200 units the average cost falls to £2,400 per unit.

The marketing department has qualified 100 customers and established that they are in the market for the product, and have currently budgeted to acquire it, but not at £3,200. The average budgeted price that the 100 customers are prepared to pay is £3,000.

In another market, a further 100 customers have been identified and qualified. They are proposing to buy the product in the near future but the price they are prepared to buy at averages out at £2,200.

On the face of it the company is unable to satisfy either segment because the costs exceed acceptable prices for each one. However, by exploiting the time factor in the buying intentions of the customers, the company can market its products profitably.

It produces at the level of 200 units at a cost of £2,400 each. It sells the first 100 units produced to the first market segment at £3,000. Subsequently, it sells the next 100 units at £3,000 discounted down to £2,200. The position is shown in exhibit 12.2.

This is the principle involved in price-cutting old models, high-pricing scarce products, skimming the market with a new product, off-peak travel, out-of-season vacations, matinée seats at theatres, school trips, off-peak electricity, periodic sales and discounting of end-of-season goods, and many other examples.

DIFFERENTIAL DISCOUNTS

Careful analysis is necessary when using different discounts for the second and subsequent market segments. If it is confined to trans-

Exhibit 12.3 Cash flow with immediate payment

	Jan	Feb	Mar	Apl	May	Jun
Sales	20	20	20	20	20	20
Revenue	60,000	60,000	60,000	60,000	60,000	44,000
Manufacturing	48,000	48,000	48,000	48,000	48,000	48,000
Cash flow +/(-)	12,000	12,000	12,000	12,000	12,000	(4,000)
Balance b/fwd		12,000	24,000	36,000	48,000	60,000
Balance c/fwd	12,000	24,000	36,000	48,000	60,000	56,000

	Jul	Aug	Sep	Oct	Nov	Dec
Sales	20	20	20	20		
Revenue	44,000	44,000	44,000	44,000		
Manufacturing	48,000	48,000	48,000	48,000		
Cash flow +/(-)	(4,000)	(4,000)	(4,000)	(4,000)		
Balance b/fwd	56,000	52,000	48,000	44,000		
Interest						
Balance c/fwd	52,000	48,000	44,000	40,000		

Exhibit 12.4 Cash flow with normal credit terms

	Jan	Feb	Mar	Apl	May	Jun
Sales	20	20	20	20	20	20
Revenue			60,000	60,000	60,000	60,000
Manufacturing	48,000	48,000	48,000	48,000	48,000	48,000
Cash flow +/(-)	(48,000)	(48,000)	12,000	12,000	12,000	12,000
Balance b/fwd		(48,000)	(96,480)	(85,445)	(74,299)	(63,042)
Interest		(480)	(965)	(854)	(743)	(630)
Balance c/fwd	(48,000)	(96,480)	(85,445)	(74,299)	(63,042)	(51,673)

	Jul	Aug	Sep	Oct	Nov	Dec
Sales	20	20	20	20		
Revenue	60,000	44,000	44,000	44,000	44,000	44,000
Manufacturing	48,000	48,000	48,000	48,000		
Cash flow +/(-)	12,000	(4,000)	(4,000)	(4,000)	44,000	44,000
Balance b/fwd	(51,673)	(40,189)	(44,591)	(49,037)	(53,528)	(10,063)
Interest	(517)	(402)	(446)	(490)	(535)	(101)
Balance c/fwd	(40,189)	(44,591)	(49,037)	(53,528)	(10,063)	33,837

actions where payment is made at the time of purchase, little difficulty will be experienced. Even with high-priced goods, if no credit has to be given, judicious secondary discounting of a product can achieve an acceptable overall profit. Consider the cash flow in exhibit 12.3 for the 200 units produced and sold at a rate of 20 a month for ten months. The first 100 units are sold at £3,000, the second 100, at £2,200.

The situation is perilous if normal credit has to be given. Exhibit 12.4 shows the same transactions as exhibit 12.3 but with payment for the product received two months after delivery. It is necessary to fund the operation up to nearly £100,000, the interest payment on the loan is over £6,000, and the cash balance remains negative until December. If one or more payments were late arriving – not an unusual occurrence – the cash position would be considerably worse.

Proposals for such multi-segment pricing with sales on credit must be supported by conservative cash flow estimates and, preferably, with allowances being made for a substantial proportion of the customers not paying on time.

RANDOM DISCOUNTING

For products and services sold for cash in different market segments at different prices, the focus is not so much on cash flow as on the discounting tactics. Using the same gross figures as in the example, a similar situation occurs where a company could manufacture 100,000 of a product at an average cost of £3.20; if it sets production at the 200,000 level, the average cost falls to £2.40. But half the customers will buy at £3, the other half at £2.20.

By producing at the higher level, the lower average cost of £2.40 enables the company to sell the first 100,000 at 20 per cent profit. After the first 100,000 have been sold, the cash and stock position would be as in exhibit 12.5.

The company could clear the debt of £180,000 by selling the stock of 100,000 at a break-even price of £180,000/100,000 = £1.80, but this would be a drastic last-ditch tactic and not sound business.

If secondary markets were interested at a price of around £2.20, the position would be similar to the gross figures in the previous example.

	£
Manufactured 200,000 @ £2.40	480,000
Sales 100,000 @ £3	300,000
	(180,000)
Stock 100,000 @ £2.40	240,000

Exhibit 12.5 Cash and stock position after 100,000 sales

The strategy is to price in the secondary market at the same as in the primary market, £3.00, but to use random discounting down to a maximum of 30 per cent. £3 less 30 per cent is £2.1.

Much will depend on the nature of the product, whether it is a repeat purchase, the buying habits of customer, and the degree of search normally associated with the purchase. The condition for adopting random discounting is the dissimilarity of customers' search characteristics, which enables customers with a good knowledge of prices to be attracted by discounts. The time, trouble and cost of search by potential customers must be at least offset by the size of the discount.

Customers not so well informed will be attracted by more modest discounts. The strategy is to implement a random discounting procedure that provides an overall discounted price of around £2.20, with £1.80 as the eventual 'end-of-line' clear-out price.

Assuming average prices of £3 and £2.20 for the primary and secondary markets, the situation would be as in exhibit 12.6.

PERCEIVED VALUE PRICING

Customers buy products for what they will do, not for what they are. It is not only the intrinsic value in a product's use that comprises the benefit; a product that is available where and when the customer wants it is a product benefit. It is the total perceived value.

Consider the benefit of being able to purchase an ordinary electric lamp when it is needed – usually when it is dark, no spares are to

315

	£	£	£
Sales 100,000 @ £3		300,000	
Manufactured 200,000 @ £2.40	480,000		
Less closing stock 100,000 @ £2.40	240,000		
Cost of goods sold		240,000	
Initial profit			60,000
Sales 100,000 @ £2.20		220,000	
Cost of goods sold		240,000	
			(20,000)
Final profit			40,000

Exhibit 12.6 Final profit from the secondary market

hand and all the shops are shut. The availability of such lamps would be a benefit. This same situation used to apply to motor car bulbs but garages now carry adequate ranges and supply the benefit of having the product available when it is needed by the customer.

In effect, customers are buying 'bundles of benefits' and the price paid is for some or all of those benefits, but not all of which will appeal to all customers.

When non-food items are offered for sale in what is substantially a food supermarket, customers are being provided with the convenience of not having to make a separate trip to another store in addition to the product. It was this thinking that led Marks & Spencer to introduce food into their stores that previously sold mainly clothes. The cost in time, transportation and trouble saved is unconsciously deducted from the price of the product in the supermarket. The price that the customer 'pays' is therefore less than that marked on product.

When a housewife buys a packet of washing detergent, she is not just buying the cost of the powder, additives and the packaging. She is buying the research that has developed the product and the knowledge of the manufacture in providing a powder that will wash her laundry clean and bright. The perceived value, the price she 'pays' is less than the price the manufacturer has recommended.

When a customer buys a boat from a shipbuilder, the price is not just for the raw materials and labour to assemble it. It is for the experience gained over many years from designing and building other boats. The price that the customer pays is, in his eyes, less than the final price on the boat builder's invoice because of the bundle of benefits being purchased.

In benefits analysis pricing, the distinction is drawn between costs and value. Traditional pricing methods gather together all the costs, add a percentage for profit, and arrive at a price. But the customer does not pay for the total of costs and profit; the customer pays for the sum of the values.

Products should be evaluated, or perhaps re-evaluated, from the viewpoint of customers and their benefits costed, rather than their constituent parts costs. First the product's attributes should be listed and those that are customer benefits marked. The cost of providing the benefit is compared with an estimate from the customer's viewpoint of its value. The form reproduced in exhibit 12.7 can be used for this purpose, one form for each product.

The price suggested by benefits analysis will probably be found to be higher than the current price. Before deciding to alter the price, a comparative analysis should be conducted with products similarly positioned, along the lines described in chapter 6.

SEGMENTATION PRICING

It was realized many years ago by the railways that all travellers did not wish to be treated the same. First, second-class and third-class compartments were made available, and the day excursion ticket for a fraction of the normal price ticket was developed. Much later, airlines learned that they could greatly improve both their appeal and their revenue by treating different segments of the market differently. Today, on any flight, with first-class, business-class, club-class, economy, mid-week travel, fixed-day travel, holiday package etc., it is normal for several different prices to have been paid for a ticket on the same flight.

The application of high technology to business has removed, almost eliminated, time-zone barriers to communications, and helped the rapid global growth of total markets. This has stimulated an enormous increase in market segmentation, and the development

Exhibit 12.7 Benefits analysis pricing

Product* _____   Date _____

Perceived Product Benefit (1)	Estimated Percentage of Total Cost (2)	Estimate of Value (3)	Compare and reprice Product (4)
_____	_____	_____	_____
_____	_____	_____	_____
_____	_____	_____	_____
_____	_____	_____	_____
_____	_____	_____	_____
_____	_____	_____	_____
_____	_____	_____	_____
_____	_____	_____	_____
_____	_____	_____	_____

Price based on benefits anaylsis _____

Current price _____

Pricing objectives for this product:

* Use one form for each product.

in the late 1980s of consumer 'micro-marketing'. Markets everywhere are becoming smaller, and even giants like Proctor & Gamble are changing their marketing techniques to focus on smaller and smaller segments of the market. Products, prices and appeals are differentiated to different market segments.

This fragmentation of markets into sub-markets has highlighted the fact that different market segments often have different price elasticities. The emphasis is on product differentiation and price.

There are three main parts to segmentation pricing: the market segment; the offer and the way it is promoted; the price.

MARKET NICHE

The first requirement is to identify the segment, or market niche. Find out who your customers and potential customers are, where they are to be found, and from where they obtain information about your product. The questions that need to be answered are these: Is what you are selling what the customer is buying? Is what the customer wishes to buy what you are prepared to sell?

Different segments will place different values on the same product; the value depending on what the customer expects from buying it, compared with buying an alternative product, or not buying at all. What the customer is prepared to pay for a product or service is not just one price, but, as was described in chapter 3, in a price bracket with an upper and lower limit.

This price bracket is for a bundle of benefits, and any particular price between the limits relates to the customer's desire for some or all of the benefits. The upper limit is a real one for the customer, and no amount of additional benefits will persuade a purchase to be made if it would mean that the limit is exceeded. In the other direction, if the price is less than the lower limit, the product is not what is wanted: it's 'too cheap'.

IMAGE

Within any particular segment are subdivisions, or niches, based on price. The product must be formulated and packaged for these niches. This means that the appropriate brand, product, or company image has to be projected to a carefully defined part of the market.

Greater use of the information gathered by supermarket checkout scanners has created a highly competitive environment within narrow operating limits in the consumer market. Pricing planning focus has moved from the cost variables to industry practices and promotional devices.

After a time, even the best products become mundane in the customers' eyes, sales decline, and the product needs a new image. For the fast moving consumer market, obviously, brand image is important; for the industrial company or service organization, company image is more important.

The best-known products and companies are not necessarily those with the highest sales. Products and companies that enjoy wide recognition and reputation in the total market may appeal only to a segment. Rolls-Royce cars and Rolex watches probably have the largest brand image in their respective categories, but they certainly do not have the highest sales.

OFFER

The development of a unique product image and its projection to the appropriate market niche will substantially lower price sensitivity. But the way the product is promoted and offered will largely influence its success.

A glance at the shape and styling of cars over the years proves the importance of image to car buyers and sellers. Yet image alone is not enough.

In 1989 Toyota launched their new luxury car, Lexus. They were concerned that the substantial investment of £1.8 billion, six years of effort, with 450 prototypes and something over 4 million test kilometres would fail if the offer was not equal to the image. To ensure that the offer was given the best chance, professionals were hired to analyse the offers made by dealers of competitive cars, including Toyota itself. The information was incorporated in the intensive training given to the sales and service people, who were drilled in the Lexus way, 'not to compete', but 'to excel', and that the Lexus goal is 'complete customer satisfaction'. The price of the car reflects its image in relation to others in the Toyota range, but is below that of other makers' cars with which it will compete.

IMAGE PRICING

Image pricing is more appropriate to consumer products with a high repeat purchase than for industrial products. The company produces a similar product but with a different name, different package and higher price. The price implies quality. It is not a premium product carrying a higher price, but an identical product with a different image. The image created justifies the price, and the increased profits subsidize the same products with the lower image.

This technique is used in the 'rag' trade, where identical dresses are sold under different brand names and through different outlets. It is also found in the toiletries market, where different names and labels on different shaped bottles can create an image to justify a higher price.

The practice is also seen in the pharmaceutical industry, where products with branded names are offered for minor ailments. The main ingredient of the chemical composition printed on the side of the package, 'acetylsalicylic acid', announces it to be common aspirin.

CREATIVE PRICING AS A STRATEGY

Pricing is not just part of the revenue generating machinery. Price plays its part in providing turnover and profit to the seller, but to the buyer it offers appeal, interest, opportunity, justification and satisfaction.

Pricing can be used creatively to define products, segment markets, stimulate purchases, respond to competitive strategies and increase revenue without necessarily eroding volume. Price has advantages over other business activities: it requires only limited investment, can be readily implemented and its results can be quickly assessed.

The key to creative pricing strategies is exploiting the differences between price-sensitive and insensitive market niches. Changing from tactical pricing to creative pricing means linking pricing strategy with business strategy. Differentiated price structures are prepared to achieve specific pricing objectives.

Let us look at an example of how one successful company is using creative pricing to increase its market share, revenue and profit. The company markets computer-aided design (CAD) software. It used to have a single price schedule for its main product and support service, marketing to 20,000 architects. The price for any of its systems was the same across vast areas of differing competitive advantage. Their business strategy was to target products to specific groups of customers. The architectural CAD package was marketed to architectural partnerships of ten and over, as it was thought that only architects of that size could afford and make full use of com-

Creative pricing

Exhibit 12.8 Price list for CAD programs

Architect Design and Support Programs		
	Complete programs (£)	Upgrades & options (£)
Cadesign Vers. 1.5	500	Upgrades:
Cadesign Vers. 2.0	1,500	Vers. 1.5 to 2.0 1,250
Cadesign Vers. 2.3	1,850	Vers. 2.0 to 2.3 400
Cadesign Vers. 3.0	2,750	Vers. 2.3 to 3.0 1,150
Cadesign Vers. 3.0 package, including full support and training of two operators	4,500	
		Modular V3.0 tablet 210
		2.5D drafting for V3.0 850
		Block & Stack program 540
		Set of advanced macros 150
		Training for two people 900

puter-aided design. Price was used mainly tactically, with many individual deals being struck with customers.

Architect practices vary widely from the large, internationally known outfits, who are commissioned to design all over the world, to the rural one-man practice working for local builders and designing the occasional shopping precinct.

The company segmented the market first by geographical location, then classified architects in public and private practice, and size. Each segment was divided into market niches by determining the strength of competition in each segment and finally classifying the work generally carried out by the architects. The initial segmentation was quickly carried out; secondary and tertiary classifications took time, and were conducted on a geographical basis. The information was entered into a computer database which has been continually updated as companies move to different premises, architects change jobs, undertake special or different tasks, and competitors' profiles change in the segment.

Pricing strategy was developed in line with their business strategy, and price was used as an incentive to each market niche. Exhibit 12.8 illustrates the incentives built into one of their price lists. These

322

products and prices have been simplified from the actual price list of the company but the structure is the same. In view of the company's wish to maintain confidentiality, fictitious descriptions and prices have been given to all items.

Note that the price list has been designed to appeal to various market niches. Architects with minimum CAD system requirements are catered for with the basic Cadesign version 1.5 program at £500. To upgrade this costs £1,250. If the improved version 2.0 is purchased, there is a saving of £250. There is an incentive to buy version 2.0 from the start, and the sales presentation for the basic version indicates that some of the 'goodies' are available only with version 2.0.

Similar savings, as incentives, are available up to the latest version at £2,750. Customers can purchase the version 3.0 program alone for £2,750, or the package that includes training and the items on the right-hand side of the price list for £4,500. If these items are purchased separately they cost an additional £900. This figure has been selected because of the psychological impact of saving 'nearly £1,000' by purchasing the complete version 3.0 package for £4,500.

The price list enables customers to segment themselves. Those who require a basic system are catered for; at the same time, such customers know that they can upgrade the system they choose without having to purchase an incompatible program. Those who want a more elaborate system, rather than purchase upgrades, can appreciate the saving of some 20 per cent by buying the total package.

WARNING SYMPTOMS

Most companies can improve their pricing policy, but many companies learn the vital role that pricing plays in profit making when it is too late. If any of the following symptoms are apparent in an organization, advice and possibly urgent treatment are needed.

- Prices are always based on costs.
- Prices are set by different people, and there is no collective responsibility for any particular price.
- Prices always follow competition.

- The new price list is a general all-round increase of x per cent over last year's.
- Prices to all customers are unidimensional.
- Discounts are standardized.
- Market share is eroded by competitors with similar products.

EFFECTIVE CREATIVE PRICING

A creative pricing strategy should be developed with due consideration of the three components of price: basic cost; oncosts; profit. It must be properly implemented in the company by being translated into attainable objectives, and delegated to responsible executives. Five key actions are suggested:

Plan the strategy in line with the company's overall business strategy. Pricing strategy should be concordant with strategic policy; sales and price planning should be within the same context.

Organize the implementation of the plan, and ensure that everyone directly and indirectly concerned with sales understands the company's pricing strategy. Those in direct contact with customers should be trained to make the strategy work, and all sales incentives must be designed to support it.

Aim to achieve a competitive advantage by maintaining pressure on basic costs. It is not always necessary to buy cheaper, but to buy smarter. This could mean forward buying, second sourcing, more effective production scheduling, or any other moves that will keep costs as low as possible. Good competitive pricing starts with constructive management and control of basic cost.

Watch the plan in action. If pricing strategy has been planned to achieve certain customer and competitive responses, there must be an adequate mechanism that enables managers to monitor all active market segments.

Watch all oncosts and keep them under tight control. Do not allow procedures to develop by default and do not acquiesce to an annual 'natural' increase. Use oncosts to get the products to the customers and product information to potential customers; part of oncosts should be used to develop the product's image. By keeping firm hold of basic cost and oncosts in this way, profit can be adjusted as needed to set price below the perceived value in the appropriate market segment.

Evaluate the results on a continuous basis against specific objectives. To ensure that the evaluation procedures signal the need for changes in strategy in good time, put all possible analyses on a personal computer.

Future pricing strategies should be accommodated by oncosts and not be taken from profit. Use part of the profit component for tactical pricing ploys, but evaluate increases in sales to see that they compensate for the loss of unit profit.

Review strategy regularly; revise rigorously. Price changes have rapid effects in the market. Flexible, corrective responses to unexpected or unanticipated competitive activities is essential to stay ahead of the game.

These five key points – Plan, Organize, Watch, Evaluate and Review – may be remembered with the mnemonic formed from their initial letters: *POWER*.

Index

Index